HOW TO WRITE A QUERY LETTER

Everything
You Need to Know
Explained Simply

Donna Murphy

HOW TO WRITE A QUERY LETTER: EVERYTHING YOU NEED TO KNOW EXPLAINED SIMPLY

Copyright © 2013 Atlantic Publishing Group, Inc.
1405 SW 6th Avenue • Ocala, Florida 34471 • Phone 800-814-1132 • Fax 352-622-1875
Website: www.atlantic-pub.com • E-mail: sales@atlantic-pub.com
SAN Number: 268-1250

Library of Congress Cataloging-in-Publication Data

Murphy, Donna M. (Donna Marie), 1965-
  How to write a query letter : everything you need to know explained simply / by Donna Murphy.
    p. cm.
  Includes bibliographical references and index.
  ISBN-13: 978-1-60138-405-8 (alk. paper)
  ISBN-10: 1-60138-405-X (alk. paper)
  1. Queries (Authorship) I. Title.
  PN161.M87 2011
  070.5'2--dc22

                        2011037246

INTERIOR LAYOUT: Antoinette D'Amore • addesign@videotron.ca
COVER DESIGN: Meg Buchner • meg@megbuchner.com
JACKET DESIGN: Jackie Miller • millerjackiej@gmail.com

Printed on Recycled Paper

Printed in the United States

A few years back we lost our beloved pet dog Bear, who was not only our best and dearest friend but also the "Vice President of Sunshine" here at Atlantic Publishing. He did not receive a salary but worked tirelessly 24 hours a day to please his parents.

Bear was a rescue dog who turned around and showered myself, my wife, Sherri, his grandparents Jean, Bob, and Nancy, and every person and animal he met (well, maybe not rabbits) with friendship and love. He made a lot of people smile every day.

We wanted you to know a portion of the profits of this book will be donated in Bear's memory to local animal shelters, parks, conservation organizations, and other individuals and nonprofit organizations in need of assistance.

– *Douglas & Sherri Brown*

PS: We have since adopted two more rescue dogs: first Scout, and the following year, Ginger. They were both mixed golden retrievers who needed a home.

Want to help animals and the world? Here are a dozen easy suggestions you and your family can implement today:

- *Adopt and rescue a pet from a local shelter.*
- *Support local and no-kill animal shelters.*
- *Plant a tree to honor someone you love.*
- *Be a developer — put up some birdhouses.*
- *Buy live, potted Christmas trees and replant them.*
- *Make sure you spend time with your animals each day.*
- *Save natural resources by recycling and buying recycled products.*
- *Drink tap water, or filter your own water at home.*
- *Whenever possible, limit your use of or do not use pesticides.*
- *If you eat seafood, make sustainable choices.*
- *Support your local farmers market.*
- *Get outside. Visit a park, volunteer, walk your dog, or ride your bike.*

Five years ago, Atlantic Publishing signed the Green Press Initiative. These guidelines promote environmentally friendly practices, such as using recycled stock and vegetable-based inks, avoiding waste, choosing energy-efficient resources, and promoting a no-pulping policy. We now use 100-percent recycled stock on all our books. The results: in one year, switching to post-consumer recycled stock saved 24 mature trees, 5,000 gallons of water, the equivalent of the total energy used for one home in a year, and the equivalent of the greenhouse gases from one car driven for a year.

Dedication

To my family, who continue to support me as I pursue my dreams.

Table of Contents

Introduction **13**

Are You Up for the Challenge? 16

The who, what, and why of a query letter 17

Basic tools to help you manage your queries 18

Mastering the Art of Querying 19

Do not proceed without these basic query tips 20

Keep it up; persistence pays off 21

Case Study: Writing Query Letters is a Work of Art 22

Chapter 1: Coming Up with Ideas for Your Query Letters 25

Write What You Know 26

Draw From Your Personal Experience 27

Read, Read, Read 28

Eavesdrop and Observe 31

Current Events 32

Regional and Seasonal 33

Friends and Colleagues 34

Interviews and Life Stories 35

Conferences, Conventions, and Trade Shows 36

Networking Events, Clubs, and Associations 37

Variations on a Single Topic..39

Researching Your Query Ideas...41

Chapter 2: Pursing the Attainable Dream of Getting Published 43

Why All the Fuss Over Query Letters?......................................44

Research Before Jumping in With Both Feet............................45

Research effectively..46

Interview artfully...46

Case Study: Research and Keep Learning..................................47

Know Your Rights..49

The six most commonly purchased rights..............................50

Query Letter Scams to Avoid 53

The recommendation letter scam..53

The notorious fee-charging scam 54

The writing contest scam...54

Case Study: Avoiding Publishing Scams....................................56

Helping writers beware 58

Chapter 3: Where to Sell What You Write 59

Knowing Your Market Options...60

Consumer magazines 60

Literary magazines...62

Trade journals 64

Newspapers 66

Online publications (e-zines)...68

Pursing International Markets..70

Repeating the rewards of spreading the news *71*

Is translation an option?..*71*

Other things to consider *72*

Chapter 4: Query Letter Modus Operandi **77**

Deciphering Writer's Guidelines 78

Sample guideline sections..*79*

Adding Creativity to Your Query Letters...................................84

Sample Query Letter: Humorous Paranormal 87

What Else to Include With Your Query 88

Photos, graphics, and illustrations *89*

Pull-quotes and sidebars..*89*

Clips when requested..*89*

Sample Query Letter: Cozy Mystery 89

Chapter 5: Query Letters, Compared and Contrasted **93**

Components of the Article Query...93

Sample Query Letter: Historical Children's Fiction 94

Components of the Newspaper Query.......................................96

Sample Query Letter: Local Newspaper Query 98

Components of the Nonfiction Book Query...............................99

Sample Query Letter: Narrative Nonfiction 101

Components of the Novel Query..103

Sample Query Letter: Urban Fantasy 104

The novel synopsis...*105*

Pitching to the right genre *108*

Chapter 6: Query Letter Basic Training...**111**

What Editors Really Think of Queries...112

Five Things That Can Impress the Editor 113

   1) Let your personality show *114*

   2) Have some relevant experience...*114*

   3) Be patient *114*

   4) Show that you have a specialty...*114*

   5) Be as perfect as humanly possible *115*

The Devil is in the Details 115

   Know whom to address and how..*115*

   Format to industry standards...*116*

   Include a SASE *116*

   Address the publication correctly *117*

   Proofread, proofread, proofread...*117*

Chapter 7: The Anatomy of the Query Letter...............................**121**

Greetings and Salutations 122

Make It a Good Closer 123

Five Core Sections of a Query Letter..124

   Section One: Now that I have your attention (the hook)......................*124*

Case Study: It is All About the Hook 128

   Section Two: Here is my story (the pitch) *130*

   Section Three: In case you need more detail (the body)....................*131*

   Section Four: The ideal candidate (the credentials).............................*133*

   Section Five: Some parting thoughts (the closer) *137*

Tailored for Success...137

Sample Query Letter that Landed a Book Assignment....................139

Chapter 8: Refining Your Query Letter Before Submission 143

Make a Lasting Impression 143

Case Study: Take Your Time 145

A Touch of Professionalism 147

Edit, Then Edit Some More 148

The Winning Edge 150

Formatting Your Query Letter 154

Special Formatting for E-mail Queries 156

The do's and don'ts of e-mail queries 159

Chapter 9: How Not to Write a Query Letter 161

Top Ten Things to Avoid When Querying 162

Things That Infuriate the Editor 164

Slush-pile worthy mistakes 165

Just plain unprofessional 165

Sure signs of inexperience 166

Case Study: From Both Sides of the Query Fence 167

Sample Query Letter: What Not to Do 169

Chapter 10: Querying a Literary Agent for Representation 171

Why You Might Need a Literary Agent 172

Advantages of Hiring a Literary Agent 173

Where to Find Reputable Agents 174

Proceed with Caution When Looking for Agents 176

Developing a Good Working Relationship with Your Agent 178

Seven ways to get blacklisted by an agent 180

Chapter 11: Submitting Your Query **183**

Planning Your Submission Strategy 184

Schedule Time to Write Your Queries 186

Query Submission Tracking Tools 189

Computer spreadsheets *189*

Desktop submission tracking software *190*

Online submission trackers *192*

The Submission Checklist 194

Chapter 12: When Query Letters Are Not Required **199**

Scenario 1: You Have Established a Rapport With Your Editor 200

Scenario 2: The Publication Guidelines State "No Query" 200

Scenario 3: Submitting to an Online, Small-Readership Publication 201

Scenario 4: Submitting Short, Out-of-the-Ordinary Pieces 201

Scenario 5: The Publisher Wants a Book Proposal Instead 201

Key elements of the book proposal *202*

Query Letter Anomalies 207

Quick-pitch queries *208*

Multiple-pitch queries *209*

Chapter 13: What to Do While You Wait **211**

Follow-Up Is Essential 211

Sample Follow-up Letter to an Article Query 213

Write and Send More Queries 213

Handle Rejections Professionally 214

What else might have gone wrong? *215*

What to glean from rejections *217*

When to respond to a rejection letter *218*

Other Relevant Correspondence 219

    Cover letters *219*

Sample Cover Letter 222

    Thank-you notes *223*

Sample Thank-You Note 224

    Complaint letter *225*

Sample Complaint Letter 226

Chapter 14: You Have Landed the Assignment. Now What?...229

Responding to an Acceptance Letter 230

Sample Acceptance Letter #1: Confirmation of Writing 231

Time to Celebrate! But Now the Work Begins 232

Be Responsive and Open 233

    Embrace idea and brainstorming sessions *234*

    Use constructive criticism as a way to improve *234*

Meeting Deadlines Is a Must..235

Getting Paid 236

How to Turn Down an Assignment Tactfully 239

Sample Letter to Decline an Assignment 241

Some Parting Thoughts on Querying 242

    Consider selling a column..*243*

Sample Response Postcard 246

    Develop a strong personal brand *247*

    Learn to write faster..*249*

Conclusion **253**

Appendix A: Writers' Associations **255**

Appendix B: Writers' Resources 263

Appendix C: Successful Query Letters and Synopses................271

Appendix D: Successful Book Proposal..............................293

Appendix E: Sample Revised Pages 321

Glossary: Letter Writing and Publishing Terminology.............325

Author Biography..331

Index..333

Introduction

Query letters are not just for the seasoned writer. Novice writers also can benefit from selling by query. The primary impetus behind the query is to save time for both the editor and the writer. Editors are bombarded daily with unsolicited manuscripts and articles, which makes it more enticing for them to read a one-page query letter instead of a ten-page story or proposal. Writers submitting a tailored query letter do not waste valuable time or energy preparing a full article that might be rejected. For these two reasons alone, the query letter has become the most effective way for a writer to break into the market and for the editors to acquire the work they need selectively.

In addition to the obvious benefit of saving time, there are several other benefits to querying:

- Queries are more cost-effective for the writer compared to spending time and money writing and sending entire articles or manuscripts that may not be accepted.

- A well-crafted query can lead to unexpected assignments that were different from the writer's original idea.

- Queries that present good ideas could produce multiple assignments.

- Multiple queries can increase the number of markets you could enter.

- Queries substantially multiply your prospects and increase your chances of getting more assignments or offers and could lead to more opportunities for your work to be published.

- Queries are easier to customize for different publications.

Instead of sending in complete articles or manuscripts, why not profit more with less? Submitting a concise, tailored letter that presents your ideas to an

editor is a more effective and productive way to solicit feedback and determine if you need to invest more time or energy into pursuing the idea. The beauty of this approach is that you can commit more of your time to submitting multiple queries to several markets simultaneously. Again, this increases your chances of landing assignments because you are submitting to several markets rather than submitting to one publication and waiting to get a response.

You can use a handful of techniques and tools to master the art of querying. Some of these techniques are industry standards while others are developed through trial and error and in-the-trenches experience. But, persistence is paramount. A good, solid query letter that lands you assignment after assignment is developed over time with practice, patience, and persistence. Crafting an irresistible query letter is a true art form, an art that involves presenting your case to capture an editor's interest, learning from your mistakes, and persevering through the rejection letters.

The following chapters in this book will cover how to:

- Attain your dream of being published.
- Use query letters to sell yourself and your ideas.
- Identify the right market for your content.
- Follow the proper etiquette in querying.
- Avoid annoying the editor.
- Use the basic framework of the query letter and include the same four elements with every submission.
- Determine whether you need a literary agent.
- Find a literary agent to represent you and your work.
- Tailor your queries for success.
- Refine your query letter before submission.
- Submit your queries.
- Identify the optimal query submission-tracking tool for you.
- Make the most of the waiting time between submission and notification.
- Handle rejections professionally.
- Prepare other relevant correspondence.
- Successfully handle landing an assignment.
- Tactfully turn down an assignment.
- Sharpen your writing skills.
- Get more mileage out of your current topics.

Are You Up for the Challenge?

If your goal is to break into the writing arena, whether for magazines, books, newspapers, or online publications, you will need to submit a query letter about 99 percent of the time. The writing and publishing industry is a competitive field that is not for the faint of heart. If you want to build a good foundation to break into this field, this is the book for you. Keep in mind that you will have to gain specialized skills, master the art of selling, develop a thick skin, and practice lots of patience and persistence.

Getting your article, book, or story published will require that you spend time learning the tricks of the trade and producing quality work. The goal is not to throw a bunch of queries out there to see what sticks. You will need to craft a solid query to pitch a handful of publications. This crafting will involve learning from your mistakes and others', doing extensive research, and reading samples of queries that worked and did not work.

If this is a new endeavor for you, I can guarantee that you will experience fear (primarily of rejection), apprehension, anxiety, frustration, and maybe other not-so-fun side effects. These all come with the territory, and they are completely normal. That is why dissecting the chapters of this book will help you prepare a great query letter and help to mitigate some of those feelings. The more queries you write and submit, the easier it will become. And remember, you will learn just as much, if not more, from the rejections as you will from the acceptances.

The who, what, and why of a query letter

The query letter is very basic. It is single-page, concise, professional, intriguing letter introducing you and your article idea, story, or book. The query letter serves three clear purposes: 1) gains the editor's attention enough to want to know more about you and your idea, 2) provides an example of your writing skills and style, and 3) outlines your idea and the strategies you plan to use for the full-fledged article.

- *Who writes query letters?* For beginners and intermediate writers, the query letter is mandatory. Until you have landed regular assignments or have a strong working relationship with an editor, query letters will be your primary means of approaching a publication or editor.

- *What is a query letter?* The query letter is nothing more than a business letter, a sales pitch of sorts that sells your idea, writing, and qualifications to an editor, agent, or publisher before they have read the entire article or manuscript. Query letters offer you a chance to make a great first impression without actually being face to face with an editor.

- *Why use a query letter?* The most obvious and straightforward answer to why use a query letter is editor and agent driven. Editors, agents, and publishers are too busy to read every unsolicited manuscript, article, or proposal that comes across their desks. For practicality sake, the query letter provides a simple solution for managing submissions. One page is much easier to read, skim, and make a first assessment of whether to pursue that writing venture. For writers, the query letter is the best, quickest, and cheapest way to present an idea to a publication without investing too much time and energy for a potential rejection.

Understanding these three questions provides the foundation upon which you will build your skills throughout the rest of the book. If you are contemplating forgoing the query letter route altogether, think again. The market can be challenging to break into, but by ignoring one of the most important industry rules of querying, you will reduce your chances even further.

Basic tools to help you manage your queries

Thanks to technology, your task of managing queries has become a whole lot easier. The technology trio of the computer, Internet, and e-mail has changed the face of the writing industry to help both editors and writers.

- Computer — Computers make the task of writing, formatting, and personalizing query letters almost automated. Word processing programs have features that allow you to easily copy and paste reusable content and create templates to standardize your professional query letter.

- Internet — The Internet will be one of your closest companions. It has not completely replaced the trip to your local library, but it has quickly become the easiest means to search for sample queries, review writer's guidelines, research the publication, and identify the correct point of contact for submission. Online research is quick and easy.

- E-mail — It is more acceptable these days to submit query letters by e-mail. However, it is not recommended to automatically send queries by e-mail without first checking the publication's writer's guidelines. Writer's guidelines are instructions a publication provides on how to submit queries or completed manuscripts for consideration. Not all publications accept e-mail submissions. Once you have identified that an editor will accept an e-mail submission, ensure that you still follow the structure and formatting guidelines you will learn in chapters 7 and 8.

In addition to these three main tools to help you manage your queries, you will also need a good supply of stamps, self-addressed stamped envelopes (SASE), and a basic spreadsheet program to track your query submissions. Once you have grown accustomed to the art of querying, you might want to consider investing in query letter management and submission software to replace your spreadsheet. For example, programs such as The Writer's Scribe professional submission tracking software (**www.thewritersscribe.com**), Write Again 2.0 business software for writers (**www.write-again.com**), the Writer's Database market and submission tracker (**www.writersdb.com**), and Writer's Market writing software (**www.writersmarket.com**) provide a variety of options for keeping track of your submissions.

Mastering the Art of Querying

So far, you have been learning a lot of background information about query letters. Do not lose heart; the chapters in this book are building blocks that will assist you on the road to your final destination of successfully landing an assignment and being published. Each chapter represents a piece of the bigger puzzle. By the time you have completed this book, you will have all the skills, knowledge, and information you need to master the art of querying with confidence.

Many writers who enter into the publishing arena assume that hard work is the key to success. However, mastering the art of querying is not as much about hard work as it is about *smart* work. Yes, the work will be hard at first, but that is primarily because you are learning a new trade. But ultimately, the goal is to work smarter, not harder. The more successful you become at landing assignments, the fewer queries you will need to write. Once you enter this stage, you will find that editors might even start querying you.

Do not proceed without these basic query tips

Regardless of whether you are just starting out or you have been writing query letters for quite some time, there is a query "code of ethics" that every writer should strive to follow. These codes of ethics are not specific details about how to write, develop, or submit the query. They are more relevant to the writer's conduct, for example:

- Always be professional.

- Spend time on the query lead.

- Know the publication and tailor your query accordingly.

- Seek to offer fresh and innovative ideas.

- Do not be shy about being creative in your presentation.

- Provide something interesting, such as photos, charts, or diagrams for the editors to look at to add weight to your article.

- Do not propose if you cannot deliver.

- Always provide a brief biography of yourself and include evidence showing that you are the best person to handle the assignment. Even though you might not have many clips to start with, you can glean from your work experience, personal experience, or a related interview with subject matter expert.

These basic query tips will be discussed in more detail in later chapters, but keep them in mind as you begin to develop each query letter. Keep this list nearby whenever you begin a new letter. After a few submissions, these tips will become second nature to you.

Keep it up; persistence pays off

Learning the tricks of the trade is definitely an important aspect of mastering the art of querying. But to reap the rewards of being published, persistence is the most important trait you will need to succeed. If you intend to see your name published in a trade magazine or newspaper, you must query continually and persistently. Many writers drop out of the race upon receiving the first rejection letter. Others fizzle out after not being able to keep up with the demand of multiple submissions, and even more change course when too much time has passed without a single acceptance or assignment.

Set yourself up for success by using a few of these hints to combine with your persistence, and soon you will find your way to publication and writing success.

- Own your title and brand yourself — You are a writer, so own it, and take yourself seriously as a writer. If you have to use a daily mantra or sticky notes on the mirror to remind yourself that you are a writer, then by all means do so. Establish yourself as an authority and work on self-branding. Remember, the query letter is not just about selling ideas for an article, short story, or book. It is also about selling yourself.

- Schedule time for writing — Writers write, so you will need to spend time writing every day. The only way to get better at something is to continue to practice and develop it. Scheduling your writing time will further solidify its importance. If you do not schedule time to write, chances are you will make up excuses for not sitting down and writing. Make a habit of blocking out time on your calendar to focus on writing with a goal in mind.

- Set smaller attainable goals — Writers, particularly freelance writers, need to be self-starters who can follow through and persevere. Most writers do not have a boss prompting them to meet deadlines and adhere to predefined schedules — that is, until they land an assignment, and then the editor becomes that boss. So, it will be up to you to set tangible and attainable writing goals to help move you closer to your ultimate goal.

And last, but not least, stay focused and keep it up, because persistence does pay off!

CASE STUDY: WRITING QUERY LETTERS IS A WORK OF ART

Lorraine Mignault
Founder and director
Positive Living Inc.
www.positivelivingessentials.com

Although Lorraine Mignault has been writing for more than five years, it has only been in the last two years that her writing has been query driven. She thoroughly enjoys writing query letters and feels that it has become a work of art.

POSITIVE LIVING INC.

Mignault's first and most memorable query letter experience that landed her an assignment was through a cover story competition for *WE Magazine for Women* (**www.wemagazineforwomen.com**). It took five months for her to hear back from the editor, but it was well worth the wait. She was selected to participate in an Internet project that served as a platform to showcase the mission of the competition — to recognize and reward women worldwide for their contributions to their professions and the communities in which they work, live, and play. As a result, Mignault became a *WE Magazine* Women's Hall of Fame honoree and her article became immediately available through print, online, and media avenues.

Mignault said, "When innovation ignites your writing ritual (whether for books, magazines, or online publications), it becomes your gift of opportunity to make a difference."

Making Mistakes and Overcoming Obstacles

As every writer knows, perfecting a craft involves making mistakes and facing various challenges along the way. "I once encountered a lack of clarification regarding the query letter submission deadline; I mistook 12 p.m. (noon) for 12 a.m. (midnight)," admits Mignault. The query could not be redirected the next day because it was past the deadline.

She also recalled her worst query letter experience in which she provided content to the editor for an article, which resulted in a follow-up interview with another writer. After investing extensive time developing the article, interviewing the writer, incorporating the writer's responses into the article, and resubmitting the article to the editor, the publication went out of print.

Mistakes happen, obstacles find their way in your path, and discouragement can set in at the most inopportune times; however, these situations are part of the learning process involved in perfecting the art of writing query letters. The goal is to learn from those mistakes, hurdle the obstacles, and persevere through the discouragement.

From Personal Experience

In general, editors, agents, and publishers are very busy people. You must strive to empower your message and their story to facilitate their project. Mignault has some encouraging words for writers who are just starting their careers:

- Be selective about where you send your query letters. Seek out reputable writing opportunities where you will receive appropriate credit for an article you write.

- Learn to be irresistible to the media by adapting your expertise to the subject matter of interest. Your scope may be broader than you think.

- Be consistent and persistent in your approach to the submission process. Develop a standard format that will facilitate productive and effective query execution.

The first quarter of 2011 has been outstanding for Mignault. Her perseverance with query letter writing and submissions will land her as a showcase in four books written by American authors and a feature in two notable health and business magazines (both print and online versions). Just recently, a veteran in the public relations industry stated it was "phenomenal" what she had achieved in such a short time.

Coming Up with Ideas for Your Query Letters

Most writers of articles and nonfiction books do not begin writing until editors have accepted their proposals and they have a signed contract. Instead of investing valuable time in work that might not sell, they send out multiple queries, carefully crafted to interest a variety of publications and publishers. Sometimes an editor will ask the writer to alter the proposed topic of a query to fit a particular theme or project or even to write about something entirely different. The more queries you send out, the more likely you are to sell your writing. This chapter offers some suggestions for finding ideas for query letters.

Ideas for queries are everywhere, once you learn to recognize them. Soon you will begin to discover potential topics in the events you observe every day, the conversations you have, and the books and articles you read. When considering a topic for a query letter, however, remember that if your proposal is accepted, you will have to write the book or article. It is difficult to write about something you are not genuinely interested in or passionate about. Look for topics that you want to know more about and will enjoy delving into. Be sure you will be able to find enough legitimate information to back up your ideas. When inspiration comes to you, research the topic, and have a working knowledge of it before you write the query letter. Your query will need to convince the editor not only that you have a unique approach to your topic but also that you are infinitely qualified to write the article or book.

Write What You Know

Make a list of everything you know. Write down your academic degrees and professional certifications, education and training, work experience, hobbies, sports, volunteer work, and personal relationships — anything you can think of. Are you a grandfather, a mother, a best friend, or a child of

an alcoholic? Are you a veteran? A Little League® coach? An accountant? A massage therapist? Do you love to bake cookies or play fantasy football? Perhaps you have been a Sunday school teacher for 20 years, spend your winters in Alaska training sled dogs, or are a regular contestant in barbecue cook-offs. You might have built your own house out of cordwood or breed canaries as a hobby. Your home might be a family farm in Utah or a tiny apartment in Manhattan. Maybe you operate a successful Internet business from your home or commute an hour every day to your job in a financial firm. Anything of which you have first-hand knowledge can become a topic for an article, a series of articles, or a book.

Think about how you can share your expertise or teach someone else to do the same thing you have done. Write about one or more problems you have encountered and how you resolved them. Write an article or book that would have helped you at some point in your life or your career. Tell everyone what you wish you had known when you started out, or what you realized as a result of your efforts. There are thousands of other people out there in similar situations that could benefit from your experience, or at least enjoy reading about it. Chances are, the deeper you delve into a topic, the more you will have to say. One query letter or article can spin off into five or six variations on the same theme.

You might write hundreds of queries, articles, and books during your writing career. When you write about something you know well, you establish your reputation as an expert in that area. You can build on that reputation through radio and TV interviews, seminars, and speaking at conferences. Soon publications will seek you out, editors will know who you are, and you will have to write fewer query letters.

Draw From Your Personal Experience

Take a moment to examine your life. In a journal or notebook, write your answers to questions such as, "What am I doing right now?" "What are my goals?" "Where have I been?" "What are my priorities?" "What am I trying to achieve?" "What is my biggest problem right now?" Other people are probably asking themselves similar questions, and a book or article exploring your personal odyssey might resonate with them. Tony Robbins, the well-known self-help guru and author of *Unlimited Power* and *Awakening the Giant Within* likes to recount how, at the lowest point in his life, he vowed to change his attitude and succeeded in transforming himself.

A story about overcoming personal obstacles or dealing with a personal crisis makes compelling reading. A number of best-selling books have originated with blogs in which the authors talked about their emotional reactions to a life event, such as the birth of a child or a divorce.

Whom do you know? Your experiences as a relative or friend of a well-known person might make an interesting story. You also could recount their stories from your point of view. You might have a neighbor or friend who is an expert in some field, and who would be willing to give an interview or collaborate on an article.

You could write an article or book about how a personal difficulty affected your life and how you dealt with it — for example, how you survived being laid off and found a new job, or how you learned to manage diabetes while playing professional baseball. Your child might have been bullied at school, or you might be caring for a parent with Alzheimer's disease. A story like this can contain facts, but your thoughts and feelings make it unique.

Read, Read, Read

You cannot write without reading. Go to bookstores and libraries and browse through books and magazines about your topic. Read new releases and bestsellers to see what is popular and what the latest trends are. When you find a book that interests you, take note of the publisher. Look on the publisher's website to see what books are scheduled for release next season. Bookstores often have free catalogs of upcoming releases on the counter — pick one up, and look through it.

Do not try to follow a trend too closely because by the time your article is scheduled for publication, a new trend will have taken hold of the public imagination. Instead, try to come up with a new take on a popular concept, such as "green" living or stay-at-home dads, and anticipate the next trend.

Look up topics on websites of online booksellers such as Amazon.com, Barnes & Noble, and Alibris. Read the book reviews and sample excerpts. Notice the other books recommended alongside your choices.

When you have identified a topic you would like to write about, look at the books and magazines in that category or section of the bookstore, and ask yourself what is missing. For example, most of the travel books for South America might be for affluent travelers with little or no information for young people on a budget. Low-calorie cookbooks might be lacking in Asian recipes. Articles on historical events might overlook the role of women.

Technology and scientific knowledge are advancing so rapidly today that some books are outdated as soon as they are in print. For example, financial advice written before 2008 has been made obsolete by the recession that followed. In the first half of 2011, several national leaders were deposed. Pluto is no longer a planet, the USDA's Food Pyramid is now "MyPlate," and South Sudan is an independent nation. It is important to keep up with the newest information by reading the most recent magazines, news articles, journals, and Internet blogs. Changes like these make good topics for queries, and you want to avoid using outdated information that makes you appear uninformed.

Set up Google "Alerts" to send you relevant information

Go to Google.com and select "Alerts" under "Specialized Search." (Get there by clicking "more" and then "even more" on the menu at the top of the Google screen.) Enter relevant keywords for your topic. Google will send you e-mail alerts every time a new article is published about your topic.

Reading blogs, comments on social media such as Facebook and Twitter, and reactions to news articles on news websites makes you aware of the public's concerns and attitudes. Seeing how individual people respond to a tragic accident or news of yet another Ponzi scheme may trigger an idea for an article. Reading a popular blog gives you insights into a particular group or community of people. When you know how people think, feel, and what worries or excites them, you will be able to engage them and the publications that market to them with your writing.

Other good sources of ideas are trade journals and magazines published by various professional associations. Some of these require memberships or subscriptions, but you may be able to find copies in your public library or access them online through your library's subscriptions or through High-Wire Press (**http://highwire.stanford.edu/lists/freeart.dtl**). Trade journals are often left out on tables in waiting rooms for customers to read. If you are interested in a particular industry, look for a contact in that industry that would be willing to pass back issues on to you. Trade journals contain articles about current issues in the industry, as well as new developments and industry news. You might even want to submit queries to these journals and magazines.

Eavesdrop and Observe

Wherever you go, listen to what people around you are talking about. Observe how they dress and what they do. For example, if you want to write articles or fiction for young adults, you need to understand their concerns, their likes, dislikes, and the language they use. Listen in on young boys bragging about their video game exploits. Ask a young girl what she texts about with her friends. When you are sitting in a coffee shop in a retirement community, a fast-food restaurant in a rural town, or a diner in a city, look around at the other customers, and watch how they interact with their friends and families. You might overhear elderly couples complaining that their children never communicate with them or that they dislike the politics of their homeowner's associations. Retired farmers might be entertaining their grandchildren while the parents are at work. Taxi drivers having lunch in the diner might be trading stories about rude customers. While visiting a Disney theme park, you might observe couples wearing matching Disney outfits and sporting Mickey Mouse tattoos. Circulate at public events and conferences, such as car shows, art festivals, motorcycle rallies, and comic book conventions, and try to identify with the visitors who have come there to indulge their passions.

Sadly, cell phone use has made many private matters extremely public. People loudly carry on personal conversations in public places as though no one can hear them. You might overhear a building contractor talking about a shortage of wood and how it is delaying construction and raising the cost of building a home. A single 30-something might be confessing how lonely she is to her best friend and describing the difficulties of finding a good male companion. An investor may be instructing his broker to buy gold. Any of these conversations could translate into a good topic for an article.

Keep your eyes open as you go about your daily business, and you will find interesting ideas right on your doorstep. Perhaps you drive by an organic dairy farm every day on your way home; you could interview the owner about his or her business and the laws affecting the sale of raw milk. You might observe pedestrians having difficulty crossing a busy local road. As you jog through your neighborhood park, you might come across park staff carefully destroying invasive plants that have spread from nearby gardens. You might wonder why tomatoes suddenly have disappeared from the produce section in your supermarket, and why lettuce is so expensive. Anything that catches your interest could have an underlying story that would interest an editor.

Current Events

Books and articles that tie in with current events typically sell well. For example, 1999 brought a deluge of articles about the dangers of Y2K (computers that were not programmed to accept dates beginning with "2___"), overviews of the 20th century, and predictions for the coming century. Natural disasters, upcoming elections, celebrity weddings, deaths and funerals of public figures, assassinations, changes in the law, fluctuations in the stock market, and political upheavals are gold mines of material for articles and books. Keep in mind that current events are time-sensitive; it could be several weeks before your query is accepted and your article is ready for publication. Magazines and newspapers assign staff journalists to cover current events, so your query will have to touch on a unique angle, such as a first-hand experience, behind-the-scenes coverage, little-known background information, or a tell-all from someone directly involved with the event.

Sales of books related to current events drop soon after public interest in that event has faded. In contrast, topics such as child-rearing, dieting, and human relationships are perennial and can be revisited repeatedly. Dale Carnegie's book, *How to Win Friends and Influence People*, published in 1937, has sold 15 million copies worldwide and is still available in bookstores. In 2005, his daughter, Donna Dale Carnegie, published *How to Win Friends and Influence People for Teenage Girls*. Dr. Benjamin Spock's *Baby and Child Care*, first published in 1946, is now in its eighth edition and has sold more than 50 million copies.

Regional and Seasonal

There is a market for books and articles on local history, travel, food, and people of distinction. Think of the books you find in a museum bookstore or a souvenir shop. Local newspapers and magazines often run feature sections about events and attractions particular to an area. Look for the qualities that make your hometown or an area you are visiting unique and interesting. Food, architecture, rare native plants, local traditions, and interviews with old-timers all make good subjects for queries. Identify regional magazines and publications, such as real estate magazines and local business directories that need feature articles. Some small presses specialize in regional material or in books about travel or natural history. An article about a colorful local tradition, such as Mardi Gras parades in New Orleans, could sell to a national magazine if it is written from an interesting angle.

Seasonal events and holidays provide endless material — Christmas crafts, Thanksgiving recipes, Easter stories, back-to-school hints, childhood memories, winter sports, and summer road trips are only a few of the seasonal topics you could write about. Remember that there is a lead time of several months for books and some articles, so you will need to query seasonal topics well in advance.

Friends and Colleagues

Your personal experiences can be a rich source of ideas for queries, but what about your friends' and relatives' experiences? Perhaps a friend is coping with the challenges of raising a special needs child, and another spent five years at sea as a navigator on a whaling ship. Their experiences might inspire you to research the topic and come up with ideas for a series of articles or a book. You can ask if they would agree to be interviewed about their experiences.

If you have a day job as a professional, and your colleagues are experts in the field, consider interviewing them for an article or collaborating on a book. You contribute your writing skills, and they contribute their credentials and their expertise. Being featured in a magazine article will add to their prestige and their public recognition. Depending on the extent of

their involvement in a book collaboration, you might have to agree to share a portion of the proceeds from the book.

Writers' groups and associations, both local and on the Internet, are another source of inspiration. Writers' groups hold regular meetings to critique each other's work and share wisdom and experience. Writers' websites abound in helpful articles, advice, and blog posts by writers about their concerns, discoveries, and frustrations. You should not steal another writer's idea, but participating in discussions and asking questions will inspire you to look in new directions. More experienced writers will be able to help you improve your query letters and might suggest publications to which you can submit them.

These online writers' communities and association websites are a good place to start:

Absolute Write (**http://absolutewrite.com**)
Forwriters.com (**www.forwriters.com**)
Goodreads (**www.goodreads.com**)
LibraryThing (**www.librarything.com**)
Mystery Writers of America (**www.mysterywriters.org**)
Romance Writers of America® (**www.rwa.org**)
Science Fiction and Fantasy Writers of America (**www.sfwa.org**)
WritersBeat (**www.writersbeat.com**)

Interviews and Life Stories

Ask an interesting person if he or she would agree to be interviewed for an article. Do not conduct the actual interview until after you have received a positive response to your query because you do not want to disappoint your subject if the article is not published. A person does not have to be a celebrity to give a good interview. A tradesman or a businessperson could reveal interesting details about his work, a doctor could talk about children's health, or an elderly person could talk about relating to his grand-children. Of course, an interview with someone famous is likely to attract immediate interest if you send it to the right editor.

A biography or an authorized life story of someone who has gone through a dramatic experience is a good subject for a query. When writing about a person, get him or her to sign a letter giving you permission to publish the story. You should never pay for an interview because that undermines the credibility of your story. Offer lunch or a drink, and if you are asked for payment, explain and remind the person that he or she will receive full recognition in the article. If you are collaborating with someone on his or her life story, you may need to acquire life story rights by signing an agreement to share the revenue from your book. Securing the rights to someone's life story typically gets you a signed release protecting you from a lawsuit based on defamation, invasion of privacy, or infringement of right of publicity. Sometimes it also gives you access to confidential documents and information and exclusive interviews with your subject.

Conferences, Conventions, and Trade Shows

Trade shows and conventions are excellent sources of ideas for articles. You can learn about the latest innovations and see the newest merchandise, listen to lectures about current issues and scientific discoveries, attend seminars and panel discussions, meet experts who can become candidates for interviews, and network with professionals to hear about their interests and concerns. Circulate and talk to as many people as possible, including sales reps that may be hanging around their booths waiting for someone to stop by and representatives staffing the tables for trade organizations. Ask questions — someone's comments or personal opinions might give you a story idea. Often the theories and concepts being talked about at a conference have not yet hit the mainstream, and you might find a topic that is breaking news.

Once you have decided to write about a particular topic or industry, visit the websites of professional organizations to find the dates and locations of conventions. You may have to register and pay a participation fee, but two or three hundred dollars buys you direct access to leading figures in the field and enough ideas for dozens of queries. Small educational seminars and workshops can be rich sources of inspiration and offer a chance to speak to experts in your topic. Government departments, public libraries, and community colleges sometimes offer free classes or seminars on interesting topics such as personal finance, water conservation, parenting, and social networking. The other participants you meet at these classes also might be a source of ideas because they already may be experienced in the field you want to write about, or they represent your future readers who want to learn more about your topic.

Networking Events, Clubs, and Associations

Meetings of professional, business, or civic associations provide an excellent opportunity to pick up new ideas for queries. You can talk to community leaders, hear lectures about current developments, and talk to others in the field about their hopes and concerns. If you do not already belong to such an association, look for some local groups that might relate to your topics of interest. Groups such as the Rotary Club, Elks, Small Business Chamber of Commerce, and Toastmasters International bring you into contact with professionals and community leaders. If there is a membership fee, consider whether the potential benefits are worth the investment.

You could be part of an informal networking group without even realizing it. Do you attend PTA meetings, or are you on a committee to plan a fall festival at your child's school? Get to know the other parents and the teachers. Are you in a Bible study group or a church committee? Do you volunteer in your community? Do you participate in a book club? Do you keep talking to the same parents at children's birthday parties or soccer games? Are you often thrown together with the same people at parties and social events? Talk — and listen — to as many people as you can. Any occasion can become a source of ideas, either because of the people you meet or because the activity itself makes a good topic.

Attend meetings of clubs and special interest groups related to your topic, such as garden clubs, vintage car clubs, or groups for parents of twins. You can find club meetings listed on community message boards, the event calendars of local newspapers, or through the websites of national associations and interest groups. Through the Internet, you can find local groups that share similar interests. Meetup.com (**www.meetup.com**) fosters thousands of groups nationwide. The people who gather may have nothing in common except a love of gourmet food, butterfly gardens, or yoga. Through groups like these, you can contact a wide variety of people who could be-

come resources for your writing. Many other types of groups, including mommy groups, support groups, book clubs, elder groups, and spiritual communities also can be found through the Internet.

Variations on a Single Topic

Creating variations on a single idea is a good way to increase your stream of income. You do not have to develop a new idea because you already have one. The goal is to take an existing idea or topic and slant it in as many ways as possible to create a feel that is fresh and new. Start with a well-written and well-researched piece you already have had published. This article, book, or story becomes the foundation for several new pieces. Here are a few of the most effective ways for creating variations on a topic:

- **Propose it in a frequently asked questions (FAQ) format.** Evaluate your current piece and assess what question it answers. Rewrite it in a way as if the reader were asking those same questions. Format the final piece by answering each of the questions.

- **Recreate it as a checklist.** If your content is written to be helpful tips or information, see if you can recreate it as a checklist. Make the pertinent items into a list of things to do or steps to follow, and write a brief description of each.

- **Present it in a step-by-step booklet.** This is similar to creating a checklist, but you can expand the list and develop a step-by-step booklet that provides your readers with more detailed guidelines to follow. Although this approach is a small shift from the checklist, it creates just enough change in the focus to produce content that looks fresh and new.

- **Tailor it to a specific industry.** Do you have content that might be more suitable to a specific profession? If so, consider developing an article or a series of articles that answer questions or provide solutions to the professionals in that industry. Although this approach has its limitations, it might provide an outlet to sell a column or for you to become an industry expert. This can open the door for future opportunities.

- **For books, consider a series.** If you have written a book, determine if you can create a series out of it. If you cannot develop enough content for another book, try pulling excerpts from you book and making smaller articles to sell to relevant publications or blogs.

- **Develop an e-book.** You might have enough content under a certain topic to gather it into an e-book. E-books can contain anywhere from ten to 70 pages. They are easy to produce and take less time to publish than traditional books.

- **Create a webinar.** Webinars and teleseminars are the latest craze in professional development. A webinar is a PowerPoint® presentation of your content to an audience that has signed in through a phone line or videoconferencing. The beauty of developing webinars is that you can run them over and over to a wider audience. You can also sell a discounted archived version of your webinar once you have conducted it.

- **Consider podcasting your content.** Podcasts are a series of digital media files released periodically through web syndication. It is similar to self-syndication but uses video streams. Create a running series of your content by creating small podcast snippets and publishing them weekly on a podcast site or on your own website if you have one.

- **Turn your content into blog posts or online articles.**
  Break your content up into a series of short, informative articles, and post them on your blog to draw more traffic or on a site that pays for content, such as Examiner.com (**www.examiner.com**) or eHow.com (**www.ehow.com**).

Once you have worked through these options for one of your pieces, gather a few more of your best articles. You can pull together a database of past content that might be suitable for repurposing. Once you have established this database, keep updating the content, especially if it was time sensitive. Freshen up the content with current examples, and eliminate old references. Group the content in your database into smaller, more focused topics.

Promoting and reselling past content can be a great way to supplement your income while keeping your current readership interested in your material. Repurposing old content can attract new readers too.

Researching Your Query Ideas

A good idea is only one element of a good query. If a hundred other writers are proposing the same idea or if a similar article was published just last month, your query will go nowhere. Once you have settled on an idea for a query, spend some time researching it. You will need to formulate your query in a way that makes your idea stand out as fresh and original. Also, you do not want to appear uninformed by including information that is out-of-date or incorrect in your query.

As with so many other aspects of writing, the Internet is your most valuable research tool:

Type your topic into one or more search engines to see what other articles have been written on the subject. If you find articles similar to the one you plan to write, read them carefully, and note the date and the publication in which they appeared. You will have to offer a new viewpoint or a deeper insight in your query. Your query can reference these articles as evidence that the topic is current and readers are interested in it.

Visit the website of the publisher to which you plan to send the query. Look at back issues and upcoming titles to confirm that a similar article has not been published recently or is not scheduled for publication. If the site has a search feature, search your topic to see if any other articles in that publication reference it. Formulate your idea and query to fit closely with the general theme and attitude of the publication.

Check and double-check all the facts in your query. Make sure you have the most recent statistics and the most current theories. If your source is more than a year old, there is a possibility that the editor has more recent information that contradicts it or alters your premise. Before making any assertions, confirm with at least three references to avoid parroting incorrect information from an unqualified source. When quoting statistics or other scientific data, cite your source in the query.

Chapter 2

Pursing the Attainable Dream of Getting Published

This chapter will challenge you to approach query letters from a different perspective. Beginning writers tend to start their query writing careers from the bottom up by focusing on the structure and elements of a query letter. A more strategic approach is from the top down. Start with the main objective of the letter (top), and work your way toward polishing the content, structure, and style (down). Begin by comparing the query letter to other business letters, such as cover letters, sales letters, or — in a broader sense — a job interview.

The reality of being a writer is that you will write more than your share of query letters over the course of your career. If getting published is truly your dream, you will benefit from having some fun with it and perfecting the art. Although you will find examples that skew the statistics about your odds of being published, the ultimate goal for you is to find a balance between the form letter and the extreme attention-getting queries. It will be about using the guidelines in this book and incorporating them into your own personal style to present a work that shines.

Why All the Fuss Over Query Letters?

Query letters have become the standard for a competitive, almost impenetrable market. Consider writing query letters as part of the dues for belonging to the society of published writers. If you do not query, your work will go into the slush pile.

Many writers feel that querying is a waste of time. What they do not realize is that writing a full-fledged article that potentially does not meet the editor's needs is a bigger waste of time. This approach is equivalent to trying to read an editor's mind. Do not do it.

Of course, there are always exceptions to the rule. In certain cases, such as short essays, an editor might want to see the entire piece to get a better feel for the writer's story and style. A few magazines ask writers (in the writer's guidelines of course) to send articles "on spec." This means the publisher wants to see the entire article before he or she decides to publish and pay for it. Either way, these scenarios are the exception rather than the rule. As mentioned previously, 99 percent of the time, you will need to write a query letter. Period.

Before throwing out the idea that query letters are a waste of your time, consider these important aspects of the query:

- **Queries get the editor's attention.** You can use the first paragraph of your query letter to captivate the editor.

- **Queries sell your work.** Your query letter can get right to the point of why you are pitching a certain topic.

- **Queries sell you.** Use your query letter to show the editor why you are the most qualified to do the proposed piece.

- **Queries allow you to ask.** Use a section of the query letter to strategically ask for the assignment and demonstrate to the editor how easy it will be for you to handle the entire assignment.

- **Queries showcase your qualifications.** Aside from briefly describing your experience and qualifications in the query letter, you can showcase your skills, writing style, and experience with high-quality clips.

Always remember that the query is a form of interest gathering. It is a brief, to-the-point sales letter intended to convince the editor, agent, or publisher to consider your idea or ideas and assign you the projects.

Research Before Jumping in With Both Feet

As exciting as it might seem to get started with your first query letter, that approach will not bring you success. Before jumping in with both feet, start by building your foundation on supporting facts obtained through research. Editors place high value on research because they are looking for information that is not only entertaining to readers, but also educational.

Do not rely simply on your personal knowledge and experience. Although both of those are good places to begin, your work always can be enhanced with additional research and interviewing.

Research effectively

Editors have a knack for spotting false or unsubstantiated information. With the unlimited resources available to writers today, there is really no excuse for not providing editors with substantiating evidence. For example, if you write about a personal experience you have had, provide examples, offer dates, and provide details (with discretion) to demonstrate why your situation is unique. Suppose you have had a personal experience with chronic fatigue syndrome, and you have researched the subject thoroughly to learn how to manage it in your own life. You could pose the idea "Living Day-to-Day with Chronic Fatigue Syndrome" to health and wellness or medically focused publications.

Interview artfully

Another great way to add weight to your work is to interview an expert. Gone are the days where you have to meet face-to-face to interview a person. Now, most interviews are conducted by phone or even by e-mail. The success of an interview is based on the script you prepare. Make the questions in your script short and easy to understand. This will elicit a clearer

and more direct response from the subject. With all interviews, be sure to get the basics: names, titles, dates, contact information, professional affiliations, and bio.

As valuable as research and interviewing can be to an editor, you do not want overkill. An editor is not impressed by too many facts or too many quotes from an industry expert. Before piling all the stats into your query letter, organize a research and interviewing plan that identifies key points to convey and a few substantiating pieces of information.

Many inexperienced writers spend too much time researching and not enough time crafting the query letter. It is appropriate to gather as much research materials as necessary, but you will need to know when to say when. Your researching and interview techniques will develop over time as you learn what is expected from the editor, agent, or publisher. For now, try to focus only on pertinent resources, and do not waste your time chasing down every possible lead.

CASE STUDY:
RESEARCH AND
KEEP LEARNING

Cy Tymony
Sneaky Uses for Everyday Things
www.Sneakyuses.com

Cy Tymony has been a writer for 20 years and has been creating home-made inventions since childhood. He has appeared on *CNN Headline News*, ABC's *Chicago Morning Show*, and NPR's *Science Friday with Ira Flatow*, and he has been featured in the *Chicago Tribune* and *Future Life* magazine.

His first introduction to query letter writing began with the purchase of a book about writing book proposals. He studied the query letter writing section, researched potential publishers, and spent a couple of months crafting a great query. All of that research and studying paid off when Tymony landed his first assignment within two weeks of submitting a query.

Tymony believes query letters work. "Even if a query letter was not necessary, the exercise is important for you to know how to sell your subject," he says. Based on his 20-year experience, Tymony provides these three tips for making a query letter stand out:

- The first paragraph, and especially the first sentence, of your query must be perfect.

- Print out and take your query letter with you to review multiple times a day for at least a couple of weeks.

- Before you complete and submit the query, start writing the article or proposal.

As a technical writer and computer specialist, Tymony understands the importance of finding unique ways to present ideas. For example, to develop ideas for a good hook, Tymony loves reading feature articles in newspapers and magazines. These resources provide him with just the right inspiration to craft his own interesting and compelling hooks. "It may not be clear where they are going at first, but they take care that the sentences are interesting enough to lead you to the next paragraph where the subject is revealed," expresses Tymony.

If you are just starting out in the writing business, Tymony recommends that you:

- Research your subject. Even if you think you know enough, keep looking up things about it; search the background of other contacts and experts.

- Keep editing your query letters until not one word can be added or omitted.

- Show your work to trusted friends. They point out issues and angles that you may be too involved to see.

Consider the possibilities of alternate media

Like other professional writers, Tymony knows that rejection is inevitable in the querying process. His advice for dealing with the rejections is two-fold: 1) Have a list ready of alternate media to submit to, and 2) continually evaluate your query ideas and keep submitting them. Tymony is a big fan of exploring other media. For example he suggests, "If it is a book idea, submit some of the material as a feature article, a column, a blog post, an MP3 audio, or an e-book." When tailoring your idea to alternate media, Tymony recommends evaluating questions such as:

- Can your idea be turned into a Smartphone app?

- Is your idea good material for a TV series episode or movie?

- Can you package your topic (i.e., article or book) with others' ideas?

- Have you tailored your idea for a local, regional, or national market?

When you are excited about a topic and finally have submitted a query, the wait can be frustrating. But Tymony says, "It is important to have other projects out there so your need for feedback is fed. Or, engage in other interests and read more. Inevitably, it will lead to more writing project ideas, especially the areas outside your subject."

Know Your Rights

Many new writers are so distracted by the excitement of landing their first assignments that they ignore the legality of the publishing rights. The goal of this section it to identify the most commonly purchased rights in the industry and to provide a layperson's description of what they mean and how they are used.

Before you sell your work, know your rights. When you are selecting publications to which you want to submit your work, investigate the writer's guidelines to see if they specify the type of rights they expect. If you are comfortable with offering the type of rights they require, then query away.

Understanding your publishing rights is the first step to protecting your work and ensuring you get the most out of the sale. Two basic things to remember: 1) When you create a piece of work, you automatically hold the rights to it, and 2) once you have sold *all* your rights, the work is no longer yours. As important as these two concepts are, many writers still do not understand the importance of negotiating rights with the editor, agent, or publisher. The goal is to keep as many rights as possible so you can get more mileage out of your work. Depending on the publication, you might not have the opportunity to negotiate the rights. They might set the precedence, but that should not come as a surprise because they publish the rights in the writer's guidelines.

Keep in mind that rights may be administered by region, but for simplicity sake, the focus will be on North American rights only. Although there are numerous rights an author may sell, for example rights for film, TV, CD, DVD, and print formats, only the most common rights will be discussed in this section.

The six most commonly purchased rights

The following is a list of the six most commonly purchased rights:

- **One-time rights** – As a popular choice for writers, one-time rights give the publisher nonexclusive rights to publish your work only once. The benefit of this type of right for the writer is that it allows you to license the rights to more than one publication at a time. Sometimes, there is a clause indicating that the writer will not sell the piece to another publication within a certain locality for a designated length of time.

- **First serial rights** – First serial rights are another good option for writers. These rights allow the publication to be the first to use your work, but after it is published, the rights revert to the writer. The catch is that you cannot sell first serial rights to multiple publications. The most common example of first serial rights is First North American Serial Rights (FNASR), which gives the publisher permission to publish your work in all of North America, including

Canada. **Note:** First serial rights sold to an online publication are not limited by geographical area.

- **Second serial rights** – Second serial rights also are known as reprint rights. These rights provide you the most mileage for your money because publications will pay you for the same article multiple times. The pay for your reprinted article will be much less than the original sale, but you will still benefit from additional income without having to redevelop the work. Second serial rights can be either exclusive or nonexclusive in nature.

    o For exclusive rights, the publisher owns the work for a specified (but brief) period, which is agreed upon in the contract. During this brief period, the writer cannot resell the rights to another publisher. At the end of the specified period, the publisher returns the rights back to the writer and allows the writer to begin reselling his or her work.

    o With nonexclusive rights, several publishers can share rights to the writer's work.

- **All rights** – All rights means you give up complete ownership of the work and allow the publication to publish this work in any format and medium without additional compensation to you. By giving up complete ownership, you are no longer allowed to reprint, sell, make profit from, or even use any part of your work anywhere. This is type of right is highly discouraged for writers, but a publisher might not work with you unless you submit all rights. Selling all rights might work for some writers on a case-by-case basis and in situations where there might not be a big market value.

- **Electronic rights** – Electronic rights cover a variety of electronic media including online publications, blogs, websites, e-zines, and streaming media. If you plan to offer electronic rights to a publisher, be sure to be specific about what type of media it covers. If there is room for negotiation, try to offer one-time rights.

- **Work made for hire** – Work made for hire, also referred to as "ghostwriting," is probably the least desirable agreement for writers because it transfers every possible right, including copyright, over to the publisher. With a work made for hire agreement, the publisher, not the writer, is considered the legal owner of the completed work.

To be successful in your writing career, you will need to learn some business savvy. Most of the agreements you will see from publications are not complicated. In most situations, you will be perfectly capable of understanding the terms of the contract. However, do make it a habit of reading contracts carefully, understanding your rights, and learning how to negotiate for what you want. The time you spend researching this area of the writing industry will be well worth it. Begin with the following resources:

- **Rights of Writers (www.rightsofwriters.com)** – This is a blog maintained by Mark Fowler about writing and the law. Fowler is a New York City attorney with 25 years experience working for media companies. He focuses on intellectual property, antitrust, and defamation aspects relating to newspapers, book publishers, and magazines.

- **Keep Your Copyrights (www.keepyourcopyrights.org)** – This website is devoted to authors and creators of work in the United States. The organization aims to inform and instruct creators about how and why to keep your own copyrights. Keep Your Copyrights encourages creators to take a more proactive approach toward copyright management.

- **Copy Law.com (www.copylaw.com)** – This site belongs to Lloyd J. Jassin, who provides counseling to book publishing, television, theater, new media, arts, and entertainment clients about licensing, copyrights, trademarks, right of privacy, and other matters relating to copy.

Query Letter Scams to Avoid

By the sheer volume of writers in the industry, this group is a prime target for scams. Many novice writers are so eager to get published that they  miss all the telltale signs of the carefully planned scam. Education is your best defense. Do not be afraid to ask questions and seek out the answers. Instead of falling prey, arm yourself by recognizing some of the most common scams:

The recommendation letter scam

In this case, you submit your work to an agent or publisher, and you receive positive feedback and encouragement for your submission. Then you are notified that your work would be published with additional editing, and the recommendation letter refers you to a specific person or firm.

> **The hook:** Pump writers up with false hope

> **The scam:** Charge astronomical fees for generic suggestions while paying literary agencies and publishers kickbacks for the referral

> **The tip-off:** The recommendation letter and the subsequent referral to one service that will fix your "supposed" errors

The notorious fee-charging scam

You submit your work to an agent or publisher, and they request a "reading fee" before they will review it. Another approach is that they look at your work free and then later request a marketing fee, retainer, contract fee, or coverage for expenses once you have signed on.

> **The hook:** The fear of not being represented
>
> **The scam:** Request for any type of upfront fee before representation
>
> **The tip-off:** Any exchange of money should be a clue because money should flow toward the author, not away.

The writing contest scam

The posing publisher promotes a writing contest where writers pay $5, $10, or even $50 for a chance to win $500. The contest ends, and the writer's story is never published. The contest promoter already has the entry fees and walks away clean.

> **The hook:** Plays on the notion that it is difficult to get short stories published and writers potentially can win money for their work
>
> **The scam:** If 1,000 authors pay $5 each to enter the contest, the publisher makes $5,000 and pays the winner $500. The publisher just made $4,500.
>
> **The tip-off:** The entry fee. Legitimate contests do not charge a fee.

Although these three represent the most common types of scams for writers, other scams are not as invasive but do a fair share of damage:

- **Paid anthologies** – Writers enter a piece of work into a contest. The entry is free, but the winners and all finalists are required to purchase a copy of the anthology when it is published. Everyone who enters the contest ends up being a finalist, and the work is published in the anthology. The anthology contest host is also relying on the fact that the entrants have told friends and family about the anthology, and they, too, have purchased a copy.

- **Vanity presses** – Usually used in a negative sense, vanity presses publish books at the author's expense and usually are not selective about what and who to publish.

- **Print on demand** – Digital printing technology that allows you receive a complete book printed and bound. It can be a useful resource for printing small quantities of books. However, POD scams do exist. This scam is when a company tries to persuade the author that printing his or her book is just like having a publisher pick it up. The scamming POD company charges you money, but they do not edit your work, and the quality of the product is poor.

- **Book doctors** – Independent or freelance editors who will read and edit a manuscript for a fee. Their primary job is to edit your manuscript for structure, technical errors, style, continuity, and grammar. However, you know this is a scam when the following scenarios happen, or the book doctors make these claims: 1) You cannot be published without their services; 2) using them will result in getting accepted by an agent; 3) they will not provide references from previous authors or agents with whom they worked; 4) they will not provide editing or critique samples.

- **Phantom conferences** – A non-reputable company is posing as a legitimate publisher. The company announces a conference and solicits attendees to register for the conference in advance. When it comes time for the conference, the attendee find out that the conference never existed.

- **Cyber-squatting** – This is when someone registers, sells, or uses a domain name that uses the name of existing businesses with the intent of trying to sell the names for profit. The cyber-squatter will approach the business and attempt to sell them the domain name back to them for a substantially increased cost. Authors can be particularly vulnerable to cyber-squatting because many either use their names or the title of their URL address. If a cyber-squatter has already secured the name of the author, then he or she might try to get the author to buy the URL back for an unreasonable price. Another downside to this cyber-squatting scam is the author cannot use his or her name as a recognizable URL address.

CASE STUDY:
AVOIDING PUBLISHING SCAMS

Jim Fisher
http://jimfisher.edinboro.edu/scams/
intro.html

Jim Fisher has been investigating the world of bogus literary agents for years. His 1998 and 1999 groundbreaking study of bogus literary agents, book doctors, and vanity publishers, The Fisher Report, helped and informed hundreds of aspiring writers. His investigative journalism has been an aid to the FBI in bringing some of these criminals to justice.

The following information has been reprinted with permission from Jim Fisher's site. For more information or more tips on avoiding scams, visit **http://jimfisher.edinboro.edu/scams/intro.html**.

"Writers in the 1990s have been confronted with changes — revolutions — in the publishing industry that have worked against their interests. Two of these changes, fewer publishing opportunities and a new trend in the way literary agents do business, are connected. Today, most of the literary agencies available to unpublished writers charge fees — up front. These agencies represent a growing number of fee-based enterprises operating within a profession traditionally dependent upon commissions on sales. Although fee-charging agencies present themselves as traditional, commission-based operations, they do not derive significant income through manuscript sales to royalty-paying publishers. These agencies mainly exist on money from unpublished writers. Fee charging is not illegal, and it is not unethical as long as the agent does not mislead the writer or fail to act in the client's best interest. Whether or not the practice is professional or good for writers is another question.

Fee-generated literary services range from one-time reading fees to expensive editing jobs. Many agents who boast that they do not charge reading or evaluation fees, require so-called contract fees for the client's privilege of being represented. A few agencies impose contract fees on a per book basis, renewing the charges annually. Other agents, in addition to reading and representation fees, collect marketing fees to cover the cost of sending manuscripts around to publishers, a practice unheard of ten years ago.

Most of the unpublished writers who contribute to fee-based literary agencies do so because they have been unable to acquire agents who work off commissions. These writers, and there are thousands of them, assume that having a fee-charging agent is preferable to being without an agent. This comes from the widely held belief that one cannot get published without an agent.

People continue to write books as the opportunities to publish them shrink. This has created an enormous backlog of manuscripts, an expanding source of income for enterprising literary agents. These agents trade off writers' hopes and dreams. The rapidly expanding pool of manuscripts also has produced more than a few charlatans, scoundrels, and thieves. It is not surprising that many fee-based agent-client relationships end unhappily. After hope has been replaced by rejection, the client's money has not purchased what he or she really wanted — to be published and to become a respected author. Writers who have paid agents hundreds, and in some cases thousands of dollars, are left feeling angry, depressed, and victimized. They have lost their money, their hope, and their self-respect. Ashamed and embarrassed, some of them, unable to trust anyone, stop writing."

Helping writers beware

Writer Beware® (**www.sfwa.org/for-authors/writer-beware**) is an organization formed to provide "warnings to writers about the schemes, scams, and pitfalls that threaten writers." Other organizations that can help identify scams affecting writers include Preditors and Editors (**www.pred-ed.com**) and Association of Author's Representatives (**www.aar-online.org**).

You cannot avoid every scam there is, but you can protect yourself by using a few general rules. Most people have heard that if something sounds too good to be true, then it probably is. That applies as the first principle to avoid being scammed. If you want someone to assess or edit your work, get it from a known or reliable source. If someone approaches you to assess and edit your work, red flags should be going up. Always ask for references of previous work sold or published, references, and proof of satisfied clients. If the posing agent or publisher claims that information is confidential, it is time to search elsewhere. Remember that reputable publishers pay writers and reputable agents work on commission. If neither of those scenarios is happening, decline and move on.

Chapter 3

Where to Sell What You Write

Before getting into the actual specifics of drafting, crafting, and submitting query letters in the following chapters, it is good to familiarize yourself with the markets to which you want to sell you your work. Knowing where to sell what you write is as important as knowing how to write.

While you are learning about the various markets to which you can present your idea or topic, think of these five questions when looking to query a publication:

- **Audience** – Does my article fit the audience in this market? Does the audience fit to my topic?

- **Market** – Does my idea or topic work best in one particular market over another? Can I cross over markets?

- **Fit** – Does the market or publication publish my type of idea or topic?

- **Acceptance** – Does the market accept freelance work, beginners, or established writers?

- **Payment** – Does the market or publication pay? How well? If they do not pay, what do they offer the writer for compensation?

There are plenty of markets for you to explore that present solid opportunities for publishing your work. The goal in this chapter is to identify a few of the most popular markets in the industry, with the understanding that you, as a professional writer, will take the liberty to do additional research and uncover more viable markets.

Knowing Your Market Options

The previous chapters have already touched on the who, what, and when of the query letter. Now it is time to look at the "to whom" aspect of the querying. It is extremely important to know to whom you will be sending your queries. Tailoring your query letter will depend on the information you uncover about the prospective editor, agent, or publisher. There is a market for almost every topic you can think of, so do not feel like you are limited. If your idea has not been successful in one market, then try another. Between newspapers, trade magazines, e-zines, consumer magazines, and literary journals, your options abound.

This section will showcase the various markets for getting your work published and the best resources to get you started in each.

Consumer magazines

When authors talk about query letters, the most common type that comes to mind is the consumer magazine article. And better yet, consumer magazines such as, *Reader's Digest, Better Homes and Gardens, National Geographic, Good Housekeeping, AARP the Magazine, TIME, Sports Illustrated,* and *Newsweek,* typically pay the best. It is the market that most writers try to break into. Observe the checkout at any local supermarket or convenience store, waiting rooms in doctor and dentist offices, airplanes, hotels, and health clubs. The selection of consumer magazines is endless.

The consumer magazine world has a language and protocol of its own. If you do not master the language and follow the protocol, you will run into many obstacles, which will lead to unnecessary frustration. To increase your odds of getting an assignment, become familiar with the publications you want to solicit. For each magazine of interest to you, study and focus on the following five areas: audience, market, article topic, freelance acceptance, and payment.

After you have studied the magazine and clearly answered those five areas, write to the publication for their writer's guidelines. Many magazines now have online versions and post writer's guidelines online. Start your search on the Web first, and if you cannot find it there, you will need to submit a letter asking for guidelines and enclose a SASE for the response.

The Writer's Market (**www.writersmarket.com**) is the primary industry resource for finding available magazines to query and writer's guidelines for each publication. You can purchase the annual print version of the publication or subscribe online to a monthly, one-year, or two-year membership.

In addition to *Writer's Market* and solicited writer's guidelines direct from the publisher, a few other resources are worth investigating. These resources include:

- *Writers Weekly* (**www.writersweekly.com**) – This is an online, freelance writing e-zine dedicated to bringing industry news and market opportunities to freelance writers.

- *Writer's Digest* (**www.writersdigest.com**) – Since 1920, this industry magazine has been devoted to helping writers develop their craft and hone their publishing skills.

- Worldwide Freelance / Writing Markets (**www.worldwide freelance.com/writing-markets**) – This website was established in 1999 with the goal of publishing a database of freelance markets around the world.

Literary magazines

Unlike consumer magazines, a literary magazine (also known as a literary journal), such as *The New Yorker, The Atlantic, Harper's* Magazine, and the *Harvard Review*, is a publication that focuses strictly on creative writing with an emphasis on projecting a "literary" feel. These magazines often are affiliated with a university or independent literary publisher.

Getting your fiction story or poetry published might be challenging, but it is possible. Although this market struggles to pay substantially, most writers submit for the prestige and look to publishing in literary magazines as a way to jump-start a career in fiction writing. The good news is that literary magazines often welcome and encourage submissions from new writers.

With literary magazines, starting small might be your best bet. Look first at colleges and universities because circulation through these avenues is usually low and regional. This type of publication generally is looking for scholarly essays, stimulating prose, book reviews, poetry, and sometimes art and photography.

Start your research online at the Literary Magazines section of *Poets&Writers* online magazine (**http://www.pw.org/literary_magazines**). *Poets&Writers* has a comprehensive, searchable database that lists more than 500 literary magazines and journals and respective submission guidelines and contact information.

Other notable resources to for finding literary markets include:

- *Publisher's Weekly* (**www.publishersweekly.com**) – This trade magazine is published weekly and is the primary resource for booksellers, librarians, and publishers. The magazine reviews on average 5,000 books annually, with the exception of reference books.

- NewPages (**www.newpages.com/literary-magazines**) – NewPages is an online resource that provides news, information, and guides to independent bookstores, literary magazines, independent publishers, alternative periodicals, and other writing outlets.

- Every Writers Resource (**www.everywritersresource.com/literarymagazines**) – This website is about writers and the passion for publishing and helping others who are dedicated to the same passion.

- Kirkus Reviews (**www.kirkusreviews.com**) – This is a biweekly prepublication newsletter for booksellers, agents, librarians, and publishers that reviews 80 to 100 books per issue. The newsletter reviews nonfiction and fiction works with the exception of poetry, mass-market paperbacks, and children's picture books.

The key to success in this area is to present yourself as a professional and have a system in place for submissions. As with consumer magazine articles, the first step to getting your fiction or poetry published is to start by researching the market. Identify the literary magazines and journals that would be most open to your work. Once you have narrowed that down, go about finding the submission guidelines for the publication. Reference *Writer's Market* at your local bookstore or library, or search online for the publisher or publication website.

Trade journals

Trade journals are publications that focus on a particular "trade" or industry. The pay for getting publishing in a trade journal varies widely. If you have a particular expertise or specialization, you can really stand out in this market. This is a great outlet to establish yourself as an expert in a specific line of business. Just as there are consumer magazines for just about every topic you can think of, there are trade journals for just about every business you can imagine — from house painting trade magazines, such as *Paint Talk* and *PaintPRO* to truck driving trade magazines like *RPM For Truckers* and *Big Rig Owner.*

Writing for trade journals is an easy market to break into. The editors of these journals are often loyal to freelancers. This is primarily because the competition in this market is not as fierce as with consumer magazines, so an editor might not have the luxury of having an overflowing stack of queries from which to choose. As a bonus, writing for trade journals provides a basis for you to cross over your articles to consumer magazines and newspapers. Foremost, you have built your credibility and clips by writing in a specialized market. Also, you might be able to use some of the articles you have written for the trade journals and to tailor them to consumer magazines (if you have retained the appropriate rights to your work). If this is the case, most of the writing is already done; so all you have to do is tweak what you have.

The general writing protocol for trade magazines is to write with a tone of facts and information rather than creativity. People who subscribe to trade journals are looking for relevant, timely information that will help them learn a new skill or provide professional development opportunities. Not often the first market to come to a writer's mind, trade journals can be a lucrative industry, and they offer a variety of other benefits including:

- Providing pertinent news and information for the industry
- Functioning as a marketplace where suppliers can reach users
- Providing a forum for people within the industry to collaborate
- Functioning as a marketplace for ideas
- Functioning as means to provide industry best practices

In most cases, writers who submit articles to a trade journal will not be familiar with the industry. Therefore, it is a good idea for writers who want to pursue the trade journal market to work with a mentor. This mentor should be a member of the industry who can advise on the issues and provide the writer with direction. E-mail makes it easier to approach an industry mentor. Start your search by looking at biographies at the end of articles related to your topic. You also can check with professional associations and networks to find a mentor. Once you have found a potential mentor, craft a professional e-mail, and send it off asking if he or she might consider being your mentor or if he or she can refer someone who might be interested in being a mentor.

Typical resources for locating trade journals include:

- *Oxbridge Directory of Newsletters* (**www.oxbridge.com**) – This directory provides detailed contact information, editorial descriptions, target audiences, and other helpful information for more than 15,000 U.S. and Canadian consumer, business, and association newsletters.

- *Bacon's Newspaper/Magazine Directory* (**us.cision.com**) – This comprehensive directory contains in-depth information about all daily and community newspapers published in the U.S. and Canada, as well as 21,700 trade and consumer magazines, newsletters, and journals.

- *The Encyclopedia of Associations* (**www.gale.cengage.com**) – This directory details more than 162,000 nonprofit member organizations worldwide and provides contact information and descriptions of professional societies, trade associations, fan clubs, and organizations.

These publications are best referenced at your local library. Because the publishers of these directories usually produce these publications annually, it might not be cost effective to purchase them outright. These directories can cost anywhere from $175 to $650, which is much more expensive than the cost of an annual magazine subscription.

Newspapers

Writing for newspapers can be another good way to jump-start your writing career, and the payoff can be great once you have landed a few assignments. The best place to get started with newspaper writing is in your local market. The key to breaking into this market involves a combination of the following:

- **Persistence** – This has been a running theme throughout this book. Get used to it because persistence is the key to when querying your ideas to the editor. Do not take it personally, because editors receive hundreds of queries weekly, sometimes daily if it is a larger circulation.

- **Reliability** – Newspapers work against tight deadlines and have a daily requirement for new, fresh, or up-to-the-minute content. You do not always need to be extra creative or have the most technically sound content. Those who submit on time, on topic, and within the allotted space requirements do the best.

- **Contacts** – This industry is built around your contact list. If you are new to the industry, start networking to build your circle of influence. A phone call or a brief e-mail to the editor of your local or regional paper could open up a world of opportunities. The amount of time it takes to make a connection will be worth it in the end.

The most important lesson you will need to learn when trying to corner the newspaper market is technique: Prepare yourself to work as efficiently as possible against tight deadlines. This type of scenario often produces some of the best writers. Very few environments can force a writer to organize, prioritize, and deliver more than a newspaper. The top industry resources for the newspaper market include:

- *Editor and Publisher*® (**www.editorandpublisher.com**) – The *Editor and Publisher* journal date backs to 1884. It is America's oldest journal, covering all aspects of the newspaper industry from business and newsroom to syndicates and circulation.

- American Society of Newspaper Editors (**www.asne.org**) – Founded in 1922, this nonprofit professional organization focuses on leadership development, innovation, policies, and journalism topics.

- Association of Alternative Newsweeklies (**www.altweeklies.com**) – AAN was founded in Seattle, Washington, in 1978 and is a conglomerate of 130 alt-weekly news organizations covering every major metropolitan area of North America

Here are a few other things to remember if you decide to pursue the newspaper market: Listen, observe, get in the field, and engage in the human experience as much as possible.

Online publications (e-zines)

Online publications, such as *Wired, Slate Magazine,* and *Fireside Chat,* are magazines, journals, or newsletters published on the Internet. The pay for this market varies greatly, but the opportunities are endless, and online publications seem to be more open to freelance writers. It is becoming more acceptable and almost a necessity to have online magazine publishing as part of your clips lineup.

Many novice writers make the mistake of having a more relaxed demeanor when it comes to online publications. Regardless of the medium, writers should approach a publication with the same enthusiasm and professionalism. Editors are editors, both online and off. Just as with any of the other markets, querying might vary greatly depending on the requirements of the publication you approach. Some submission guidelines are more stringent than others.

If you decide to explore the online publishing option, consider these differences between online publications and print publications:

- **Word count might not be limited.** Because online publications do not have space restrictions, articles can be much lengthier than printed counterparts.

- **Keywords will become relevant.** Many online publications will ask you to provide keywords with your article to accommodate search engine optimization.

- **Your target audience is global.** When writing for a print publication, your audience is clearly defined, and you can tailor your query accordingly. However, when it comes to online publications, you are writing for a larger audience that is tuned into the social media trend. You will have to be more media-savvy when you query a publication and be sure to include relevant photos, videos, and sound clips.

- **Keep the reader interested.** The Internet audience reads much differently than the print audience. Online text is scanned more often than read, so you will need to organize your information more succinctly and in small bites.

- **There is no excuse for sloppiness.** Because the Internet is a dynamic environment and content can be updated quickly, it is tempting to relax on fact checking. Whether writing for a print or online publication, keep your facts razor sharp. For example,

Wikipedia is considered an unreliable source for information. Linking an online piece back to Wikipedia or using Wikipedia as a cited source easily can deem your work invalid and unprofessional.

Writing for an online publication is another worthwhile endeavor if you do your homework before querying the publication. The approach to an online publication is the same as a traditional publication. Nevertheless, publishing your work online might require you to be more flexible by writing for different online markets. Start with some of these valuable resources to learn more about getting your work published in online publications:

- *Writer's Digest* University (**www.writersonlineworkshops.com**) – Writer's Digest provides an online, state-of-the-art learning environment dedicated to writing instruction. The web-based university combines world-class writing courses with on-demand training.

- *The Writer Magazine* (**www.writermag.com**) – This monthly industry magazine is considered an essential resource for writers. It provides advice and inspiration for today's writer through feature articles, literary markets, practical solutions, tips from famous authors, and profiles of selected literary magazines.

If you are just starting out and looking for a flexible market, online publishing might be a reliable source. Focus your attention on smaller, local publications (after ensuring they are reputable) and work your way up to the more well-known publications. Build your clip file and your earning potential by writing for a variety of markets and publications.

Pursing International Markets

Many writers shy away from international or foreign markets because they are not familiar or comfortable with international publishing rights. However, with additional research and assistance on international publishing rights, writing for international markets can be a great way to increase your income as a writer.

Repeating the rewards of spreading the news

First rights along with serial rights in different foreign territories can dramatically improve your writing income and your writing time. You can write an article, nonfiction book, or novel once and then promote and sell it in an international market.

Is translation an option?

As you are deciding whether you want to write in the international arena, you also will need to determine if you intend to write in the country's native language or in English. Writing in English has an advantage because it is understood in many countries, and translators are easily accessible. This makes English a good base language from which to work.

If you decide to write in English, here are a few points to keep in mind:

- **Remove errors.** Ensure that your work is free of errors, which is something you should do regardless of the audience. Analyze the grammar closely, particularly for subject-verb agreements, as these can translate over incorrectly into other languages.

- **Write clearly.** Your writing, especially technical or scientific information, needs to be as clear and succinct as possible. A perfect example of this is "warning messages" in assembly instructions or medical indications. Unclear descriptions can lead to serious, unwanted outcomes.

- **Be consistent.** Use consistent terminology and grammar. Changing terms and using colloquial phrases lead to confusion. The goal is to help readers find information quickly and recognize terms and ideas they have seen before.

- **Make it translatable.** Write your content so it will be easily translatable for the international market. Making your article or book translatable can be accomplished by following the tips mentioned previously. If you reduce and remove errors in spelling, facts, and grammar; if you write clearly and concisely; and if you are consistent, chances are your work will be easier to translate.

There are numerous things to consider before venturing into the international market. If you are serious about pursuing this option, start your research with these best international writing markets:

- Worldwide Freelance Writer (**www.worldwidefreelance.com**) – Worldwide Freelance Writer is a website established in 1999 with the goal of publishing relevant information about freelance writing markets around the world. The Worldwide Freelance Writer database lists more than 2,400 publications from all over the globe.

- Publist by Infotrieve (**www.publist.com**) – Publist has a large database containing more than 150,000 magazines, journals, newsletters, and various other periodicals that provide document delivery, procurement, and staffing solutions for libraries, information managers, and product and marketing managers.

Other things to consider

If you think you are ready to expand your reach beyond what you already know, international markets might be the choice for you. The benefits to writing for overseas publications include: new opportunities, increasing your income, adding clips, and increasing your reputation on a global scale. You will find advice from both sides of the fence regarding the ease of entering the international market. However, by taking advantage of the resources outlined above and using the following tips, you can strategically entrench yourself in the global writing arena:

Research the various markets. Read about the countries you would like to target. Determine whether they will accept English submissions. It might be easier to enter a British or Australian market than an Italian or Chinese market. Once you have determined which country to pursue, hop online, and start finding publications related to the country and the type of stories you want to write. Libraries are an excellent resources to research global markets. Many libraries have subscriptions to international databases, magazines, and newspapers.

Write for the location. It is extremely important that you develop not just good topics, but also relevant topics when addressing an international audience. It can be a challenge to start thinking globally when you have been accustomed to pitching nationally or even locally. Your article topic on the best sites to visit in Colorado obviously would not be relevant or suitable for an Ethiopian reader. However, if you have written work for a publication in the United States that you believe would be suitable for an international audience, then use it again. Repackage it, and market it to a comparable publication abroad.

You will be playing by different rules. The primary difference between U.S. and international markets will be in grammar and style. A classic example that is easy to understand is the difference between American English and the Queens English in the U.K. Words in American English, such as favor, color, and neighbor, will add a "u" in the Queens English and become favour, colour, and neighbour. Another example of a slight variation between these two countries is the use of words in American English such as elevator, line, and apartment. In the U.K., these words would be lift, queue, and flat, respectively.

Other things to consider when writing for a global audience are colloquialisms, humor, and sarcasm. International audiences do not always understand American humor, even if the humor relates to the same product or service or is addressing the same target market. A way to overcome this particular hurdle is to communicate effectively and often with your editor. It will be extremely helpful if you take the time to explain American cultures, dialects, colloquialisms, humor, and sarcasm with your editor so he or she can see if there is a comparable phrase or word for it in his or her native language.

Negotiate payment before assignment. If possible, try to negotiate the form of payment you will receive before accepting the assignment. Although it is becoming easier to receive payments from abroad, you will still need to be aware of bank fees and exchange rates.

- International money transfers can be a convenient form of payment, but bank fees vary greatly; so do your homework before opening an account.

- PayPal (**www.paypal.com**) is a free and easy form of payment for national and international works. Fees through PayPal (e.g., 1.9–2.9 percent +.30 USD per transaction) tend to be lower than bank fees, but research PayPal's offerings before you make your decision.

- Western Union (**www.westernunion.com**) now provides online accounts from which you can transfer and receive funds. However, fees with Western Union can be relatively high compared to other services available on the market.

Modern technologies, such as the Internet, e-mail, satellite, cable TV, 3G, and 4G networking have facilitated a bridge for writers to tap into international markets more easily than ever before. You have the option to write for publications in countries you have never visited, which will expand your research and your sphere of influence.

You easily can acquire an in-depth knowledge of the marketplace by devoting an hour or two each week to do research and study the markets discussed above. This due diligence quickly will be rewarded with the increase in opportunities where you can present your ideas. And while you are conducting your research on the various markets, remember the five topics to consider: audience, market, fit, acceptance, and payment.

Now that you have some valuable information about the potential markets for your queries, it is time to learn about the ways of the query letter. Before actually crafting your query, you will learn how to decipher submission guidelines, how to add creativity to your query letter, and what other bits and pieces you can add to your query to capture the editor's interest.

Query Letter Modus Operandi

lthough the query letter must be professional and create a great first impression, it can, and should, demonstrate creativity and a personal style. To be a successful published writer, you must master the ways of the query submission. This chapter will discuss how to decipher writer's guidelines, develop your personal style, balance your writing tone, and become familiar with the query letter modus operandi.

Even before you spend any time on query letter modus operandi, you must devote an hour or two a week to conducting market research on your area of interest. After you have identified the potential markets (health, finances, business, cooking, fiction, self-help, women's interest, boating, golfing, men's health, etc.) to which you are planning to submit, gather and read at least one sample of the publication to which you intend to query. Spend time studying the publication and learning everything you can about it.

Study the format, the advertisement (if applicable), the editor's page, the masthead, and any other aspect of the publication that will give you an indication of its personality. Once you have a better understanding of the tone and style of the publication, you are ready to work on your query letter.

Deciphering Writer's Guidelines

It is critical that you learn to decipher and follow the writer's guidelines for each publication. Anything less is considered inexperienced and un-professional. The guidelines are the rules of the publication. The primary purpose is to help writers determine whether they want to approach the publication and how. Depending on the source you use, writer's guidelines can vary. Fortunately, the guidelines contain the same information; it just may be presented in a different order.

Sample guideline sections

To give you an idea of what to expect, the following elements are being used as examples from the *Writer's Market*, which is the primary resource for magazines, trade publications, and journals.

- **Point of contact** – You are looking for the person to whom to send the query. Some entries include the publisher and editor at the beginning and then provide another name as the point of contact. When you are not sure to whom you should submit the query, look at the masthead of the publication, and query the assistant editor or someone comparable.

- **How to contact** – Mail, fax, or e-mail, which one is the best way to send your query? Do not assume that every editor would gladly accept an e-mail submission. Look to the guidelines to be sure. If it is not specified, then default to either fax or e-mail to save on postage costs. Not only is this section about how to submit the query, but it also indicates whether to submit a query or a complete manuscript. If the guidelines do not specify either way, be safe and send a query.

- **Type of material accepted** – Read this section carefully. Publications often will list the various types of materials they do not accept rather than what they will accept. If followed, this guideline can set you apart from the competition.

- **Percentage of freelance material accepted** – You want to look for publications that have a high percentage of freelance material, usually about 80 percent or more. This means your chances of being accepted are higher than publications with a lower percentage. You still can query publications with lower freelance acceptance percentages; it just means your chances of securing an assignment are significantly reduced.

- **Publication frequency** – It is important to know how often the publication publishes an issue. You want to ensure your query is relevant to a particular topic, season, or issue. Knowing the frequency of a publication allows you present a timely query, which shows the editor you are familiar with the publication.

- **Pay rates** – On average and at a glance, you can get a feel for what the publication pays. *Writer's Market* rates the publication on a scale of one to four. A single dollar sign means a low-paying market, and four dollar signs mean a high-paying market. You will also see dollar ranges such as $250 to $500, which for the novice writer might seem like a dream. But be selective; getting paid $250 for a 2,000-word article might not be worth the time you put into acquiring the assignment.

- **Payment terms** – Become familiar with the two types of payment terms, which are "pays upon acceptance" and "pays upon publication." If you have the option to negotiate this, choose pays upon acceptance because, typically, you will receive payment sooner. Acceptance means the editor likes your article and will use when it comes times for publication, which can happen several weeks to months later.

- **Rights purchased** – Reference Chapter 2 to refresh your memory about the different types of rights a publication can purchase. This will be an important section to reference when you are making your selection of publications to query.

- **Photo submissions** – Submitting photos with your query can improve your chances of acceptance, but only if you follow the publication guidelines. This section provides specific details on how to and what kind of photos to submit including photo size, resolution, rights, and format.

- **Columns or departments** – Review several copies of the publications you intend to query. You might notice that many of the publications divide the content into several columns and departments. Check this section carefully to see if a particular column or department accepts freelance pieces. You might find that the column you wanted to pitch to might be slotted for a regular industry expert.

- **Editor's notes** – If you want more hints on how to approach an editor, spend time reading the editor's notes. This will help you tailor your query even more, or it can help you rule out the publication before spending time developing the query.

- **Byline or bio credits** – A byline or bio credit provides additional credibility for your clip file and is another way for you to promote your business, products, or services. Although bylines are commonplace, confirm that the publication offers a byline or bio; it can enhance your prestige and add to your credentials when submitting queries.

- **Lead time** – This time will vary greatly depending on the size of the publication and circulation. The larger the publication, the longer the lead time, which is the amount of time an editor needs to review manuscripts for a specific issue. For example, there usually will be a cutoff date for submitting manuscripts intended for a particular month. For query letters, it is best to try to submit your ideas well in advance of the publication's editorial calendar, particularly if your topic is seasonal.

- **Acceptance of simultaneous submissions** – You are engaging in simultaneous submissions (SimSubs) when you query several agents, editors, or publishers at the same time. Some publications refuse to review your query if they know it is a simultaneous submission. It often can create confusion and complications when it comes time for publication. Be careful about the publications that accept simultaneous submissions. Say you submitted your work to two publications, and one publication wants to publish your piece. Unfortunately, you have already agreed to have it published with the other publication, or the publication already ran the piece. Simultaneous submissions can make it difficult for you to refuse an editor. When you sent out simultaneous submissions, you will most likely offer exclusive rights to the publication that accepts your topic. If more than one publication wants to use your piece, you will have to choose which one and withdraw your submission from the others. It also makes it harder for an editor to secure new ideas from you. Inadvertently, you have created a more competitive environment, which can discourage editors. Writers and editors have had differing opinions on SimSubs for decades. For writers, simultaneous submissions offer the increased chance of getting your work published quicker. However, most editors do not like simultaneous submissions for the simple reason that they make their buying decision based on how a piece will fit in with a specific theme for an issue. Once the editor makes plans for a story, they do not like the idea that a piece is now unavailable because it has been sold to someone else.

- **Requesting a sample copy** – Whether the publication provides a free sample copy or not, you will need to send a self-addressed, stamped envelope (SASE) along with your request. Publications will not pay the postage to send you a sample copy. Check this section carefully because many publications charge a fee for sample copies. If the publication has a website, check to see if you can find a sample copy there and spare yourself the postage.

- **Kill fee** – A kill fee is not as bad as it sounds. It can actually be an advantage for you, especially because you put the time and effort into finishing the assignment. A kill fee generally represents 25 to 50 percent of the original payment promised. You would receive this if the article you wrote was scheduled for publication but then was canceled. If the article was canceled, the writer receives the kill fee regardless of whether the payment was on acceptance or publication.

- **Response time** – A good piece of information to know after you submit your query is how long you will have to wait before hearing the news. Similar to lead times, response times will vary depending on the publication size. The larger the publication, the longer the response time. If you have not heard back from the publication after the response time has elapsed, it is okay to follow up.

- **Acceptance of reprints** – The use of reprints is specific to each publication. Reprints are advantageous for the writer, but some publications do not use them at all. Although the price for reprints is reduced dramatically from the original fee, it still can be a profitable outlet because you do not have to do any rewriting.

- **Word count** – If a publication has different departments, they might require varying word counts. You can easily determine the average word count for each section of the publication by investigating a few issues. Generally, feature articles can run between 1,000 and 6,000 words, whereas editorials between 500 and 750.

- **General info** – This is a great section to reference when you want to learn more about the publication. It often can shed some light on what the publication is all about without you having to purchase a copy from the library, newsstand, or send off for a sample copy.

- **Founding date** – The longer the publication has been around, the better your chances are for getting an assignment. That is not to say newly established publications do not provide opportunity. Unfortunately, many new publications have to deal with the reputation of underpaying freelancers or not paying at all. It is a generalization, but often, the more established publications typically are more stable and pose less risk for you.

- **Circulation** – This is the number of readers a potential advertiser could reach by advertising in the publication. This number is important to you because it can indicate a couple of things: It can help you determine whether the publication is regional or national, and it can give you an idea of pay rate and prestige.

Do not let this list overwhelm you. The more familiar you become with the terminology, the easier it will be for you find what you are looking for. Writer's guidelines exist to increase your chances of getting published because editors easily can weed out the writers who submit queries that do not follow guidelines. Another reason these guidelines exists is to prevent you from wasting your time. It takes more time to try to mind-read a publication's needs than it does to look up and follow the instructions.

Adding Creativity to Your Query Letters

Some writers have a difficult time imagining that they can be creative when writing query letters. Although there are protocols to follow when crafting and submitting query letters to editors, agents, and publishers, there is nothing that says you cannot be creative in your presentation.

A common misconception is that the only creativity allowed in writing is in fiction novels or poetry. Writers often think that somehow in these writing genres, the writer is allowed to be more expressive and have more creative liberty. You can add creativity to your query letters by selecting tantalizing words, providing colorful descriptions, adding relevant quotes, and sharing personal anecdotes.

The approach you take in developing the query easily can set you apart from another query from a writer who stuck strictly to the rules by paying close attention to the writer's guidelines and submission instructions. The tone you use in your query can exude creativity as long as it is appropriate for the publication. The way you present your information in the query, whether in a bulleted or numbered list, a true-false quiz, or bolding and italics for emphasis, can demonstrate your ability to be creative in your approach to communicating your idea or story.

Here are a few essential tips for adding some creative elements to your query letter and increasing your chances of landing an assignment:

- **Tailor the content to the publications mission.** After researching the publication, identify the slogan, tagline, or mission statement. Include that somewhere in your letter to show subtly that you have done your homework, and you have become familiar with them.

- **Add a thought-provoking quote.** Whether it is a quote or a statistic, start your query letter with something that will provoke thought in the reader. Ensure the quote is relevant to the target audiences' needs and to the pitch. Adding a quote or statistics is an effective strategy that immediately can attract the attention of an editor, publisher, or agent.

- **Add testimonials.** Another effective approach for adding creativity to your query letter is to add a testimonial from an industry expert, another author, or a person who has had experience with the topic you are pitching. The purpose of the testimonial is to support the claims you make in your query. It provides additional evidence to why you are the best candidate to handle the assignment.

- **Do not forget the P.S.** It has been shown that many letter readers start with the postscript section. It is one of the most important elements of a letter, and it draws the most attention. It is not a common element of a query letter, but you can decide if it will add or detract from your query. If you decide to use the P.S. section, make it something important and relevant. Do not waste the reader's time on impertinent information in this section.

- **Create your own tagline.** You will learn more about personal branding in Chapter 14. But for now, think about a personal slogan or tagline to add to your correspondence (business cards, stationery, website, social media sites, etc.) that will help set you apart from other writers. This will become part of your professional persona and branding strategy; it ultimately will help build and solidify your reputation as a professional writer.

Sample Query Letter:
Humorous Paranormal

Dear Ms. Faust,

Straight-laced preschool teacher, Lizzie Brown, never lies, never cusses, and doesn't really care much for surprises. When her long-lost Grandma Gertie shows up on her doorstep riding a neon pink Harley Davidson wearing a "kiss my asphalt" T-shirt and hauling a carpet bag full of Smucker's jars filled with roadkill magic, Lizzie doesn't think her life could get any stranger. That is until her hyperactive terrier starts talking and an ancient demon decides to kill her from his perch on the back of her toilet.

Lizzie learns she's a demon slayer, fated to square off with the devil's top minion in, oh about two weeks. Sadly, she's untrained, unfit, and under attack. Grandma's gang of 50-something biker witches promises to whip Lizzie into shape, as long as she joins them out on the road. But Lizzie wants nothing to do with all this craziness. She simply wants her normal life back. When she accidentally botches the spell meant to protect her, she only has one choice – trust the utterly delicious but secretive man who claims to be her protector.

Dimitri Kallinikos has had enough. Cursed by a demon centuries ago, his formerly prominent clan has dwindled down to himself and his younger twin sisters, both of whom are now in the coma that precedes certain death. To break the curse, he must kill the demon behind it. Dimitri needs a slayer. At long last, he's found Lizzie. But how do you talk a girl you've never met into going straight to Hell? Lie (and hope she forgives you). Dimitri

decides to pass himself off as Lizzie's fated protector in order to gain her trust and guide her
toward this crucial mission. But will his choice
to deceive her cost them their lives, or simply
their hearts?

THE ACCIDENTAL DEMON SLAYER is an 85,000 word humorous paranormal. I'm a member of RWA and the partial
manuscript placed first in the Windy City RWA's Four
Seasons contest. The judge for that contest, Leah
Hultenschmidt of Dorchester Publishing, has just
requested the full. As an advertising writer, I've
won multiple awards for my work in radio dialogue.

I would be happy to send you the complete manuscript. Thank you for your consideration and time.

Sincerely,
Angie Fox Gwinner

Be careful not to sound too gimmicky when you are trying to add some creativity to your query letter. You want the publisher, editor, and agent to take you seriously; you want them to be confident that they will be working with a professional.

What Else to Include With Your Query

Aside from the standard query letter and self-addressed stamped envelope (SASE), you may want to add something extra and different for the editor, agent, or publisher to think about. Some of these additions can be considered eye candy to break up the monotony of an editor's engulfing query pile. When crafting your query to a specific publication, consider including the following with it:

Photos, graphics, and illustrations

Even if you do not have the photos or graphics at the time of submission, it is still a good option to offer to send them as soon as you secure them. You will save the editor valuable time by doing the research to find which illustrations, graphics, or photos would complement your article idea.

Pull-quotes and sidebars

Recommending sidelights, sidebars, and pull-quotes is a sign that you understand readers. These can function as selling tools or factoids to help the reader gain a quick understanding of the article idea before delving deep into the content. Suggesting these small enhancements sometimes can earn you more money for the article. Remember, it is all about saving the editor time.

Clips when requested

If a publication request clips, then send them along. Clips are great way to substantiate your credentials and provide proof that you can do what you say you can do. If an editor tells you not to send clips, and you really want to highlight them in some way, then you can mention them in your query. Just remember to be brief and succinct about it.

```
Sample Query Letter:
Cozy Mystery

Dear Ms. Faust,

I enjoyed meeting you at the conference in Austin
this past weekend. As I mentioned, I have had my
eye on BookEnds for quite some time; when I discov-
ered you would be at the conference, I knew I had
to attend. We met during the final pitch session and
discussed how the series I am working on might fit in
with your current line of mystery series. Per your
request, I have enclosed a synopsis and the first
```

three chapters of *MURDER ON THE ROCKS*, an 80,000-word cozy mystery that was a finalist in this year's Writers' League of Texas manuscript contest and includes several bed-and-breakfast recipes.

Thirty-eight-year-old Natalie Barnes has quit her job, sold her house, and gambled everything she has on the Gray Whale Inn on Cranberry Island, Maine. But she's barely fired up the stove when portly developer Bernard Katz rolls into town and starts mowing through her morning glory muffins. Natalie needs the booking, but Katz is hard to stomach – especially when he unveils his plan to build an oversized golf resort on top of the endangered tern colony next door. When the town board approves the new development, not only do the terns face extinction, but also Natalie's Inn might just follow along. Just when Natalie thinks she can't face more trouble, she discovers Katz's body at the base of the cliff and becomes the No. 1 suspect in the police's search for a murderer. If Natalie doesn't find the killer fast, she stands to lose everything – maybe even her life.

I am a former pubic relations writer, a graduate of Rice University, a member of the Writers' League of Texas, and founder of the Austin Mystery Writers critique group. I have spent many summers in fishing communities in Maine and Newfoundland and escape to Maine as often as possible. The second Gray Whale Inn mystery, *DEAD AND BERRIED*, is currently in the computer.

If you would like to see the manuscript, I can be reached at (phone number). Thank you for your time and attention; I look forward to hearing from you soon.

Sincerely,
Karen Swartz MacInerney

These type of extras sent along with your query can add significant weight and substance. Editors like to have some variety in their day and what better way to give it to them than by adding a few of these extra special touches to your submission?

Ideally, you are developing a solid image or impression of what it takes to develop a good query letter. Like good writing, a query letter evokes a sense of urgency and clarity. It does not reek of boredom, and yet it gets straight to the business at hand. By now, you understand that the query letter should be a passionate sales pitch that does not overtly send the message that you are either bragging or begging. For a query letter to be effective, it will need to follow a few basics: It needs to sound interesting; it should never be longer than a page; it should not be about you except when you are briefly stating your credentials; and it should not state the obvious.

Now that you have read about some of the basics of query letter modus operandi, continue to the next chapter to learn about the similarities and differences between the various types of query letters.

Chapter 5

Query Letters, Compared and Contrasted

query letter is your basic introduction to an editor, agent, or publisher. Although the approach and the format of the letter follow the same general theme, querying to an editor of a national magazine will have a few different aspects than querying to a book publisher.

The rules of the game are pretty much the same regardless of the industry you approach. Editors are always looking for professionalism, experience, and fresh ideas.

Components of the Article Query

There is no magic formula for getting your work published in magazines, but there is an expected format to follow for queries. Use a standard business letter format. Your name and full contact information should be at the top either centered or right justified. The contact person's full name, title, and contact information should be just below yours, left justified.

This single-page letter uses the following four-paragraph structure:

- **Paragraph 1: The hook** – The hook is an opening paragraph that piques the editor's interest in the idea you are pitching.

- **Paragraph 2: Supporting details** – The supporting details answers the five Ws (who, what, when, where, and why).

- **Paragraph 3: Qualifications** – This paragraph will focus on your qualifications to write the piece you are proposing. It does not have to be lengthy; it merely needs to explain why you are the right person for the assignment.

- **Paragraph 4: Closing remarks and thank you** – Generally considered the closer, this paragraph needs to tie up the loose ends. It should address how soon you can write the piece, and it should mention that you are enclosing a SASE.

Sample Query Letter: Historical Children's Fiction

Dear Ms. Adams,

I attended the SCBWI National Conference in New York in February and was delighted to hear of your interest in historical fiction. Please find the first three chapters of SELLING HOPE, a historical novel, attached.

Hope McDaniels wants to break free from the vaudeville circuit, and she sees opportunity blazing toward her in the nighttime sky: Halley's Comet. On May 19, 1910, Earth will pass through the tail of Halley's Comet. Many believe this to be the end of days. Hope believes this to be her jackpot. The passing of Earth through the tail of Halley's Comet has been described as the world's first case of mass hysteria. The "abundant" media, combined with the clashing of holdover Victorian sensibilities with Industrial-age objectivity, created a spark that made May 1910 one very interesting month.

My middle-grade historical novel, *Autumn Winifred Oliver Does Things Different*, will be released this October by Delacorte Press. I've also penned more than a dozen activity books for children, many for licensed characters like Scooby-Doo, Lisa Frank, PowerPuff Girls, and Holly Hobbie. I won the *Highlights Magazine* Pewter Plate award for Outstanding Arts Feature for "They'll Be Back," a story that appeared in the June 2005 issue of *Highlights*. My work has also appeared in *Guideposts for Kids* and *Spider Magazine*.

After reviewing your website, I was excited to see that your goal is to represent authors, not books. In that regard, I feel our goals are similar, and hope that we'll have the opportunity to work together.

All the best,
Kristin O'Donnell Tubb

The quickest way to find the possible magazine markets to break into is by referencing *Writer's Market*. This is the top industry resource for writers looking for writing markets. For general markets, you will want to reference general consumer magazines. For more specialized or technical content, a good place to start will be trade magazines.

Querying is a craft, and you will need to discover your own style with words. This process takes time and initiative; it is evolutionary. You must accept the fact that your queries will be rejected, and you will need to be persistent. With each query, strive to learn why it missed the mark and what you can do to improve the next time around.

Components of the Newspaper Query

There are thousands if not millions of newspapers circulating, all of which require a large amount of content. Most of the current staff of these newspapers cannot fulfill the large content requirement, so chances are very good that they are accepting submissions from writers, experienced and novice alike. Newspapers reach a far greater audience than most publications; so, they are always looking for fresh material every day.

An advantage to querying newspapers is that simultaneous submissions to different newspapers are not frowned upon. The rule is to submit to newspapers that are 100 miles or more apart. This is because most newspapers are local — with the exception of national newspapers — therefore, running the same or similar article in two different newspapers more than 100 miles away from each other does not cause too much threat to the editor and publisher.

The advantage to you as a writer can mean making money several times for the same article. That is strategic querying at its best. In addition, newspaper articles can be used as reprint material for trade publications, magazines, or even books, as long as the information is relevant.

As you have been learning, the first step is to research the publication and study the writer's guidelines. Unfortunately, newspapers rarely have guidelines. But that should not prevent you from picking up the newspaper and dissecting the masthead. The masthead is the section that identifies the editor-in-chief, editor, assistant editor, publisher, staff members, and contributing writers. This information should provide a point of contact for submitting your query. Without writer's guidelines, it can be difficult to know which section to pitch.

Because newspaper articles usually run fewer than 1,000 words, many editors will ask that you send the article along with the query, which means your query letter will function as a cover letter to the article.

- **Improve your chances with a local slant.** Your chances for publication greatly improve when you write your story for the local audience. This does not apply to national newspapers such as the *Wall Street Journal* or *USA Today*. However, if you are just breaking into the market and have decided to start with your local or regional newspaper, focus on slanting your topic to something that will resonate with local readers. For example, if your specialty is in the food industry, you might suggest an article such as "Five Things You Probably Did Not Know About Peaches" and recommend running it during the city's annual Peach Festival.

- **Tie it in to a current event.** Search the headlines of national and local news to see what types of current events are circulating. Try to tie in your article topic with one of these current events, a particular holiday, or a national event. A great resource to use to find national holidays and events is *Chase's Calendar of Events* (**www.mhprofessional.com/templates/chases**), which is a comprehensive and authoritative reference guide on worldwide events, holidays, festivals, anniversaries, famous birthdays, and more.

- **Enhance your story with photos.** Although photos are not mandatory, they can definitely enhance your story. If you have a decent photo to offer with your pitch, be sure to state that in your query. Do not automatically send in your photo with the query, because you most likely will not get it back. When you submit your query, mention that photos are available upon request.

Sample Query Letter: Local Newspaper Query

Dear Ms. Hammond,

Amanda Smith helped to deliver her mother's baby in their home last week while waiting for paramedics to show up. Amanda is 7 years old.

Mary Smith was not expecting to go into delivery five weeks before her due date while alone at home with her daughter. Amanda rose to the challenge, however, by not only calling 911, but also delivering her new little sister after being told that an ambulance would not reach them in time. Following the instructions of a 911 operator, Amanda even tied off her sister's umbilical cord. Newborn Sarah Smith is thriving, and the happy parents are amazed at how Amanda responded to the situation.

Would you be interested in the attached article about Amanda's experience with delivering her sister along with her mother Mary's take on the event? I currently work as an English teacher at Local High School and my article "Off to College… at 15" was published in *The Local Tribune* last year.

Thank you for your time and consideration.

Sincerely,
Michelle Pearson

Writing articles for newspapers can be one of the easiest markets to break into. If you are still lacking confidence about submitting query letters to newspapers, you can submit an article to the newspaper's special section that openly solicits readers' stories. These sections are usually the letter to the editor, opinion, parenting, traveling, or personal interest. Once you become comfortable in your local market, look to expand into regional markets and ultimately, national markets. All the while, you will be building a strong clip file.

Components of the Nonfiction Book Query

The book query will be an important tool if you intend to write a nonfiction book. Some publishers might skip the book query request and go directly to the book proposal. If this is not specified in the writer's guidelines, then you can find out either from your agent (if you are working with one) or the editor will tell you in their response to your query. If that is the case, then revisit the information covered in the previous section. But for now, this section will focus on the components of the nonfiction book query, which is different from a query for a fiction book or a novel. That will be discussed next.

Your nonfiction book query will break down into a paragraph structure that is similar to the article query. You will notice, however, that there is an additional paragraph required for the nonfiction book query. The summary, the fourth paragraph of the query, provides insight into how the book will be structured, or it can speak to the type of audience to which the book caters. This paragraph may vary in its contents, but the intent is to provide information to the editor about how the book will be received.

This one-page query will include the following paragraph structure:

- **Paragraph 1: The hook** – Instead of crafting the hook for the editor's sake, a hook for the nonfiction book query will be tailored more toward what the reader might see on the book cover. This paragraph will set the stage for the tone, style, and message of the book.

- **Paragraph 2: Supporting details** – Similar to the supporting details in an article query, this paragraph for the nonfiction book query will provide information on how you plan to research and develop the content for the book. The real details (i.e. facts and figures) are not as important as stressing to the editor your approach for developing a story around the hook. Those specific details will be needed for the book proposal.

- **Paragraph 3: The summary** – This is the component of the nonfiction book query that differs from the article query. It is the one paragraph where you can be a little more creative. In this paragraph, you want to show the editor, agent, or publisher that you have put more thought into how this book will be marketed, whether it will have spin-offs (e.g., sequels to the current title, publishing additional books, or producing an accompanying newsletter), who will buy the book, or if the book will be a good fit for the publisher's new series. Provide enough information for the editor or publisher to want to know more. This will prompt a request for a full book proposal.

- **Paragraph 4: Qualifications** – Once again, it is time to impress the editor with your experience and expertise. And if you cannot impress with published clips or relevant credentials, at least present a strong, solid case for why you are the perfect candidate to write the book.

- **Paragraph 5: Closing remarks and thank you** – Similar to the article query, keep your closing remarks and thank you short and professional. After thanking the agent or editor for taking the time to review your query, be sure to mention that you have a full proposal available upon request.

Sample Query Letter: Narrative Nonfiction

Dear Mr. Mosely:

It was a pleasure meeting you at the Writer's Digest Conference last month and learning that you represent historical nonfiction.

There's one oddity of western history; it is that it is often difficult to tell the difference between the good guys and the bad guys.

Billy the Kid and Pat Garrett straddle the line between good and evil… and misunderstood. History tells the story of William H. Bonnie as a homicidal psychopath and Sheriff Pat Garrett as the dirty coward who shot him in the back. But that's not the real story. *ETERNAL DESPERADO* will explore the myth and the folklore surrounding these two men and analyze the crimes of the Lincoln County War in the context of the political corruption of the New Mexico Territory in the late 1800s.

The book will reveal how the legends were deliberately manufactured and manipulated to divert attention from larger crimes committed by politicians and powerful businessmen. *ETERNAL DESPERADO* is a 90,000-word narrative nonfiction that will set the record straight and introduce readers to the outlaws and lawmen of the Old West. These stories are as relevant today as they were 125 years ago.

I am the author of 12 published books, recipient of the Western History Alive honor and the award for Outstanding Achievement in Western History, and I hold a master's degree in history of the Southwest. I write the popular blog "Western Outlaws and Lawmen," which receives more than 50,000 visitors each month. I also host the weekly television program "Welcome to the Old West" that is syndicated nationally, and I lecture at universities throughout the U.S. and Europe, speaking to more than 250,000 people each year.

Thank you for taking the time to ready my query. I have a completed book proposal and manuscript available for your review, should you be interested in the project. I look forward to the possibility of working together.

Sincerely,
Thomas Tyler

Finding markets in which to submit your query is best done by visiting your local bookstore to scan the sections where your book would fit. After you identify the market, reference *Writer's Market* and the Internet to determine what writer's guidelines to secure and learn about the publisher's guidelines. Get to know more about the publisher by browsing the website and finding out whether the submission guidelines are available online. Once you receive the guidelines, follow the direction carefully, submit your professional query or proposal using the techniques you have learn throughout this book, and send it off. Waiting can be the hardest part, but if you want to find out what you can do while you are waiting to hear back, skip ahead to Chapter 13.

Components of the Novel Query

Can you imagine drudging your way through hundreds of 60,000-word novels to determine whether it is a good story or provides interest for your readers? Neither can editors, agents, or publishers. That is why the novel query is as important, if not more so, as the article and nonfiction book query. Unless the publisher's guidelines specifically say you should not send a query, make it a point to always do so. Your query letter is the first introduction to the agent, acquisition editor, or publisher. It is your chance to make a great first impression that leaves the editor wanting more.

The novel query is a one-page letter written to answer one simple question: What is the book about? Another element that sets the novel query apart from the nonfiction book and article query is synopsis. The synopsis is a condensed version of your entire book. It does not provide all the details your book ultimately will; however, it demonstrates to the editor how the book's plot will develop, and it will showcase your writing ability, style, and voice.

The novel synopsis will be covered more in-depth in the next section, but for now this section will focus on the components of the novel query:

- **The target** – At the top of your novel query letter, you should have the name, title (optional), and contact information of a target literary agent, editor, or publisher. This person, ideally, should be someone who has recently handled or specialized in managing books similar to the one you are proposing.

- **The grabber** – The grabber is exactly what it sounds like: the element that will grab your attention. What grabs your attention when you are browsing the shelves of your local bookstore? You might notice the cover first, but you also notice the title of the book. This is what you want to include as your grabber in the query letter. To improve the grabber, add a subtitle or hook to the title.

- **The "wow" factor** – Use this section of the letter to "wow" your reader. It should not be used to provide details about how you will develop the plot or the characters. Write this section to match the style and tone of the genre for which you will be writing the book.

- **Stress to impress** – Now that you have the editor's attention, stress some additional facts, statistics, or pertinent research information to beef up your image and show the editor that you have done your homework.

- **Qualifications** – Provide appropriate and relevant qualifications that clearly show why you are the ideal person to write this book.

- **The closing and P.S.** – Close your letter respectfully and encourage the agent, publisher, or editor to respond by noting that you can provide sample chapters or a completed manuscript upon request.

Sample Query Letter: Urban Fantasy

Dear Ms. Pepus,

I found your website on WritersDigest.com and thought you may be interested in my novel. After reviewing your wish list, I thought you might enjoy this slice of urban fantasy.

In brief, Shiarra Waynest is a private detective working in an alternate, present-day New York City. Less than ten years ago, creatures such as vampires, werewolves, and magi (collectively called "Others") came out of the closet and are now

vying for equal rights and the same protection under the law as any other human being. As most any
human would be, Shiarra is trying to come to grips
with these changes while still making ends meet.
A mage contacts Shiarra and essentially gives her
an offer she can't resist. For a good sum of money
that just may be enough to save her failing PI
firm, she agrees to work with a coven of magi to
find where a local vampire, Alec Royce, has hidden
a powerful artifact.

What Shiarra doesn't count on is the depth of corruption in the mage coven, how the vampire Royce
is not what he seems, and having to deal with and
solve the murder of supernaturals that seem to come
in contact with the focus. It is primarily about
her getting in way over her head, far too fast, and
having to find a way to save herself, and later her
friends from the corruption of the focus.

HUNTED BY THE OTHERS is an 83,000-word work of
mystery/urban fantasy with a touch of humor. I can
supply a full transcript at request. This is my
first novel, and I anticipate being able to expand
into a series.

Thank you very much for taking the time to read my
query. I have included the first couple of chapters
for your consideration below. I hope to hear from
you soon.

Best regards,
Jess Haines

The novel synopsis

If you accomplished your goal with the novel query letter, then you will be
happy to start preparing the next piece of the puzzle for the editor, agent,
or publisher who has requested a synopsis. The sales pitch, the query letter,

got you in the door. The synopsis is the final tool that will help you close the sale and, eventually, lead the reviewer to request the entire book.

The novel synopsis is a condensed version of your 400-page novel. You have to tell the whole story in ten to 25 pages. The synopsis offers you a chance to describe your book to the editor, publisher, or agent as accurately, completely, and dramatically as you can. There are no hard and fast rules or guidelines to follow when preparing your synopsis. However, do keep these few tips and hints in mind as you proceed:

- Detail each chapter of the novel.

- Content should be written in narrative form, not outline form.

- Use the style and tone that is used in your novel.

- Do not tease the editor; include the ending.

- Examine movie summaries or reviews to see how they condense a two-hour movie into a single paragraph without losing the excitement.

- Parallel your synopsis to the same chronological sequence of events as in your novel.

- Describe characters and events creatively, but leave most of the details for the full novel.

Whether you are starting your query with a dramatic opening or a straight-to-the-point approach, you will want to address a number of questions when developing your synopsis. For example:

Why did you choose this particular publisher, editor, or agent? Make it clear to the reviewer of your proposal that you have spent a substantial amount of time researching the right market to shop your manuscript and that you selected the editor, agent, or publish with care.

What is your book about? Start with the basics: genre, word count, and working title. The next step is to place your book in the category matching the publisher's guidelines. If you are unsure about the categories, take a trip to the bookstore, find the section where you think your book would fit, and take note of the section label. Letting the reviewer know where you have categorized your work demonstrates that you have thought about how to market your book. Reviewers appreciate this because they do not like reviewing books that do not have a clear market.

What is the plot or major theme of your book? Briefly describe the main plot of your work. A common approach seasoned writers take is to prepare this as if they were writing the copy of the cover of the book. Do not feel that you have to summarize your entire manuscript into two paragraphs. Remember the query letter is a pitch, not an outline or chapter summary.

Who will read your book? Spend some time thinking about your book's audience. Who will read your story? Do not attempt to write a novel or say that your novel appeals to everyone. That is a sure sign of a naïve and inexperienced writer. Start by looking at what is currently being sold in a comparable market, and see who is reading those books.

What makes you the best person to write this book? It is extremely important that you choose your credentials wisely for a fiction book. Unfortunately, nonfiction clips do not offer much substance for fiction queries. Even though nonfiction writing credentials can demonstrate your professional writing skills, they do not help to market and sell your fiction story. The upside of this is that your writing will dictate what makes the sale, not your credentials. The downside of this is that you will need a completely polished manuscript to land a book deal.

If you are a novice writer and this is your first experience with writing a synopsis, do not become discouraged at the exercise of cramming your 80,000-word novel into 25 pages and successfully capturing the entire essence of your story. It is impossible, and your editor knows it is impossible. Nonetheless, it is a submission requirement and a necessary step in the process of final publication. The editor is trying to get the big picture to see how you develop your plot and characters, how you structure the story, and how it all comes together at the end. So stay calm and focused when preparing your synopsis, and most important, do the best you can.

Pitching to the right genre

No two queries are alike. Particularly for novels, each individual genre will have specific query requirements that are different from the other genres.

When writing a fiction novel, the first thing you will need to decide is to which genre you intend to pitch. Although there are numerous fiction genres and subgenres, the common categories are described in the following table:

GENRE	DESCRIPTION	AVERAGE WORD COUNT
Mystery and crime	Focused on a crime, usually a murder. The premise is usually a "who-done-it" type of story in which the writer's job is to create a puzzle for the reader to investigate and solve. The answer is not revealed until the end, and it is usually an unexpected outcome.	50,000 – 65,000
	For more information about writing a mystery or crime novel, reference the Mystery Writers of America (**www.mysterwriters.org**), the premier organization for mystery and crime writers.	

GENRE	DESCRIPTION	AVERAGE WORD COUNT
Thriller and suspense	The plot focuses on a hero and a villain. Often, the story is about a crime committed by the villain who puts obstacles in the way of the hero, making the odds for the hero to win seem unattainable. It creates an underdog feeling for the reader who continues to the end in hopes that the hero is victorious.	65,000 – 120,000
Speculative	Based on speculation rather than factual or historical events. The common subgenres of the speculative fiction, that we are familiar with, include horror, sci-fi, fantasy, and paranormal. There is the Speculative Literature Foundation (**www.speculativeliterature.org**) that provides a hub of information for speculative fiction readers, writers, editors, and publishers.	75,000 – 100,000
Romance	The most popular form of fiction, the primary focus is on a relationship between a couple that finds themselves in the middle of various obstacles, challenges, and precarious situations. The end is usually a happy reunion, leaving the reader with the feeling of "happily-ever-after." The romance genre has several subgenres including romantic suspense, romantic company, inspirational romance, historical romance, and time-travel romance. A great resource for romance writing and genres is the Romance Writers Association (**www.rwa.org**).	40,000 – 140,000
Historical	A fictional story that is often based in a setting, which is actually historical and true. This setting usually takes place in the past and commonly occurs more than 100 years ago.	100,000 – 140,000

GENRE	DESCRIPTION	AVERAGE WORD COUNT
Juvenile	These fiction novels cover topics for children and young adults ranging from picture books to full-length novels. A good resource for writing juvenile novels is the Society of Children's Book Writers & Illustrators (**www.scbwi.org**)	10,000 – 50,000
Inspira-tional	Written with a spiritual theme (usually Christian-based) and covers topics such as religious prophecy, daily walk with God, spiritual warfare, or the global mission of the church. The primary professional organization devoted to helping Christian fiction writers and publishers is the American Christian Fiction Writers (**www.acfw.com**).	80,000 – 100,000

Check your local bookstore to see how they categorize fiction novels. You might find a category not listed here, but it could be relevant to your subject matter. However, if you write a good query, the editor, publisher, or agent will be able to clearly determine under which genre your manuscript will work best. Remember, no two queries are alike; so do your research, and develop the best pitch you can to make the right fit.

Query Letter Basic Training

elcome to query letter basic training. First, you will learn what editors really think of query letters and what to include that will impress them. This chapter stresses the importance of style and mechanics and explains the key elements of a query. Once you have the basic elements intact, you will want to include supporting documents to enhance or validate your presentation. This chapter shows you what those supporting documents are and how they can help your query submission.

Just as persistence is paramount to the success of your writing career, proofreading and attention to the details are paramount to the fate of your query letter. Editors are looking for two primary things when reviewing a query letter: 1) a reason to stop reading and 2) a reason to keep reading. Your job is to give them a reason to keep reading.

What Editors Really Think of Queries

There seems to be a love-hate relationship between editors and writers. Editors have rules and standards, and writers have the responsibility to follow these rules while also showing creativity, freshness, and simplicity. It seems like a tall order to fill, and yet that is what editors expect. As mentioned, the query letter is an editor's preference over receiving an entire manuscript or fully written article.

Editors, agents, and publishers are bombarded every day with queries, proposals, manuscripts, and other information to read. If you were in that position, what tools would you want to use to help you get through all the piles? For editors, queries are one of the most effective tools available to help manage the ideas coming in from countless writers looking to break into the industry. And at a glance, reviewing a query letter allows the editor to assess whether a writer can:

• Write well and concisely

- Craft well-thought-out ideas
- Demonstrate the expertise and/or credentials to write the assignment
- Follow instructions and guidelines
- Construct grammatically correct sentences and paragraphs
- Proofread the query for typos and grammatical mistakes
- Research and learn about the publication and its reader
- Develop a topic that can fit into the publication's style and tone

Publications and the representing editors, agents, and publishers are different. As you work with different publishers, agents, or editors, you will find they all have different opinions, backgrounds, preferences, personalities, and procedures. This is all part of the "art" of querying and working in the writing industry. One of the best skills you can have as a writer, besides the ability to write well, is the ability to listen to the agent, editor, or publisher and determine what works best for each. This will not be an easy task, but it will pay off for you in the end.

Five Things That Can Impress the Editor

When you first begin to query, you probably will not know what exactly the editor wants. However, editors are no different from writers in the sense that they are looking for things and ideas that spark interest. Although editors, agents, and publishers have differing opinions, backgrounds, preferences, procedures, and personalities, there are special tastes editors have for presentations. Although these five things are not a standard, they will give you an idea of things that can impress an editor. Your job will be to find out what works best for each editor you establish a relationship with. But for now, think about these possibilities:

1) Let your personality show

Even though it is only a one-page letter, your personality needs to come across in your query. Editors are looking for personalities that make them chuckle, inspire them, or make them think. Work to make your query letter exude a sense of style and personality. Here is a word of caution though: try not to sound too casual, gimmicky, or over-the-top. Your goal is to give editors an idea of who you are while maintaining a sense of professionalism.

2) Have some relevant experience

This is a difficult angle, particularly for the newbie. With the increasing demands on editors, agents, and publishers, it is refreshing to come across a query letter that shows a writer with experience. That is not to say that a novice cannot land an assignment without experience. It is saying that editors appreciate it when their jobs are made easier. Writers with experience can do that for them.

3) Be patient

Inexperienced writers let anxiety get the best of them. Many publications have a long lead time (i.e., the time between receiving an assignment and publication of the final piece), and responses often can take up to a month. Editors appreciate it when a writer shows some restraint by not contacting them until enough reasonable time has elapsed. Be particularly sensitive to this when the response time is clearly stated in the writer's guidelines.

4) Show that you have a specialty

Few writers can write for every topic. There is still much controversy over whether a writer should specialize or write as a generalist. One can see how from an editor's perspective it would be extremely helpful if the writer had a specialty. Editors, agents, and publishers often already have ideas in mind of what they need. Writers who send in queries and show the editor they have a special knack for the topic of interest will more than likely win the interest of the editor.

5) Be as perfect as humanly possible

Editors definitely are not perfect, but somehow you are supposed to be with your submissions. Of course, you know that nobody is perfect, but the expectation is that you need to be as perfect as humanly possible with your query letters and submissions. The devil is in the details.

The Devil is in the Details

One of the basic skills of querying is to look, act, and sound professional in every way possible. This requires acquiring a command of the rules and paying attention to the details. Think about it from your perspective: what would you think if you received a five-page packet addressed to the wrong person, with blatant spelling errors, and on canary yellow paper? Would that make you want to contact that person right away, or would that make you cringe in disgust? This is what editors, agents, and publishers deal with on a daily basis.

Writers abound who feel that the details should be overlooked because we are human and mistakes happen. However, although we are human and mistakes happen, it is within your control to try to put your best foot forward and make a lasting impression. So, what exactly are these details? Take a look:

Know whom to address and how

Even though staff assistants will most likely forward your query to the right department, do not use that as an excuse not to address the right person. Do your research to find out to whom you should submit your query. This small detail will show the editor that you can do your homework, and you will go the extra distance. Try not to make gender assumptions. For example, if you are sending a query to a women's magazine, do not assume the editor will be a woman. Also, if you are unsure of the gender of the editor whose name could be either a male or female, call the publication to get clarification, or do some digging on the Internet. This does not just apply to names. It is professional not only to know whom to address but also to know the person's correct title.

Format to industry standards

There is no excuse for writers to send query letters formatted in a substandard manner. Typewriters and handwritten queries are no longer acceptable because they clue the editor to the fact that the writer has not written much, or even lately. Clean, smudge-free, white paper is the professional standard. Check the writer's guidelines to determine if they have specific formatting guidelines. If they do not specify, follow these industry standard letter-formatting guidelines:

- Print on white paper.
- Use black ink.
- Use Times New Roman font.
- Set the font size to 12 point.
- Set all margins to 1 inch.

It might be tempting to add a little creativity to your formatting, but you will need to refrain until you land the assignment and get to know the editor, agent, or publisher better.

Include a SASE

If you are sending a query by regular mail, the professional thing to do is send a self-addressed stamped envelope along with it. Only an amateur does not include a SASE, so remembering this detail will differentiate your submission from theirs. One of your goals as a writer is to show the editor that you intend to make it as easy as possible for him or her. A good way to demonstrate this is by including a SASE, especially because no company is going to pay postage to send you a rejection. Also consider this: Sending a SASE with every query can get expensive. Unfortunately, it is part of the protocol, so be sure to budget for it in your business expenses.

Address the publication correctly

It is getting more challenging to identify the correct address of a publication or publishing house. Many of the larger organizations have multiple addresses, and some of those addresses are even international. Use the Internet and the writer's guidelines to determine the correct address and name of the company to which you are submitting your query. This detail often irritates the editor and will label your query a waste of time. If you are not willing to take the time to pay attention to the details of the address of the publication you are submitting the query to, can the editor really expect you to pay attention to the details when you are writing an article slotted for publication?

Proofread, proof-read, proofread

Double and triple-check your query, particularly for spelling errors, grammatical mistakes, typos, and incorrect facts. These imperfections signal to the editor that you lack professionalism and are not willing to spend extra time doing things right. Here are a few tips to help you ensure you have an error-free query letter:

- **Sleep on it.** One of the best techniques for dealing with the details of your query is to let it stew overnight and come back to it the next day with a fresh perspective. You will be amazed at the number of things you notice with a good night's rest.

- **Get help from a friend.** Enlist the help of a friend to read your query letter. Often, a fresh set of eyes from an unbiased person can pick up typos, inconsistencies, and other errors you may not have noticed yourself.

- **Read aloud.** Either have someone else read your letter aloud or read it aloud to yourself. This exercise often identifies unclear statements or thoughts and poor grammar or sentence structure.

- **Look up the rules.** Proofreading can be easier with the help of a handbook or style. If a phrase does not seem right, or you are not sure about punctuation, look it up in common stylebooks such as *AP Stylebook* or the *Chicago Manual of Style*.

- **Read bottom to top.** Our brains get used to nonexistent letters, words, and punctuation, which allows us to skip over blatant errors. To trick your natural tendency, read your query letter from the bottom up. Also, try reading the text in a sentence backwards, which breaks up the rhythm and flow of your writing. This approach helps your brain focus on the letters and words.

- **Focus on punctuation.** Uncover errors in sentence structure by focusing on the punctuation in your query letter. Circle every instance of punctuation: comma, period, semicolon, colon, quotation marks, etc. If you are working in a word-processing program, bold or highlight all punctuation.

The spell-checker feature in your word processing program can help, but it is not foolproof. With the increasing acceptance of typos and grammatical errors, taking the time to fix the mistakes in your query letter is essential now more than ever. A clean, properly written, edited piece projects a professional image and will go a long way to ensuring you are taken seriously in the world of writing and publishing

After finishing this chapter, you have completed your query letter basic training. Now that you have know how to query an editor, it is time to review the anatomy of a query letter a further dissect the core elements.

The Anatomy of the Query Letter

rom an editor's perspective, query letters come in all shapes, sizes, and colors. Some are amusing, others are amateurish, and even more find a home in the slush pile. A good query letter, one that can quickly grab an editor's attention, provides a writer with the possibility of future assignments and a long-term, profitable relationship.

What was it about the letter the editor selected that made it stand out from the rest?

This chapter will dissect the query letter from beginning to end and uncover various aspects that can produce a winning query in the right shape with the right content. The main components of the query, in general, do not change. Most industry experts who write about the query letter will use the same formula when talking about the anatomy. You have to achieve two goals with this letter. The first goal is to hook the reader, reel them in, and guide them through the letter. The second goal is to make your query letter so compelling the editor, agent, or publisher will want to read more or make an assignment.

But before getting into the meat of the query letter, consider the book-ends: the salutation and the closing. These two elements often are over-looked because writers can become obsessed with getting the in-between items correct.

Greetings and Salutations

The salutation sets the tone for the rest of the letter. Look at the following salutation scenarios to see the message the editors receive when you are not careful with your greetings and salutations.

If your salutation addresses the wrong gender, "Dear Mr. Jamie Benson" [Jamie is a woman],

then the editor knows you did not dig deep enough to find out if Jamie was a man or woman. If you did not research this one small point, how will you research information to substantiate your claims in an assigned article?

If your salutation addresses the person incorrectly or you spell the person's name wrong,

then the editor will know that you are not willing to pay attention to the details. If you do not take the time to proof your one-page letter, will you take the time to proof your article before submitting it for publication?

If your salutation reads, "Dear Sir or Madam:"

then the editor knows you are too lazy to figure out to whom to address the query. If you are too lazy to look up a point of contact, then chances are you probably will not meet the article deadline.

If your salutation is too relaxed, "Hey Pam,"

then the editor knows that you probably are not going to be very professional in your future dealings.

Aside from the address, the salutation is the first line of the official query. If you get that wrong, the rest is downhill from there.

Make It a Good Closer

On the opposite side of the salutation is the closing statement. How you close your letter also sends a specific message to the editor. If you do not have a rapport with an editor, agent, or publisher, it is best to go with a more generic, professional closing rather than a more relaxed closer. Take a look:

PROFESSIONAL	RELAXED/FRIENDLY	UNPROFESSIONAL
"Sincerely yours,"	"Take care,"	"Goodbye,"
"Respectfully,"	"Warmest regards,"	"Godspeed,"
"Regards,"	"Cheers,"	"Later, alligator,"
"Best regards,"	"Best wishes,"	"Peace,"

PROFESSIONAL	RELAXED/FRIENDLY	UNPROFESSIONAL
"Kind regards,"	"Hope to hear from you soon,"	"Talk to you later,"
"Cordially,"	"Looking forward to your response,"	"Shine on,"

You can use plenty of other closing statements, but with those demonstrated above, you have an idea of how to send the right message with your closer.

Now that you are familiar with the bookends of the query letter, it is time to dive into the specific elements of the query.

Five Core Sections of a Query Letter

At the core of this small, yet powerful, one-page letter are five main sections. The first three sections will discuss the piece you are pitching. The last two sections will cover talking about you and establishing a rapport with the decision maker. This chapter breaks down each of these sections, so you can learn the purpose of each and how to successfully develop each section, so at the end, you have a solid and irresistible query letter.

Section One: Now that I have your attention (the hook)

Is it the hook or the lead? The answer: it is both or either. Many people referenced the opening paragraph as the lead, which is intended to hook the reader. Others just refer to it as the hook because that is what you are trying to do, hook the reader. If there is one place in your query where it is worth investing your time, it is best to spend it crafting the hook. The hook should be a concise, one- to two-sentence tagline for your entire piece. It is intended to captivate the reader's interest and motivate them to ask for more. Use these first few lines to prove that you are a skilled writer and have a saleable idea.

You can approach the hook several ways; the following are just a few of these commonly used techniques:

- **Solve a problem.** Start your query by defining a problem or situation that is common to the audience of the publication you are addressing. Next, propose a piece that will solve that problem.

- **Use the five Ws.** The foundation of the lead/hook is constructed using the five Ws: who, what, where, when, why. Although this approach often can result in a dry question and answer banter, it functions as a good rule for starting a query.

- **Use the inverted pyramid.** This technique is another valued aid for structuring your hook. The concept is simple: Start with strong points first, and end with the details. Trying to tell a story first will lose the reader's interest. Start strong with an attention-grabbing statement or question, and then develop the main points later.

- **Provide useful information.** When using this approach, start by presenting two to three lines of pertinent information (i.e., statistics, facts, figures, etc.). Then close the hook by explaining how your proposed piece is relevant to the target audience.

- **Use a quote.** Begin your query letter with a saying or quote from a famous person or expert in the field. A good strategy is to obtain a quote from a subject matter expert, prominent figure, or person with first-hand experience in your subject.

- **Add a personal touch.** Anecdotes can be a solid hook for an editor. Many well-established writers like to use this approach because it immediately establishes credibility by experience. However, proceed with caution when you add a personal touch. First, ensure that the publication uses a more relaxed tone for the targeted audience. If they do not, you want a more professional style.

- **Provide shock value.** The goal with this approach is to make the reader sit up and pay attention. Maybe you want to provide something bizarre or so unbelievable that it makes the editor, agent, or publisher want to request more out of curiosity.

- **Compare and contrast.** Do a comparison of how two companies are using a technique or product to provide a solution to their end users.

Things to avoid in the hook

Take heed and avoid these common hooks, which are most often submitted by amateur writers:

- **Too personal** – Stay away from hooks that introduce yourself ("Hi, my name is Sally, and I would like to submit this letter for your review…") or provide too much or irrelevant information. ("I am a long-time fan of the Grateful Dead, and much of their music inspired my writing career…")

- **Brown nosing** – Do not just give lip service to an editor. They want evidence by your writing style, your attention to detail, and your ability to follow through on your assignments. Avoid brown nosing and "kissing up" to the editor. ("I have an entire bookshelf full of issues of this magazine; I have been a subscriber almost all my adult life.")

- **The sympathy angle** – If you have never been published before, the editor will not care, and chances are, they might even discard your letter just because you tried to pull the sympathy card. ("Even though I have never been published before, I know I can do a good job with this assignment.") Stick to what you know, present a clear, concise, professional letter, and you will get a lot farther.

- **The perfect fit** – Everyone thinks they are the perfect fit when trying to land an assignment. Even though you might be a good fit for the article, avoid singing your own praises. ("I would be a perfect fit for this because I have the right experience and credentials for your magazine.") Again, editors want proof with a good query, substantiating facts, and supporting credentials.

- **I am just an amateur** – You might be an amateur, but no one else needs to know about it. Do not call attention to your lack of writing experience or your lack of credentials. Write your query letter in a manner that makes the editor want your work regardless of your experience.

You can use numerous hook techniques to pique an editor's interest. Study samples of successful queries and learn why those hooks worked. Then get to work crafting your own successful hook.

Examples of hooks:

- If Adrian Thompson had left his house but two minutes earlier, he would have made it to work this morning.

- Helen Walden thinks she has successfully hidden from the government. What she does not know is that agents were waiting to expose her at the opportune moment — today.

- Thirteen-year-old Greg Foster is the heir to the throne: He just has not been told yet.

- They took my sister last night. They say I am next.

Start your "hook" research using these online resources:

- QueryTracker.net Blog (**www.querytracker.blogspot.com/2009/ 01/writing-query-letter-hook.html**)

- Archetype — Writing the Query Letter Part 1 — The Hook (**www.archetypewriting.com/articles/QTers/letter1_EJ.htm**)

- Adventures in Writing (**www.adventures-in-creative-writing. blogspot.com/2009/07/example-query-letter-hook- summary.html**)

- Rachel Heston Davis — Best Query Letter Hook (**www.rachelhestondavis.com/?p=62**)

CASE STUDY:
IT IS ALL ABOUT THE HOOK
Leigh Court
Author/romance writer
www.leighcourt.com

"Query letters are a lot like advertising," says Leigh Court, published author/romance writer. "You have to get a buyer (or in the case of query letters, an editor, agent, or publisher) interested in your product right off the bat. So, it is always best to start with a hook."

The query letter hook that helped Court sell her first romance novel, *The Disciplinarian*, read like this:

"What happens when a headstrong young Victorian wife is sent to be tamed by London's notorious Disciplinarian?"

Her advice on crafting a good hook is to make the first sentence so interesting or so surprising that an editor needs to read more. Court has a best friend in public relations who has a knack for writing catchy opening lines and is a great resource. "I am always picking her brain," says Court of her friend. If you do not have a resource like Court's, she recommends that you participate in a critique group where you can enjoy the benefits of a brainstorming session or two.

Court is no stranger to writing. Like many writers, she always has told stories. For her, writing goes back to age 11 when she used to write wild adventure stories for her elementary school newspaper.

Court encourages writers to wow an editor with your opening line to entice them to read more of your story. She also recommends thinking outside of the box, even for nonfiction material, to craft a unique angle describing the premise of your topic.

"Query letters absolutely work, in my opinion," claims Court. With so many writers wanting to be published, the competition is fierce, and a great hook in a query letter is a valuable tool to make your story stand out from the hundreds of other submissions editors receive weekly.

From Personal Experience

The biggest tip Court has for an up-and-coming writer is to never give up. Writing can be a lonely, rejection-filled process, but with every book, novella, essay, poem, or article you write, you are honing and improving your craft. She also recommends finding a critique group. This group can give you valuable feedback on your writing and support you through all those inevitable rejections.

Remember that the following writers were rejected many times before finally selling their work: Stephen King, John Grisham, Jack London, Louis L'Amour, Dr. Seus, Alex Haley, Mary Higgins Clark, Norman Mailer, Pearl Buck, George Orwell, and Joseph Heller.

"Rejections are frustrating and discouraging, but unfortunately, they are part of the writing life," confirms Court. Once, she verbally pitched an editor during a writer's conference and only managed to tell her the hook before the editor stopped her and exclaimed, "Been there. Done that. Next!" After several years of rejections, Court sold her first story just two weeks after sending the query for *The Disciplinarian*, along with the opening chapter. It took Court about five years before she sold her first story as a result of a query letter.

So remember, if you get a rejection, you are in good company.

Section Two: Here is my story (the pitch)

Once you land the hook, now it is time to make the pitch. The pitch is where you explain what exactly it is you are proposing. Editors want to know a little bit about how the piece will work in the publication. This is a good time to show the editor that you have really thought this through. You will want to address questions such as:

- Why does the editor care about this topic?
- Is this a timely and relevant idea?
- How does the idea fit with the publication's mission?
- What approach will you take to convey your idea and message?

Now that you have told the editor *what* you intend to write, this is where you demonstrate *how* you intend to write about it. Here are a few ways you can show how you plan to cover your topic:

- **State the purpose.** Approach this pitch with a lead-in such as, "This article will focus on helping career-minded women develop their own brands." Or "The goal of my book is to provide step-by-step, visual instructions on how to build a birdhouse like the pros." Putting these types of statements early in the pitch ensures that you have clearly conveyed your subject and slant.

- **Outline your plan of attack.** A good rule is to choose three to six interesting topics you will cover and write a couple of sentences for each topic. Try to avoid the standard school outline format; it shows unprofessionalism and lack of creativity. Instead, use bulleted or numbered lists or indented paragraphs to create a sense of hierarchy and order.

- **Prove it with numbers.** There is no better way to validate your idea than with facts, figures, and/or statistics. Even better, provide the facts from a reliable source. For example, you query can include something like, "The *Journal of American Medical Association* recently published a study confirming that the percentage of overweight Americans has gone from 30 percent to 35 percent in the last five years," and your credibility has just increased two-fold.

The purpose of the pitch is clearly to explain why you are proposing this idea and how you intend to develop the story so the targeted audience can benefit from it. What you discuss in your pitch will be dictated somewhat by the publication to which you are querying. How you develop your pitch will be the difference between the top of the heap or the slush pile.

Section Three: In case you need more detail (the body)

This is the meat and potatoes of the letter. This section is where the selling really begins. If query letters and creativity converge, this is the place. In section three, you want to develop your idea further to provide enough detail for the editor, agent, or publisher to get an idea of where you are going with your proposed work. Your support details can come in a variety of shapes and sizes, but most of them will fall into one of the following categories:

- **Just the facts** – A good way to substantiate your story is to provide facts, figures, and statistics. Citing some relevant facts provides good evidence and supports your claims.

- **From the source** – Interviewing relevant, well-respected experts is a great way to establish credibility with the editor and ultimately, with the readers of the publication.

- **Case histories** – Reuse the anecdotal approach in the summary section. They are just as effective here, but now you can add more detail.

- **Predicting the future** – Creating a reference point for your subject can be an effective way to provide context to your idea. Predictions of the importance of this topic in the near or distant future can be a strong selling point.

- **Timely events** – This is a simple and often fun approach when selling ideas. A good strategy is to try to tie your piece in with a seasonal event such as Christmas, Fourth of July, National Doughnut Day, or Take Your Daughter to Work Day.

- **Nuts and bolts** – You also can use this section to detail things like: word count (rounding to the nearest 500), to which issue the piece should be tailored, and a working title. Before confidently stating the word counts, be sure to check the publication's guidelines to confirm the average length of pieces they require. Be flexible about your title. State that this is a proposed or working title because editors, agents, and publishers frequently change titles.

- **Visual aids** – Maybe you do photography on the side or know someone who is a good illustrator. At the time of the query, you do not have to have visual aids ready or included, but if you can state that you can secure photos or provide diagrams or illustrations, that will add weight to your pitch. Describe in as much detail as space will permit the type of visual aids you can provide — charts or diagrams, illustrations, black and white or color photography, pencil sketches, cartoons — and the reason the visual aid is important to the content. Using a caption best conveys the goal.

If you do not intend to provide visual aids, you definitely can provide suggestions. The editor, agent, or publisher will be happy to know that you have taken time to think through how the final piece might work.

The creativity should be demonstrated in your writing style, how you intended to present the material using bulleted lists, call-out boxes, quizzes, spin-offs, and subsequent subtopics. If after you have developed your summary, you find that you have more than one page of descriptive information, your query is probably too long. It may be necessary for you to use that length to develop the supporting details, but keep this in mind: Editors are busy; they would prefer not to have to read more than one page.

A strong, well-crafted summary is the heart of your effective sales piece. Once you have gone through your details, edit it down to remove wordy phrasing, clichés, awkward sentences, and impertinent information. You can be creative with your summary, but do not overdo it and lose the essence of your idea.

Section Four: The ideal candidate (the credentials)

As you have learned in previous chapters, editors, agents, and publishers want to know why you are the best person to handle the assigned project. Whatever you do, do not lie or try to cover up your qualifications. This will be a bad career move and can often be difficult to recover from. You do not have to be modest either in your query letter. You do not want to come across sounding arrogant or braggadocio, but there is nothing wrong with expounding on your credentials to show that you can do the job.

A good approach to this section is to start by writing a biography. This is a good exercise because you can write it once and then craft smaller versions of it for each query. To ensure you are putting your best foot forward, try a few of these tactics:

Use a little bit of life.

Start with your education or professional experience as a way to gather credentials. If either of these is related to your pitch, they can be used to substantiate the claims you make in your query. For example, if you write content for the company newsletter, provide technical content for business proposals, or write copy for the corporate website, these are examples of a writing background. If you write any material that could possibly connect to the query topic, include photocopies with your query.

Any degree, even if it is not related to your query topic, can provide credibility in your bio. If you attended relevant courses or obtained a license or certification that pertains to the topic of your query, be sure to include that as well. Writing courses should be excluded because they potentially can emphasize your lack of writing experience. Instead, mention courses you have taken to enhance your understanding of the topic you are pitching. Any teaching or speaking you have done could prove interesting to editors.

Another way to use a little bit of life is to add life experiences, either your own or someone else's. Life experience can add depth to your story and a feeling of authenticity.

Emphasize the positive.

Instead of calling attention to your lack of writing clips or your previous rejections, work toward making a more positive impression. Try not to use language that will emphasize your shortcomings. Instead, rework the language in your query letter to stress more of what you *have* done rather than what you have not done.

For example, if you are submitting a query to a book publisher and you do not have any book credits, list magazine or newspaper credits if you have them. If you do not have any publishing credits to offer, focus on crafting your credentials to emphasize years of experience in the topic you are presenting. Do an honest assessment of what you bring to the table, and find a way to present it in the best possible fashion, so you can show your strengths as a writer.

Use the right endorsements.

Having your family, colleague, or best friend endorse your work will not impress an agent, publisher, or editor. Of course, if Stephen King happens to be your uncle and he recommends your work, your chances have just improved. Nevertheless, if you can acquire just the right endorsement, it can give your query the added leverage you need to get the reader's attention. Endorsements more commonly are recommended for book queries than article queries. So, if you can tout the right endorsement, you can enhance your query.

Who is the best endorser for your query? First, that will depend upon the topic you are pitching. If your book project is about health and fitness, then it would be ideal to gather an endorsement from Jillian Michaels.

Although third-party, expert, or famous endorsements might be hard to solicit, you also can enhance your query by getting an existing client, previous boss, or former teacher to refer you and your work. Think of it as providing references during a job search. In either case, be sure to have the endorser's full and complete permission to use his or her name and reference or quote.

Honors and awards.

If you have been recognized for outstanding performance or other relevant achievements, this is a good place to include that information. Carefully pick the honors and awards that are important and add weight to the topic you are pitching in your query letter. Touting an award for "IT Training Specialist of the Year" will not impress an editor, publisher, or agent if your topic is about making a career change. On the other hand, if you are writing a book about the benefits of training and certification in the information technology field, then your award becomes very relevant. It can quickly establish you as an expert on that topic. Consider the letter you are pitching, think of the audience who will be reading the article or book, and start pulling together accolades that match or complement that subject.

Professional and social memberships.

Another valuable way to enhance your credibility is to add your participation or affiliation with professional and/or social memberships and networks. This credential functions as another way to establish you as an expert quickly.

Media and publicity.

If you want to make an editor, agent, or publisher happy, show that you are promotable. If you can show that you have experience with personal appearances through radio, newspapers, magazines, television, speaking engagements, or teaching, this can work to your advantage. The more often you get your name out and heighten your profile, the better impression you can make on editors, publishers, and agents.

After you have gathered all the pieces together and drafted a preliminary bio, try to edit it down to one paragraph. If you have an extensive background, two paragraphs will do. Do not be discouraged if you do not have credentials starting out. You can gain relevant qualifications from a variety of sources, including professional experience, academic training and background, teaching experience, expert interviews, and personal experience. Just start working toward your goal, and the credentials will come.

Do not forget this most important element

Before ending your query with the closing statement, be sure you include a paragraph thanking the editor for his or her time and consideration. Most editors greatly appreciate this small attention to detail and are surprised how many writers miss this part in the query. A simple sign of appreciation can yield big results.

Section Five: Some parting thoughts (the closer)

Be professional and respectful. Ideally, you have been getting that message loud and clear as you dissect the contents of these chapters. The purpose of this last section of the query letter is to thank the editor, agent, or publisher for reviewing your proposal. You also can use it to offer one last attempt to encourage the reader to respond and let them know you have provided a SASE for that convenience.

Never make the editor work harder than he or she already does. Have your contact information easily accessible so the editor knows exactly where he or she can follow up with you. Include a brief reference to any clips you have included. If you have a website, make it highly visible. And above all else, be professional and respectful.

Tailored for Success

Editors are used to seeing the same ideas pitched query after query. Then your query pops up with an idea that seems similar, but you have taken extra special care to delve deeper into the idea and tailor it specifically for what you think the publication needs or the reader would like to know. You have captivated the editor, and your article will most likely be published. How did this happen? Well, you most likely:

- Provided a specific word count of your article and showed that you understand the publication's requirements

- Pointed out a particular section of the magazine or publication and demonstrated how your idea would be a good fit

- Were spot on with the style, tone, and voice of the publication's past articles

- Referenced an article that was published in a previous issue and illustrated how your writing style is similar

Attention to the details is what can set your query apart from the rest. Tailoring is a technique that experienced writers use to demonstrate to the editor that they have done the research.

Whether you are writing a query for an article, nonfiction book, novel, or writing to an agent, do not stray from this basic anatomy. Developing your own set of rules for a query format will not impress an editor, publisher, or agent. Play by the rules, be professional, and write a good piece. Before you know it, you will find yourself one step closer to a sale. Keep these simple tips in mind to increase your chances of reaching the top of the heap:

- Short is better; if you can capture the essence of your story in 250 words or fewer, you will make an editor happy.

- Make your query letter stand out with charm and flavor.

- Match the subject of your piece with the language and style of your letter.

- Demonstrate that you understand the economy of language.

- Be deliberate in your word choice.

The query is not a résumé or a rambling tome of your writing life. It is a simple, one-page letter introducing you and your work. Keep it simple and stick to the basic anatomy.

Sample Query Letter that Landed a Book Assignment

Dear Mr. Ladd,

How often do you think — REALLY think — about transforming commonplace items you use everyday into the extraordinary? If you have read *Sneaky Uses for Everyday Things* and its sequels, then you know how to start a fire with water, make plastic with milk, activate devices with your ring, turn a penny into a radio, and make a gadget jacket with ordinary things.

But, all of the possible Sneaky adaptations have not been exhausted. *SUPER Sneaky Uses for Everyday Things* reveals even more bizarre, out-of-the-ordinary ways of adapting everyday things.

For lovers of self-reliance and gadgetry, *SUPER Sneaky Uses for Everyday Things* is a fun assortment of 40 fabulous build-it-yourself gadgets, science projects, and more sneaky strategies.

The book's uniform format makes it easy to follow. All projects begin with a few introductory remarks and a list of materials needed. Detailed step-by-step instructions then allow one to complete most projects in just a few minutes.

Perfect for putterers, would-be inventors, or just those with inquisitive minds, *SUPER Sneaky Uses for Everyday Things* is packed with high- and low-tech projects that are simple, safe, and quick to assemble. There are projects made from items found in every household. After finishing the book, readers will revel in their newfound powers and glance around the room with a sneaky grin.

SUPER Sneaky Uses for Everyday Things avoids projects or procedures that require special or expensive materials that are not found in the average home. No special knowledge or tools are needed.

Currently, books that deal with resourcefulness cover only wilderness survival, decorative crafts, or household hints. Beyond what competing books have offered, *SUPER Sneaky Uses for Everyday Thing*s actually empowers the reader to get up and do something about his situation.

Whether readers use the book as a practical tool, a fantasy escape, or as a fun science and trivia guide, it will be a popular reference favorite for years to come. "Things" will never appear the same again.

SUPER Sneaky Uses for Everyday Things will be 175 pages with an introduction, 40 projects, and take 10 months to complete.

About The Author

Before *MacGyver*, before The Professor on *Gilligan's Island*, Cy Tymony was making extraordinary use of everyday things. By reading comic books as a kid and studying scientific techniques, he bridged science and fiction to amaze and protect his friends.

In grade school, he defended himself from bullies with the help of a spring-loaded shocker gadget hidden up his sleeve. As a teen, Tymony developed other gadgets including the Magne Power Ring, which he uses to start his car. He started a mail-order business and sold gadgets and booklets via advertisements in comic books and science fiction magazines.

Cy compiled many of his inventions and techniques into a 60-page project book titled, *Super Powers Made Simple*. His marketing, publicity and book promotion resulted in a guest spot on ABC-TV's *AM Chicago Show*, a two-page story in the *Chicago Tribune* and a feature article in *Future Life* magazine.

Cy Tymony has written ten books including seven Sneaky Uses titles for Andrews McMeel.

He has more than a dozen articles in print in publications such as *Make* magazine, *Byte*, *LAN*, *Computer Edge*, *Popular Computing*, *Computer Based Training*, *Kitplanes*, and *American Fitness*. His website, **www. sneakyuses.com**, provides free conservation and re-use projects, articles, and science resource links.

His publicity work for *Sneaky Uses for Everyday Things*, a science bestseller, landed him on CNN Headline News, PBS's *MAKE Television*, NPR's *Science Friday*, more than a dozen local TV news programs, and feature articles in *U.S. News & World Report*, the *Los Angeles Times*, *Orange County Register*, *Las Vegas Review-Journal*, and other publications. He also has appeared on more than 100 radio talk shows and performed author events at dozens of bookstores, libraries and schools.

Chapter 8

Refining Your Query Letter Before Submission

s you get closer to the final stage of licking the stamp or pressing the send button, you might grow weary of looking at your query, but do not let your enthusiasm wane just yet. The end is near, and you need to cover a few finishing touches before submitting your query to the identified publisher, agent, or editor. This chapter will reiterate the importance of making a lasting impression, exuding a touch of professionalism, performing judicious editing, sharpening your style, and formatting your query letter for submission through the right medium.

Make a Lasting Impression

By now, the message should be clear or getting clearer for you: A query letter is a combination of a written sales pitch and a summary of your topic idea. The main goals of this query are 1) to sell the editor, agent, or publisher on you and your ability to write well and complete the assigned task and 2) to help the editor, agent, or publisher make a good first impression of you.

It is not uncommon for an editor, agent, or publisher to receive up to 500 query letters in a two-week period. It is your job to make the reviewer's life easier while also making it difficult for him or her to reject your work. A lasting impression can begin with five to seven drafts of your letter before you achieve the polished result.

It only takes about 15 seconds for an evaluator to form a durable, fixed impression of you and your work. With every query submission, another editor, agent, or publisher evaluates you, and the publishing industry is more connected than you realized. These impressions often are difficult to reverse, which makes first encounters (whether in person, on the phone, or by e-mail) extremely important. If you do not land an assignment, do not be tempted to retaliate or send a snide response. The editor might have made the decision to reject you this time but might be contemplating using your work in the future. If you have burned that bridge by taking the rejection personally or skimping on making a good impression, you will have closed a door of opportunity with that particular publication and possibly others.

Here are a few helpful hints to help you make that lasting impression so the editor, agent, or publisher will appreciate working with you:

- **Be open and confident.** This does not mean you should reveal all and tout your accomplishments incessantly. Keep the balance. Show that you are human and approachable, but project a sense of confidence in your writing that will make the editor, agent, or publisher feel he or she can rely on you.

- **Project positivity.** Your attitude comes across in everything you do, and it can come across through e-mails and your writing tone, too. Project a positive attitude regardless of the circumstances. If you are nervous, still project positivity. If you have been criticized, project positivity. If you have been asked to rewrite a specific section, project a positive attitude.

- **Good manners, a lost art.** Being polite and courteous can help tremendously when making a lasting impression. It should be obvious what kind of things can help you be on your best behavior, but a few of them are worth repeating here: Say please and thank you; give the editor, agent, or publisher your undivided attention; and avoid using slang or derogatory comments as a joke. Anything less will not do.

Remember, you have only a few seconds to make this lasting impression, and it is almost impossible to change. Spend a lot of time getting these areas of your query letter and your professional approach to writing perfected, and you definitely will make a positive, lasting impression on the prospective editor, publisher, or agent.

CASE STUDY: TAKE YOUR TIME

Carol Hoenig
Publishing Consultant, Inc.
www.carolhoenig.com

Carol Hoenig has been writing for as long as she could hold a pencil and has been writing professionally for about 20 years. She has extensive experience writing query letters and knows what it takes to get the agent, interviewer, or reviewer's attention.

It has not always been like that, however. When Hoenig first tried to figure out how to write query letters, she would scour books at the library and research as much as she could to find out what agents were looking for in a query.

Hoenig's first successful query letter experience was for an anthology that was looking for stories about a writer's childhood. The anthology accepted Hoenig's query and accepted the story; unfortunately, the anthology was never published. Nonetheless, Hoenig is reaping the fruits of her labor, perseverance, and diligence as the same story is now being included in another anthology titled, *Lost Lessons of Life on a Farm*.

Through her extensive research and years of experience, Hoenig uncovered valuable information to help hone her craft. She offers these three tips for making your query letter stand out from the slush pile:

- Ensure the person you are querying is the correct contact.

- Include exactly the nature of your query in the first or second sentence. Do not try to be cute or unique; just get to the point.

- Provide the word count for the piece you want to submit.

Hoenig believes a good query letter works. "If the agent or editor finds the query letter to be poorly written, even if the idea is intriguing, they quite likely will reject the submission."

Hoenig speaks from experience. It took her about six months to land her first assignment by query. "Writers must take time to write an impressive query letter, one that mirrors their writing style, voice, and topic," claims Hoenig. She urges other authors not to give up or take things too personally. "When those rejections start including personal notes, know that you are on the right track and getting closer to publication." If you are just starting out, Hoenig suggests you:

- Hone your craft.

- Take your time before submitting.

- Know the interest of the editor or agent to whom you are submitting; otherwise, if you submit to a publication that is not right for your work, you will be wasting their time and yours.

Hoenig has had her share of challenges and discouraging experiences, mostly related to sending out queries with errors in them. She realized she was sending out query letters too soon without really taking the time to edit and re-edit them. Hoenig had not gotten into the habit of proofreading her queries and double-checking all the details. She became frustrated with herself for rushing the query, and in turn, eliminating a possible opportunity.

Through her personal experiences and her perseverance, Hoenig now realizes what it takes to get responses from her query letters — taking the time to prepare a good solid query. "Even if the response is a rejection," she says, "it is comforting to know that my query was read, for what it is worth."

A Touch of Professionalism

The importance of professionalism cannot be repeated enough. This is not something you do once and then forget about. Professionalism is a state of mind; it is the way you conduct yourself whether you have the credentials or experience. An up-and-coming writer without any credits can appear just as professional as a writer who has dozens of published works. Professionalism is such an important aspect of writing, but it can be adopted into your career modus operandi very simply by remembering these two primary things:

- **Learn the business.** Take time to learn about the writing business and how things are conducted. There is no excuse for being naïve about this because there are so many available and valuable resources on the topic. A simple keyword search on the Internet would yield numerous websites to research. Numerous resources are listed in Appendix A: Writers' Associations and Appendix B: Writer's Resources. To get a jumpstart however, you can begin your research with sites such as: **www.writersmarket.com, www.writersweekly.**

com, **www.writersdigest.com**, and **www.literarymarketplace. com**.

- **Control yourself.** No matter how many rejection letters come or how difficult an editor, agent, or publisher might be to get along with, keep your cool and stay professional. Whatever impression you make, you can be sure it will spread around the industry.

- **Hone your skills.** Take an honest assessment of your current skill level, and start working to develop the skills you need to perfect your craft. To reach this level of professionalism requires practice, hard work, and a true respect for the industry.

- **Grow thick skin.** Rejection is a part of the business, so get used to it. It is part of the querying business, and your willingness to persevere through rejections can set you apart more than you realize.

Edit, then Edit Some More

After multiple revisions, your query letter is finally complete. You have the pitch solid and feel that it will make a good first impression. But that first impression will turn sour in an instant without further proofreading and editing. It is your responsibility to check, double-check, and triple-check your letter for sloppy spelling, incorrect facts, grammatical errors, random punctuation, and any blatant signs of unprofessionalism. Consider these tips for editing your query:

- **Keep it short and sweet.** Do not forget to step back and look at the query letter as a package. Pretend that you are an editor, publisher, or agent and review your query. Trimming the fat is always a good idea. Editors prefer concise, punchy, short pitches. Eliminate minor ideas and hyper sales promotions.

- **Fill the holes.** After you have done the fat trimming, review your query to see if there are any gaping holes in what remains. Keeping your writing brief does not mean you should leave the major points out for the sake of space.

- **Solidify the structure.** You have hit the major points, you have removed the fat, and you have filled the holes. Now, it is time to revisit the structure of your content. Review your query to see if you have organized the material in a logical manner and that the information is clear and easy to understand. *Revisit Chapter 6 to ensure you have prepared the letter in the industry format that is expected.* Bulleted lists often help to create an easy-to-read layout while providing clarity.

- **Let it sit.** For the best proofreading and editing results, let your query sit. If you can spare the time, let it sit for a few days. If you cannot spare the time, at least let it sit overnight. Coming back to your query with a fresh set of eyes allows you to see things you might not have before.

Even though judicious editing and proofreading are not enough to win the assignment, editors agree that it is a key factor in standing above the competition. If you need help with editing, proofreading, and grammar, refer to industry grammar and style guides, such as *Chicago Manual of Style* Online (**www.chicagomanualofstyle.org**), *AP Stylebook* Online (**www.apstylebook.com**), Grammar Girl™ (**http://grammar.quickanddirtytips.com/**), and William Strunk's *Elements of Style* (**www.bartleby.com/141**). You also can have a friend or family member review or consider hiring a professional editor until you can improve those skills yourself. But remember that some of these editing services can be the scams mentioned in Chapter 2. First, ask other writers you know if they can recommend an editor. Otherwise, you can reference the Literary Market Place (**www.literarymarketplace. com**™) under the category of "Editorial Services and Agents."

The Winning Edge

Whether you are a novice or a seasoned writer, you will need to continue doing things that set you apart from the pack. The more successful you become in your writing career, the fewer queries you will need to write. Once you become part of the circle of influence in the publishing arena, your work and reputation will speak for itself. At this moment, you might not be at the place where you can turn down work or write fewer query letters. But, you can start laying the foundation and begin building the steps that will land you right in the middle of the editors' lair. Here are a few ways to begin laying that foundation:

- **Start small, but think big.** There is nothing wrong with thinking that you want to land a published article in *Woman's Day, Time,* or *National Geographic.* However, think wisely and practically so you do not get discouraged too early. Start small and grow steadily, but continue to have your big thoughts and ideas in front of you. The big goals are not reached without first taking the smaller steps. Stay focused, start small, but continue to think big.

- **Set small and manageable goals.** If you set big goals and make long to-do lists, you will soon find yourself discouraged and unmotivated. The idea is to set small, manageable goals and tasks. If something is taking longer than two weeks to accomplish, your goal is probably a bit too big. Break it down into smaller pieces, and start accomplishing mini milestones to help you complete the larger one.

- **Encourage yourself.** Ask any writer who has been in this business for a while; writing can be a lonely business. You can network and attend writer's clubs and conferences, but ultimately, it comes down to you and the keyboard. Practice the art of encouraging yourself and developing your own cheering section. One of the best ways to do this is to create an "Atta Girl/Atta Boy" file that contains all the kudos, accomplishments, and milestones you have received or reached as you progress through your career.

- **Make submissions mandatory.** The crux of the query letter process is the submission. To succeed and develop that winning edge, you must make submissions a mandatory part of your daily or weekly activities. Once you have a good query letter, send it off, and get busy on the next one. Sitting too long on queries stops up your submission flow. Seasoned writers understand the importance of query standards and guidelines, but they do not stress over it to the point that it creates blocks in their cycle. It should get to the point where submitting queries is like second nature for you.

- **Network.** Even though writing itself can be a lonely endeavor, you should not remove yourself completely from the industry. Networking is an important part of developing your winning edge. Getting yourself in front of industry experts, other professional writers, agents, and publishers is part of laying the foundation for future opportunities. There are numerous ways to network. Start with associations and organizations relevant to writing and the type of markets you want to pursue. Subscribe to industry publications, and join online writing blogs and forums.

- **Selling once leads to more sales.** This book has focused on the importance of developing a good query letter, and for good reason. The query letter is the item that will be the most fundamental to your success. Having a large berth when you are first starting out is good. It helps you identify markets that might be lucrative and provide steady work. It also can help you weed out the markets that show little to no promise. As you sell more of your work, you learn on which publications to expend more of your time and energy. Your ultimate goal is to narrow your circle down to a handful of productive publications and then spend your efforts marketing and building relationships with the editors, agents, and publishers in these markets.

- **Look for opportunities everywhere.** Do not just limit yourself to the writing industry or the publishing industry. If you do, you are bound to miss an opportunity that would be a perfect fit. For example, you might be working out one evening at the gym and run into a colleague who just returned from a conference. That colleague got a tip about a publication that was looking for writers who could write about the subject in which you specialize. If you were closed to the idea that you could get a lead from going to the gym, then you would have missed an opportunity like that.

- **Develop your own personal brand.** It is very important these days to set yourself apart not only from the writing competition, but also from business world competition. One of the best ways to develop the winning edge and stand apart from the rest is to develop your own personal brand and image. You can work with a personal branding coach or a branding firm to start with a basic branding package. You do not need something extravagant at first, just come up with something that is the best version of you.

- **Increase your writing speed.** It is simple mathematics. If you can write faster, you potentially can make more money. The key to increasing your writing speed is to keep writing. When you first start writing, it can be extremely laborious because you are worried about every detail. However, as you continue to write and grow in your career, you will learn to let the ideas flow and go back and edit accordingly. Set aside a specific amount of time for writing, and stick to that schedule. The minor pressure of the deadline will help you increase your speed and challenge you to cover only the major points.

- **Take advantage of reprint rights.** A writer with the winning edge has learned how to get more mileage out of each idea. It takes less time to change the slant of a piece than it does to completely write a new one. If you already have a few ideas developed and a working draft of the piece — or even a published one — use it to your advantage, and try to sell it to other markets. First, be sure you still have the rights to reuse these articles. Do not forget to consider international markets, which might open up a completely new playing field for income and opportunities.

- **Develop longer pieces.** It is more challenging to write longer pieces, but it can be more lucrative because many publications pay more for full-length features (4,000+ words) over shorter articles (750 – 1,000 words). A full-length piece requires research on one subject; two or more smaller pieces require research on many potentially different subjects. Some writers also prefer to write longer pieces because it gives them the opportunity to fully develop their ideas and stories.

- **Write all the time.** Writing often functions as a 24/7/365 career. If you are not at your computer typing a 1,000-word article, you will find yourself thinking about writing or even carrying around a notepad or tape recorder with you so you can capture your thoughts and ideas. Writers with the winning edge immerse themselves into their profession. They hone their skills and educate themselves continuously to the latest trends, releases, and industry news. Writers are also chronic readers. Skimming every bit piece of information you can get your hands on might just spark a creative slant to a query, a unique hook, or a multiple-pitch idea.

With a combination of technique, the right attitude, follow through, and perseverance, you can accomplish just about anything. But there is something to be said about your internal dialogue and demeanor. As a writer, or an aspiring writer, what is on the inside usually finds its way to the outside. If you focus too much on the outward elements and techniques of the query, you might lose your personal flair and style, which comes from the very essence of you as a writer.

Formatting Your Query Letter

How you present your query letter can be just as important as what is in your letter. Coffee stains and pizza smudges on your letter will not inspire an editor to take notice. And this unkempt appearance of your query letter sends booming messages to the reviewer that you do not pay much attention to the details. So, place your java away from your query letter for a moment, and save the pizza for after your submission. A well-formatted query letter is of utmost importance now, and the elements required to successfully execute include:

- **Professional-looking letterhead** — This is easily accomplished with the software available on today's computers. You do not need to spend a lot of money having a design firm create professional-looking letterhead for you. Use a standard, simple template from an application such as Microsoft® Word.

- **Paper etiquette** — Choose a 20-pound or heavier bond paper to print your query letter. However, be sure not to use a cardstock paper, which is typically a 70- or 80-pound weight. Because the goal is to exude professionalism, stay away from brightly colored paper and paper with decorative borders or speckles. You may be tempted to use this type of paper to make your query stand out from the rest, but it really does not impress your target audience.

- **Format traditionally** — Traditionally, this type of formatting has been called "block" or "modified" format. It mimics the formal, traditional business letter. Be sure to include spacing between paragraphs. Keep your font clean and simple (e.g., Arial, Times Roman, Cambria, or Calibri), and use standard black ink.

- **SASE included** — The #10 full-sized business envelope is the standard size used for a SASE. You will need to fold your query letter into thirds to make it fit in this envelope. Ensure you have enough postage on it; if the agent, editor, or publisher is left with the responsibility of adding postage to your envelope, chances are good that you will not receive a response.

- **Clips** — If the writer's guidelines requests clips, be sure to include copies of your published clips. Do not ever send "unpublished" material as a clip; this is unprofessional and amateurish. Include published clips that are relevant to the topic you are pitching. If you do not have related clips, then send your best and most prestigious clips. If you have numerous clips from online publications, provide the URL address to the clip, but also include a printed copy with your query.

Query letter formatting is extremely important. Although you might argue that appearance should not be a factor in the execution of querying, the reality is that appearance does matter. An editor, agent, or publisher wants to work with professional writers — writers who can handle the basics, which include formatting query letters that adhere to industry standards.

Special Formatting for E-mail Queries

It might seem obvious to most why an e-mail query would be the most accepted submission practice for editors. Although it is evident that e-mail queries have several benefits, including savings on postage, submission time, and decreased response times, it is still important to look at this process from the editor's perspective. Although most editors, agents, and publishers have an e-mail address, many still prefer paper queries sent by regular mail, so make sure you check their guidelines before sending in any queries.

A major hiccup for editors when receiving e-mail submissions is the lack of attention to preparing a professional query. Somehow, writers assume that because it is e-mail, professionalism and formatting standards can be pushed aside.

When preparing a query letter for e-mail transmission, you will want to follow the same process as you do with traditional paper queries but with a few special tweaks here and there. You will need these elements to prepare for a successful electronic submission:

- **The header** – You only have three lines with which to catch an editor's attention in the e-mail header. With a hardcopy query letter, you often can save the details for later in the letter. However, for an e-mail query, the header is used primarily for the most important information about yourself and the query. The three elements of the e-mail header include:

o   **To:** It is important that you address your e-mail to the correct person.

o   **From:** Include your real name along with a "professional" e-mail address. For example, jane.doe@gmail.com is viewed to be more professional than geekygirl@hotmail.com. If you conduct your writing through a business, use that business name as part of your e-mail address (i.e., john.doe@writingplus. com).

o   **Subject:** Do not forget to include the word "query" in your subject line along with a three-word description of your pitch. Be careful of using phrases that are similar to spam. Refer to the SendBlaster Blog for a comprehensive list of spam words and phrases to avoid (**www.blog.sendblaster. com/2009/10/19/200-spam-words-and-phrases-to-avoid-in-your-email-newsletters**). They list more than 200 words and phrases including, "free offer," "full refund," "order now," and "no gimmick."

•   **The text** – Treat this area of the e-mail in the same fashion you would a traditional query letter. This is the safest and best approach. *Include all the essentials discussed Chapter 7.* Because the length of the e-mail is not limited, it might be enticing to create the same amount of text or even more than you would with a traditional query. Remember, one of the advantages of e-mail submissions is the ability to save time. Therefore, many editors prefer e-mail queries that are even shorter and more concise than regular mail submissions. So, consider crafting a one- to three-paragraph query when submitting by e-mail.

- **Credentials and clips** – Do list your credentials directly in the e-mail query. You can provide a link to your website or online portfolio. If you do not have a website, consider creating a very basic site that functions as your résumé for the editor, agent, or publisher to review. Whatever you do, do not attach your clips to the e-mail. Attachments often carry viruses. It can be difficult for an editor to determine whether the attachment is safe, especially if your e-mail address is unfamiliar. Also, the recipient's mail server can reject large mail attachments.

- **Address block** – The address block, which includes your mailing address, phone numbers, and e-mail address, is still relevant in e-mail submissions. The only difference is that the information is now at the bottom of the page below your name as part of the signature block.

- **Signature block** – This section of your e-mail is an extension of the address block. It can include additional information about you that would not normally appear in the address block. You may want to include a link to your website, book titles, or other special credentials. Refrain from using graphics or personal icons in your signature block. This detracts from your professionalism. It is common for people to include an electronic signature in their e-mails, but be forewarned that not all editors' e-mail clients may be able to view the image. To be safe, keep your e-mail as simple as possible.

The do's and don'ts of e-mail queries

It is difficult to be creative in the standard e-mail format, but editors are not evaluating your creative design abilities; they are looking for writing ability and credentials to perform the assigned task. Instead of trying to add color, emoticons, or special graphics to improve the look and feel of your e-mail

submission, focus on trying to format your e-mail query as closely as possible to the traditional query. And definitely do not do anything to your e-mail query that will make it harder for the publisher, editor, or agent to read.

Follow these helpful hints to reduce the number of problems you potentially could have with your submissions:

DO:	DO NOT:
Include a relevant subject	Use HTML formatting for your e-mail
Use large, readable fonts	Use color
Keep a copy of all correspondence with the editor, agent, or publisher.	Use emoticons
Keep queries as simple, short, and concise as possible	Send your clips as attachments
Ensure you are sending the query to the correct e-mail address	Send your submission as an attachment unless the guidelines specifically request it
Proofread your query before sending	Expect the editor, publisher, or agent to respond instantly to your submission
Include your complete contact information	Use special characters (i.e., tildes or accents)

DO:	DO NOT:
Use a formal, respectful, polite tone	Indent your paragraphs, not even the first line
Single-space your text	Insert graphics
Use short- to medium-length paragraphs	Bold, italicize, or underline the text

Chapter 9

How Not to Write a Query Letter

he goal is to make your query rejection proof. Queries usually go through editorial assistants first before reaching the intended editor. These assistants often are given the green light to do a superficial inspection of the query to uncover any blatant flaws, omissions, or lack of following instructions. By learning about and sidestepping some of the common pitfalls to querying, you will make your query ready for serious consideration from the editor.

The mishaps discussed in the following pages of this chapter give the impression that you are an amateur. Do not undermine your efforts with these common, but almost unforgivable, mistakes.

Top Ten Things to Avoid When Querying

The more you evolve your writing skills, and the longer you remain in the writing world, the better you will get at learning to read your editor. Editors have a reputation for being picky. They have to select just the right article and just the right author for just the right editorial calendar. There is a lot of pressure on editors to produce quality over and over and over again. So, be sure to avoid these ten things when querying a publication:

1. **AVOID being unable to deliver on the final assignment.** Editors lose complete respect for the writer who receives an assignment, accepts the assignment, and then fails to deliver. This hurts your relationship with that editor and reduces your chances of being able to pitch to that publication in the future.

2. **AVOID not following submission guidelines.** Assistant editors are skilled at weeding out queries from writers who have not followed instructions carefully. Many times, when you refuse to follow the submission guidelines, the intended editor will never see your query.

3. **AVOID unprofessionalism.** Editors only deal with professionals. Unprofessional behavior is unacceptable to almost every editor in the business. Avoid being viewed as unprofessional, do your homework, and put your best foot forward.

4. **AVOID forgetting to include a SASE.** Amateurs often forget the self-addressed stamped envelope. Remember, companies are not going to pay postage to send you a rejection letter. More important, if the publication specifically asked for a SASE in the guidelines and you did not include one, consider your idea tossed.

5. **AVOID leaving out your credentials.** Just because you do not have a list of credentials a mile long does not mean you should leave this section out of your query letter completely. It suggests to the editor that you are hiding something. Instead, be creative, and show why you are perfect for the assignment. This could be because you have personal experience in your topic or because of nontraditional writing experience, such as writing for a company newsletter or website.

6. **AVOID not including enough facts.** When you fail to support the facts, figures, and statistics or you provide or have too few facts to substantiate the claims you make, you are missing the point. Editors will not publish pieces that have unsubstantiated facts and statistics. That puts a publication's and editor's reputations on the line. It is easier for the editor to reject the query than to jeopardize a reputation.

7. **AVOID submitting unfocused queries.** With the assistance of the submission guidelines from the publication, there really is no excuse for a writer not to be able to tailor a query letter to be relevant to the market. Editors appreciate when a writer has done some digging to uncover the needs of the audience.

8. **AVOID including irrelevant information in your query.** As much as you and your family are proud of your honors and awards, if they do not relate to the topic at hand, your editor, publisher, and agent will not care, and it will turn them off.

9. **AVOID nagging about guidelines and response times.** Editors have a protocol to being approached, and they follow the protocol of the publication. When you need to talk to an editor or ask a specific question, be sure to follow this protocol. Nagging or

complaining about the guidelines and response time will not win you very many points with an editor, publisher, or agent.

10. **AVOID being impatient.** Editors are busy people. They know you are eager to land assignments and make money; however, selecting the best writer for the assignment can take quite some time. Editors cannot make that choice overnight. Following up after the response time has elapsed is allowable. E-mailing and phone calls on a daily or weekly basis, however, are highly discouraged.

Things That Infuriate the Editor

You might be getting afraid of editors at this point, but try not to be too nervous. They are people too, but they are often busy, overworked, under tight deadlines, and regularly in a position to produce high-quality content. As you read the following scenarios, you will see that dealing with editors is just common sense. Some of these things you might have to practice getting out of the habit of doing. Others will be so blatantly obvious that

you would be embarrassed at the thought of doing them yourself. Learn from others' mistakes, and try not to infuriate the editor with these things:

Slush-pile worthy mistakes

Clichés – It is difficult for editors to get the whole sense of where you might be going with the cliché in a one-page pitch. Cutesy, corny, and cheesy rarely impress an editor.

No end in sight – Editors, agents, and publishers want quick and to-the-point queries. Avoid boring the reader with extensive or irrelevant details. Provide just enough information to spark interest and not a word more. A query letter longer than a page is not recommended. Condense paragraphs, cut excessive adjectives and adverbs, eliminate wordy phrases, and get rid of anything else that makes your query sound like a run-on sentence.

Too many topics – You may think that presenting several topics at once will be helpful. Unfortunately, the opposite is true. When you present too many topics in one query letter, there are a few things that come to an editor's mind: 1) lack of confidence in your idea, 2) too lazy to separate out your ideas, or 3) lack of focus. All these scenarios can be confusing to the editor, and if it is confusing to the editor, you can bet that it will be confusing to the target audience. The result can be negative feedback from the publication's readers or loss of reputation for the overall publication.

Just plain unprofessional

Threatening an editor – Trying to force an editor to do something outside the industry guidelines is a big mistake. Editors run the show, and you have to play by their rules.

Phone calls and drop-ins – Both of these send the message that you do not understand editors or their rules. Editors are busy people, and calling or dropping by tells them you do not respect their time or space. If you need to contact an editor, regular mail or e-mail is the best method. Call only as a last resort, and forget the drop-ins altogether.

Unsubstantiated facts – A quick way to infuriate the editor is to present unsubstantiated or faulty facts. With all the available resources today, it is essential for a writer to research and validate the facts they present. Not all resources are reliable, so be sure to recheck all your facts. Do not rely on hearsay or second-hand resources; stay away from unreliable sources such as Wikipedia, advertorial sites, personal blogs, websites that have shady content, and sites that do not have a clear point of contact.

Sure signs of inexperience

Not enough details – Leaving out the details of your idea signals to the editor that you either do not have an idea, or you have not really thought it out. If either of those scenarios is the case, consider yourself flagged as a newbie.

Writing on spec – Writing on speculation/spec means you write and submit an entire article or story without a contract in place with the editor, agent, or publisher. The writer creates a piece and submits it "on spec" hoping that the agent, editor, or publisher will accept and publish it. Any writer willing to offering writing on spec in a query letter has to be a novice. Established and experienced writers do not give this option; they even cringe at the thought of the editor asking them to write on spec.

Bragging – Editors do not care who thinks your writing is great. If they do not think it is great, it does not matter if your aunt, cousin, or sister thinks you are the best writer of all time.

Military style – New writers have a tendency to be so worried about messing up that they try to follow every rule and guideline down to the last crossed "t" and last dotted "i." Editors appreciate your attempt to follow the rules of the trade for structuring and formatting your query letter and following the publication guidelines, but relax, and try to add a little bit of your personal style.

Editors are looking for clear, telltale signs that you have honed your skills, researched the market, read and followed the guidelines, and are ready to join their team. They do not want to hire someone who demonstrates lack of experience, lack of credentials, and inability to produce. Do not forget that query letters are basic business or sales letters. They function as your first impression to editors, so make sure that first impression is a good one.

CASE STUDY: FROM BOTH SIDES OF THE QUERY FENCE

Danielle Ackley-McPhail
Author/editor
www.sidhenadaire.com
www.badassfaeries.com
www.literaryhandyman.com

Danielle Ackley-McPhail has been writing for 20 years and has been a published author for 10 years. As a successful genre fiction writer, Ackley-McPhail has a more unconventional process for querying her work: "My process often can be a lot more informal, as many of my opportunities surface during informal conversations as I network conventions."

Not only is Ackley-McPhail a published author, she is also an anthology editor, so she regularly receives queries. Some of the common things she sees when writers query are 1) the writer does not follow the submission guidelines; 2) there is missing information; and 3) writers use an informal tone. From this experience as an editor, Ackley-McPhail suggestions that you:

• Pay attention, and research what an editor is looking for before you query them.

- Keep it simple and be professional.

- Highlight one or two successes you have already had, such as a noteworthy title or award.

Ackley-McPhail notes, "These three things are paramount, and yet, with the increase of Internet queries and submissions, they are most often not employed. The Internet seems to foster a false sense of intimacy that can kill opportunities for an author when he or she approaches someone too informally."

Because most of Ackley-McPhail's experience is with fiction, she spends time crafting her queries to read similarly to the back cover copy of a book. She believes a good approach for writing good hooks and pitching a good story is to look at the back covers of some best-selling mass-market paperbacks. Ackley-McPhail notes, "They are usually an excellent example of an economic, but gripping, description about a book. If you look at the top of the back covers, there are usually one or two lines of catchy text before they go into the actual description of the plot."

Ackley-McPhail agrees that query letters work, but it depends on how well they are crafted. "If they are short, to the point, and well written, then they can be very valuable, particularly if you have already accomplished something noteworthy in your career," says Ackly Mc-Phail. On the other hand, if your letter is dry, has typos, poor grammar, or contains irrelevant information, you can hurt your chances of getting an editor's attention.

As seasoned writers can attest, the goal is to sell the editor on your idea. Ackley-McPhail believes that selling your query topic is comparable to back cover copy selling the book to the reader. She says, "Get them interested, but do not give everything away."

And, Ackley-McPhail would know. She has been on both sides of the query fence as a writer and as an editor. Although her journey as an author has been somewhat unconventional, her experience in the industry has proven to be productive, successful, and rewarding.

Sample Query Letter: What Not to Do

Dear Mr. Miljler,[1]

Killer robots are taking over are planet![2]

I just finished my 150,000-word fiction novel about killer robots taking over the world.[3] After a programming malfunction in their factory, millions of robots are being sold to the public with a mission to kill instead of to assist.[4]

My mother thinks my book will be the next big thing. It is sure to be a #1 New York Bestseller![5] My novel is a cross between *The War of the Worlds* and *I, Robot*. I know it's a perfect fit for your company to publish.[6]

I have included my entire manuscript with my query.[7]

Thank you for your time. I look forward to doing business with you really soon.[8]

Sincerely,
Arthur Jones

---

[1] Do not misspell the editor's last name.

[2] Proofreading your query letter is a must. The correct phrase is "our planet." If there are too many grammatical errors in your query letter, an editor will stop reading it.

[3] The editor does not want to hear you just finished writing. He or she wants a fine-tuned and reworked piece of literature that is the best work you can produce. NEVER say "fiction novel" because novels are always fiction — that is what the word means. It is redundant and shows inexperience.

[4] This synopsis is too short to establish any sort of plot. Why are robots being manufactured and sold in the first place? Who is the protagonist? What makes your book unique? What makes someone want to publish this, let alone read it?

[5] Never reference family members. They are biased and often not familiar enough with the publishing industry to know what they are talking about. Do not pretend to foresee the success of your book. Let your work speak for itself.

[6] Do not compare your work to best sellers. It sounds pretentious and is probably incorrect. And how do you know what book is a good fit for this editor? Do not insult the editor by assuming you know more about his company than he does.

[7] Do not send your entire manuscript without being asked for it. Include an excerpt from your novel if the guidelines say to and a SASE for the editor to request more if he so chooses.

[8] Never assume that by sending your query an editor will want to publish your book. Just thank him for his time.

Querying a Literary Agent for Representation

At some point in your writing career you might determine that you need a literary agent. Writers, especially up-and-coming writers, can be reluctant to take on an agent because the industry average fee for agents is 15 percent. Many writers are struggling to land assignments and pay the bills, so it can be difficult to justify hiring a literary agent.

Before you make a rash decision either way, learn more about what a literary agent is and what he or she can do for you. This is as important as the research you have been conducting to craft the perfect query letter.

By definition, a literary agent is someone who represents a writer and the writer's work to publishers to help negotiate the sale of the work. These agents are paid a fixed percentage (usually not more than 20 percent) of the clients' profits. This is an important point when considering whether to seek out an agent for representation. Up to 98 percent of an agent's profits come from what you make. So, for a reputable agent, it is worth the time and effort to land you a good deal, because the agent wins if you win.

Why You Might Need a Literary Agent

The primary role of an agent is to find a publishing house that will publish your work. Agents usually work only with book-length projects, either fiction or nonfiction. So, if you are looking for an agent to represent you for

shorter pieces, such as short stories, articles, or poems, you will most likely have to represent yourself.

There are two primary reasons to work with an agent if you are looking to publish a book-length manuscript. The first is that the agent you work with is your representative to the industry. He or she has the incentive to find the best book deal possible concerning money, rights, and exposure. The second reason is that many of the larger publishing houses these days will not work with an unrepresented author. This makes working with a literary agent almost mandatory.

A literary agent functions as your advocate in the book-publishing world by negotiating your contract and ensuring you get the optimal deal. As far as book rights are concerned, a literary agent can market subsidiary rights to your book and is often the best person to sell translation rights, international rights, electronic rights, audio-book rights, and even movie rights.

Advantages of Hiring a Literary Agent

If coming out of your research about literary agents you decide that getting an agent to represent you is advantageous, it probably is good idea. Reputable agents are experts at saving time and making better decisions from a more objective and strategic position. If you still are unsure and need some help to back up your decision, read this list of advantages for hiring a literary agent:

- **Literary agents know books.** It is the job of a good agent to know about books and the publishing industry. The experienced agent will know what kind of books sell, what kind of topics are in-demand, and what kind of markets are best for your particular work.

- **Agents are highly regarded by editors.** To increase your chances of being considered for publishing, having an agent represent you is a good move.

- **Publishers almost expect it these days.** Trends in the publishing community are moving more toward publishers not accepting unsolicited manuscripts at all. With an agent to back you up, you often have direct entry into the editor's office.

- **Agents are expert negotiators.** Even if you feel confident in your negotiating abilities, it might be more advantageous for you to leave the negotiations up to an agent. An agent often has ulterior motives when negotiating your work. They make more if you make more. Also, agents are familiar with the boilerplate contracts for the publishing houses with which they work. These agents can assess your offer quickly and decide what is in your best interest and how to proceed in negotiations with the publisher.

- **Literary agents can become a valuable "coach."** Agents are not only sales representatives for writers, but they also can become your partners to success. The advice you receive from your agent can be a valuable resource for you. The relationship you build often can lead to future endeavors that will benefit you both.

- **Agents ensure timely payment from the publisher.** Once your manuscript has been completed, submitted, accepted, and finalized, agents will conduct the necessary follow-up to ensure any outstanding financial balances are handled. The publisher works through the agent, so any money you receive will come directly from your agent, after he or she subtracts the negotiated percentage for services rendered.

Literary agents definitely can give clients a much-needed edge over the competition. But keep in mind that agents cannot perform miracles. Your work has to be good, relevant, and have the ability to sell. It is your job to research the resources identified in the previous section diligently and ensure you land an agent who will be a good fit for you and your work.

Where to Find Reputable Agents

The key word here is "reputable." As you learned in Chapter 2, literary agent scams run rampant and are at the top of the list of the most common types of scams. Unfortunately, these scammers mostly succeed where new writers are concerned. You can begin your search by referencing the following industry resources:

- **AgentQuery (www.agentquery.com)**: Agent Query offers the largest, most current searchable database of literary agents online.

- **Writers Net® (www.writers.net)**: WritersNet is the Internet directory of writers, editors, publishers, and literary agents.

- *Publishers Marketplace* **(www.publishersmarketplace.com)**: *Publishers Marketplace* is the dedicated resource for publishing professionals to find critical information and unique databases, find each other, and to do business better electronically.

- *Publisher's Weekly* **(www.publishersweekly.com)**: *Publisher's Weekly* is a U.S. weekly trade news magazine targeted at publishers, booksellers, literary agents, and libraries.

- **Guide to Literary Agents (www.guidetoliteraryagents.com)**: The *Guide to Literary Agents* is the complete resource for writers who need representation — to get their writing published or to take their publishing goals to a new level.

- **Association of Author's Representatives (www.aar-online.org)**: AAR is a professional organization for literary and dramatic agents. It was established in 1991 through the merger of the Society of Authors' Representatives, founded in 1928, and the Independent Literary Agents Association, founded in 1977.

- **Search engines:** Do not forget to browse the major search engines by typing in relevant search keywords. Search engines can return countless links to excellent online resources, directories, and industry experts' blogs.

Another good approach to finding a reputable agent is to visit your local bookstore. Seek out books similar to the one you are interested in publishing. Go straight to the acknowledgments page to see if the author has acknowledged his or her agent by name. If so, you can go straight to the source. If he or she has not acknowledged the agent by name, jot down the name of the publisher. You can contact the publisher to get the name and contact information of the agent. Start with the assistant editor and explain that you are a writer and would like to contact the agent associated with the specific book. Assistant editors are used to working with a variety of authors, even newbies. If that approach does not work, try going through a writer's organization or writing group.

Other creative approaches to finding agents include: asking another writer to recommend you, attending writer's conferences to get direct access to agents, or sending your work directly to an agent — by query, of course.

Proceed with Caution When Looking for Agents

Try to stick with the resources provided in the previous sections when doing your research to find a reputable agent. Literary agents often get a bad reputation because of scammers posing as agents who prey primarily on up-and-coming authors as well as seasoned authors. This scam was touched on briefly in Chapter 2, but experienced writers warn others to stay away from:

Agents asking for a reading fee – This is the classic agent scam. If an agent charges you any kind of fee to review your manuscript, steer clear. This practice is considered legal, but agents who do this are considered unprofessional and are making money from the writer, not the publisher.

Agents asking for a retainer – Reputable agents are able to pay for their own expenses. They can determine whether a book is marketable and do not consider up front fees or retainers as a valid expense to request from a writer.

Agents offer to edit your manuscript for a fee – As mentioned previously, agents are not editors. They should not be asking you to pay for any kind of editing. Reputable agents will accept only market-ready materials. Do not confuse the editing fee with a reading fee mentioned previously. The reading fee is charged with the notion of simply reviewing your manuscript to see if the agent will represent you or if they think it will be marketable. The editing fee is charged with the understanding that the agent will actually edit your manuscript.

Agents asking for a commission higher than the industry standard – Reputable agents know the going industry fee, and if they try to convince you they need more to place your book, tell them thanks but no thanks. Sometimes a scamming agent will tell a writer that because he or she is new and does not have a solid track record in the industry, he or she will need to pay a higher fee. If this is the case, look for another agent to represent you.

Agents not belonging to AAR – Although membership to this organization does not guarantee you will land the best agent, it does provide some peace of mind because the agents who belong to this association have to agree to a certain standard of ethics and professionalism.

Agents who sell mostly to smaller, less reputable publishers – Do not waste your time pursuing agents who have a large percentage of sales to small, electronic, or subsidy publishers. This does not help your reputation as a serious author, nor does it provide opportunities for you to pursue avenues that normally would not be available to you without representation.

Keep these in mind as you are looking for agent representation. The goal is to find an agent who appreciates and understands your material. Do not limit yourself to only the previously listed industry resources; also seek out other writers and join high-quality, online discussion groups for writers. Establish your reputation in the writing world, and you will develop the confidence to approach writers about their agents.

Developing a Good Working Relationship with Your Agent

As you have been learning with editors, agents also have a few preferences of their own. This is why it is important for you to do extensive research to find the right agent. Your next task is to work on developing a good relationship with your agent. An agent also sizes up their clients, so be sure to have these standards when presenting yourself to a potential agent:

- **Know a bit about the business.** Writers easily can forget that they are in a business; they can be so focused on writing that they lose sight of the fact that getting published involves a lot more than just their literary masterpiece. Your agent is an expert in publishing, but it would help them more if you also knew a little bit about the publishing industry, too. Knowing the guidelines for crafting a good query letter, understanding the components of a book proposal, and knowing how to approach editors and agents will go a long way in strengthening the relationship you develop with your agent.

- **Understand that rewriting is inevitable.** Ideally, as a writer, you have come to accept that part of writing and getting published involves rewriting. Your editor invariably will ask you to rewrite your article, and your agent will ask you to rewrite sections of your proposal or manuscript. Manuscripts rarely go to the publisher on the first submission. Do not take the rewriting personally; your agent is trying to ensure you produce the best possible book to ensure the best possible return on both of your investments.

- **Be open to your agent's advice.** Remember, your agent is an expert in the publishing business. He or she will know the publisher, the market, and the genre that matches best with your project. Being open to your agent's advice is a sign of professionalism and business savvy. You do not have to agree all the time, but at least give him or her due respect because it just might be the best advice you receive that is relevant to reaching your dream of being published.

- **Have a plan past one book.** Agents enjoy working with authors who have a plan for a series or a goal to be a multi-published author. One-time authors are a risk for agents, so to build a solid working relationship with your agent, plan for more than one or two books. If your goal is to be a career writer, then be a prolific one, and let your agent help develop your reputation in the industry.

Seven ways to get blacklisted by an agent

Today's writing market can be tough to navigate and penetrate. Most traditional publishing houses will not work with a writer without agent representation. Agents are just as busy as editors, so you inevitably will come up against rejection from literary agents. To avoid this, learn and commit to memory these seven ways you can get blacklisted by an agent:

1. **Sending generalized queries** – Agents are specialists. They help writers place work in a specific market and with a specific publisher. If you are sending an agent generalized or unfocused queries, he or she will not take you seriously.

2. **Providing irrelevant information in your queries** – This is boring to an editor; so, you can bet that it will be boring to an agent. Providing irrelevant information in your queries tells the agent you did not do your homework. That does not motivate an agent to do the homework on your behalf.

3. **Missing deadlines** – This is one of the major blunders for a writer. If you cannot meet deadlines while working with your agent, do you think your agent should expect you to complete the book on time, or at all? Publishing is a deadline-driven industry. It is unprofessional to miss deadlines chronically.

4. **Dishonesty** – Agents have heard all the stories, and they are good at uncovering dishonesty and exaggerations. Be upfront and honest with your agent, and you will reap the rewards in return.

5. **Complaining** – You are not the only client your agent has. Agents often have to manage deadlines, contracts, manuscripts, and queries from a handful, if not more, clients. If you are constantly complaining or nagging to your agent, he or she will consider you more trouble than is worth the 15 percent he or she is hoping to receive by working with you.

6. **Being a control freak** – You are the writer, and your agent is the expert. If you have done your homework and selected well, you should be able to allow your agent to do what he or she knows to do. Having a tight rope around your agent will not create a good working relationship; it will have the opposite effect. Be respectful, and let your agent do his or her job.

7. **Unrealistic expectation about being rich and famous** – The percentage of writers who strike it rich on the first attempt is low. Agents do not appreciate when a writer has unrealistic expectations about getting published. Publishing is a business and a very competitive industry. Agents are good at what they do, but they do not work miracles, and they cannot promise you stardom and wealth.

Be realistic about your goals for publishing and working with an agent. You can benefit from a great working relationship that can lead to many future successes. Just be sure to learn, study what to do, and what not to do when trying to establish a working relationship with your agent.

Submitting Your Query

J ust as there is an art to developing and writing a query letter, there is also an art to submitting queries. The right editor or the right publication can be one send button or stamp away with the right strategy. One of these quickest and easiest ways to know how to submit your query is by thoroughly reading the submission guidelines for the publication or publisher you are planning to approach. Each publication and publisher will have different guidelines, so you will not be able to standardize your submissions completely.

It is possible to land an assignment on your first query submission, so you will need to be prepared. This chapter will focus on submission strategies and techniques to optimize querying. You will learn how to develop a query submission schedule, how to schedule your query letter writing time, and the protocol regarding regular mail and e-mail delivery methods.

Planning Your Submission Strategy

The art of query submission is a balance between the number of queries you send (quantity) and the amount of money you can make on a given assignment (profitability). The following strategies will help you acquire the fastest possible outcome while ensuring that you do not sell yourself short by pursuing the least lucrative markets for your work.

- **Know the market you are approaching.** As you learned in Chapter 10, reputable agents are experts because they know their markets. They are entrenched in the industry and know what the publishers are looking for. But you do not have to become an agent to acquire the same savvy. Conducting the right amount of research with the most reliable resources can have the same result. The primary resources to begin with are the *Writer's Market* and the *Literary Marketplace*. These two industry standards will provide you with a wealth of information and lead you to other reputable outlets to pursue.

- **Do not overlook the obvious.** Novice writers have a tendency to overthink the intent of a query. They can spend too much time trying to come up with an idea that has never been pitched before, which is a perfect equation of disaster. It is difficult to come up with something completely new — something that has never been done before. Seasoned writers understand that the goal is to present a sellable material to a specific market. That is not very innovative, but it is the foundation of querying. The first strategy was to know the market you are approaching. This particular strategy is about understanding the needs of that market. Do not overlook the obvious in your attempt to come up with something no one has ever done before.

- **Pursue the most optimal market first.** It can be tempting to pursue markets that are less prestigious because you lack the credentials, confidence, or clips. However, if you have identified your market, done the appropriate research, and crafted a sellable idea, you can find yourself published in one the top publications in the industry. If it is optimal for you to present your idea to *Golf Digest*, then do not waste another minute trying to talk yourself out of it. Use the information detailed in this book, prepare a good query letter, follow the writer's guidelines, and pitch your idea with confidence.

- **Learn from your rejections.** A writer must review rejected queries and make appropriate improvements before sending the idea to another publication. If any of your rejection letters have constructive comments or contain detailed critiquing, consider that an invitation to submit additional ideas. Editors, agents, and publishers rarely spend time offering detailed comments to a writer who does not show promise. Learn to turn rejections into opportunities for growth and improvement.

- **Increase your odds.** Sending out many queries to different publications will keep you in practice and increase your chances of publication. As your experience level rises, the number of queries you send out might increase, primarily because additional writing credits and experience in querying will streamline the process, and you have more opportunities for placement with those publications that require past writing experience. A good rule is to keep your submission process going by sending out at least one new query per week. You can send either the same idea to multiple publications — though be careful when doing this in case more than one publication accepts your submission; this does not look professional — or you can send out a new or different idea out each week to a targeted list of publications. If you have more time, increase the number of submissions. It is simple math; the more queries you send out, the more likely you are to sell something.

- **Query the right editor, agent, or publisher.** This cannot be stressed enough; send your query to the right person. This will ensure the fastest results. You do not want to waste your valuable writing and submission time waiting unnecessarily for an agent, editor, or publisher to respond when it went to the wrong person. If that is not clear from the magazine's masthead, the submission guidelines, or the website, call to get further guidance and clarification.

- **Exhaust all possibilities before moving on.** Some publishers, editors, or agents are harder to pitch to than others. Do not completely give up on a publication if you cannot crack the code the first time. Sometimes, it might require a six-month to a year breather before submitting a query to them again. Remember, editors, agents, and publishers are looking to fulfill an already-defined need. If your idea does not fit their need today, it might fit later. If multiple editors reject your query because of a technical flaw in your writing, then make the correction, and try resubmitting to another outlet.

Schedule Time to Write Your Queries

Writers have to write. There is no way around it. Ask any professional writer and he or she will confirm that one of the hardest things to do is find time to actually write. As you progress further in your writing career, you will learn to balance all the activities that are required of you as a writer. But starting out, it can be daunting to balance the business aspects of writing and the writing parts. Submitting queries is what drives your income, so, it will be a mandatory part of your day-to-day schedule. It almost seems inevitable that when you schedule time to write or think about sitting down to write, a variety of things can pop up. Your task is to tune things out for your allotted writing time and sit down, focus, and write your queries. It can seem like a large obstacle sometimes to try to fit writing in among all the other priorities you face, but do not lose heart. Here are a few helpful hints you can follow to developing a writing schedule:

- **Keep track of your time.** For a week, write down all the activities you performed in a given day. Document how much time you spent on each activity. Do not leave anything out, even if it was not related to writing. Your list should include time spent shopping, surfing the Internet, going to the gym, sleeping, taking classes, etc. Each day has 24 hours in it, which mean in a given week, you have 168 hours to spend. At the end of the week, you will have a good idea of where your time is being spent.

- **Cut out what you do not need.** If you need to schedule writing time, you now should be able to identify which activities can be removed. If you are having trouble cutting out what you do not need, then start prioritizing the activities into "A," "B," and "C" categories with "A" being the highest priority. Once you have prioritized them, try to remove all or most of the "C" activities temporarily (or at least cut back on them significantly), recalculate your hours, and see how much time you have recovered for writing. If you have cut out everything you can and still need some more time, try combining tasks.

- **Combine tasks if you can.** There are activities that will be impossible or very difficult to cut from your schedule. So, look at the activities that remain and see if there is anything left on your list that could be combined and done simultaneously. In other words, see if there are two or more things you can multitask on to save yourself more time for writing. For example, you could read the newspaper and work out at the same time.

- **Take advantage of extra time.** A few minutes here, a few minutes there can add up to some extra time you can allocate to writing your queries. A common problem with finding extra time is that it might not be used productively. If your extra time is only ten minutes, it is probably not a good idea to work on a 1,000-word article. However, in those ten minutes, you can probably research another market, send off an e-mail to request a sample copy of a publication, or jot down a brief outline for a query topic. If you have an extra hour or two of time, then you can dedicate that time to flushing out your query letter. Every minute counts, so, do not wait to get a large block of time to sit down and write. Use the time you have found, schedule writing time on your calendar, and be sure to start with small, manageable activities.

The closer you get to publication, the more your writing work increases. A writing schedule is imperative to be successful. If you have mastered your writing schedule and figured out how to make it work with your other responsibilities, you are well on your way to developing a winning edge.

Query Submission Tracking Tools

Next to scheduling time for writing, tracking submissions is another critical activity that will require your attention. Believe it or not, submissions do get lost in the mail and editors inadvertently can delete or misplace your electronic query. So do not rely on editors, agents, and publishers to help you manage and keep track of your markets, submissions, and contacts. This responsibility is solely up to you, and a variety of tools are available to help you successfully keep track of your submissions. The most commonly used methods for tracking queries submissions are:

- Computer spreadsheets
- Desktop submission tracking software
- Online submission trackers

Computer spreadsheets

Computer spreadsheets are one of the simplest tracking tools available because nowadays, most everyone has a spreadsheet program on their computers. The most common program is Microsoft Excel®. Another increasingly popular spreadsheet is Google Docs, which offers an online spreadsheet in the lineup. The most important aspect of creating a tracking submission spreadsheet is to design it with the correct and most useful headers. The headings listed below are generic. You might find that you need more fields tailored to your genre or personal tracking preferences. This list provides a place from which you can start to develop a simple tracking tool for your queries:

- Title of piece
- Length/word count
- Genre
- Market type
- Pay rate

- Date sent
- Response time
- Responded? (Y/N)
- Accepted? (Y/N)
- Due date
- Publish date
- Expected pay date
- Paid? (Y/N)

Spreadsheets are the simplest and most cost-effective way to track your query submissions. Once you have established the fields, you can quickly fill in the information relevant to each query. As you add more queries, the spreadsheet allows you to sort your information on any of the fields.

Using the spreadsheet approach offers you basic functionality, which can be a good way to track your submissions as you are first starting out. However, the more queries you submit, the larger your spreadsheet will become. Ultimately, it might become unwieldy, and you might need to consider another option, such as specialty submission tracking software or online submission trackers.

Desktop submission tracking software

Desktop submission tracking software often is developed by a software company that specializes in products for writers, publishers, and agents. You can purchase this software on a CD or download it from the company's website. As mentioned in the previous section, there might come a time when you outgrow your spreadsheet and need to move to something more robust to manage the size of your growing submissions. Several good — and free — software programs have been designed specifically for the needs of writers. A few of the common programs are listed below:

APPLICATION	DESCRIPTION	PROVIDER	COST
Sonar 3	Sonar 3 is a manuscript submission-tracking program that tells you which market has each piece, whether a piece has been sold or rejected, and which stories are on hold.	Spacejock Software (**www.space jock.com/Sonar3. html**)	Free
PowerTracker™	PowerTracker is a submission, file management, and expense tracking software.	WriteBrain (**www.write-brain. com/power_ tracker_main.htm**)	$49.95 US
SAMM	Sandbaggers Automated Manuscript Management software allows for easy storage and retrieval of your manuscript and query information. You can maintain a complete history of everything you write and submit.	Sandbaggers (**www.sand baggers.8m.com/ samm.htm**)	Free
Writers Project Organizer	This manuscript software helps you organize your ideas, thoughts, submissions, and contacts. With the Writers Project Organizer, you can track word and page counts, the date you started, the date you finished, and the date your piece was sold.	PinderSoft (**www.pinder soft.com/wpo. htm**)	$24.99
The Writer's Scribe	The Writer's Scribe is a professional submission-tracking software for writers that allows you to view all your activities with a standard calendar format.	The Writer's Scribe (**www.the writersscribe. com**)	$25.00

APPLICATION	DESCRIPTION	PROVIDER	COST
Writer's Database	The Writer's Database is a submission tracking system that helps you keep track of work you have written and tracks related information about submissions to publishers and magazines.	Simon Kevin (**www. simon kewin.co.uk/writ- edb.htm**)	Free

Online submission trackers

Online submission trackers are usually Web-based communities where the user creates an account (free or at a monthly subscription rate) and manages their submissions in the "cloud" — a Web-based environment. The primary benefit of online submission trackers is that you can access your information while you are away from your home or office computer. These online tracking applications offer services that allow you to track the markets you approach, the status of queries you have submitted, estimated response times, publication guidelines, query titles, money earned from each sale, editors' comments, and pay rates.

APPLICATION	DESCRIPTION	PROVIDER	COST
Writer's Database	Writer's Database is a submission tracking software that helps you keep track of all the relevant markets for your writing and the status of your submissions to each of those markets. The information you can manage includes contact information, rates, estimated response time, submission guidelines, titles of what you have written, money earned from each sale, editor's comments, and manuscripts and queries you have sent.	Luminary (**www. writersdb.com**)	Free

APPLICATION	DESCRIPTION	PROVIDER	COST
Duotrope™ LLC		Duotrope's Digest (**www.duotrope. com/subtracker. aspx**)	Free
QueryTracker	QueryTracker is an online database that helps you keep track of query letters sent to literary agents and publishers	QueryTracker (**www.query tracker.net**)	Free
Submission Manager	Submission Manager is an online system that allows you to accept and manage written submissions for magazines or publishers.	CLMP (**www.clmp.org/ about/sub_mgr_ form.html**)	$300-$600
Writer's Market	The Writer's Market is an online database of more than 8,000 listings for book publishers, magazines, contests, literary agents, newspapers, online publications, and syndicates. This system allows you to organize your top markets, manage submissions, manage your freelance rates, and stay abreast of the latest publishing news.	Writer's Market (**www.writers-market.com**)	$5.99/ month, $39.99 for 1-year membership, $59.99 for 2-year membership

Any submission tracking system you use, whether a spreadsheet, desktop submission tracking software program, or an online submission tracker, will need to offer the same basic features that answer the following questions:

- What was the piece?
- When was the piece submitted?
- When will you hear back?

- Have you heard back yet?
- What was the response?

From these five basic questions, you will need to expand your features to include information about what market you sent to, which ideas worked and which ones did not work, and what payment you can expect and how much.

The Submission Checklist

It might seem like the odds are stacked against you when you research the metrics of how many writers are submitting queries to editors, agents, and publishers. You might wonder how you will ever get through to an editor or agent who is wading through scores of submissions. To help put your brain on a more positive line of thinking, think of the query submission as a project for a client. The client has a need for your writing services and specific content for their publication. So, what fundamental elements are required to make the client's shortlist? Besides having a great topic of idea and presenting it in a way that will make an editor, agent, or publisher come asking for more, you will also need to follow this 11-point checklist to ensure your submission is ready to send:

❑ **I have read the publication.** You would be surprised how many writers have submitted queries without ever reading one sample of the publication to which they are pitching. Do not fall into the same habit. It is imperative that you read at least one, if not several samples of the publication to which you are submitting ideas. Nowadays, because most publications have a website, there are very few excuses left for not studying the publication before you query the editor.

❑ **I have double- and tripled-checked the publication guidelines.** The first hurdle is to ensure they actually have guidelines. A good place to start is the publication's website to see if they have a link to "Writer's Guidelines" or "Submission Guidelines." If you do not find these types of links, continue your search on the "About" or "Contact" pages. Sometimes this information will be buried in a location that is not always intuitive. If all else fails on the website, then you will need to resort to requesting a sample copy of the publication by mail. Continue your search until you have exhausted all possibilities. If you find the guidelines, be diligent about reading them and reading them thoroughly. If you do not find guidelines, try sending a brief and polite note to the editor or assistant editor asking if they have writer's guidelines.

❑ I **have included a SASE (if sending by regular mail).** Be sure to include a self-addressed stamped envelope so the editor, publisher, or agent can send you a response. Remember to include an envelope that is large enough to hold your materials (e.g. Use a #10 business envelope for short queries and a 9x12 envelope for novel queries, finished articles, or manuscripts). As you become a more experienced writer, do not forgo the SASE even when you have established a rapport with a particular editor. Let the editor dictate this and notify you when you no longer need to send as SASE. After an editor purchased two or three pieces from you, it would be more appropriate not to send a SASE. Always ask to be sure.

❑ I **have included the correct postage on each submission.** Check with the post office to see how much postage you will need to send the query, as well as the postage on the envelope being returned. If you do not include enough postage or an envelope, do not expect a response from the editor, agent, or publisher.

❑ **I have included copies of my published clips (if requested).** Many editors will request clips. These clips will consist of previously published materials — the key word being "published." The rule is to send the most relevant clips for the topic you are pitching. If you do not have clips that are related to your query, then send the best and most prestigious clips you have.

❑ **I have proofread and checked my content for grammatical and typographic errors.** Do not rely completely on your software to check for spelling. Do your own proofreading and editing if you can. If you do not have the time or do not feel confident in your abilities to do a good job, consider asking a friend or family member to review your query letter. Depending on your budget, you even might consider hiring a freelance editor to assist you with your grammar.

❑ **I have followed the correct submission method.** By referencing the writer's guidelines, you will have an idea of the publication's preference for submissions. Several editors, agents, and publishers still do not accept e-mail submissions. Be careful about how you send your queries; many editors refuse to open attachments because of the proliferation of computer viruses. Sending a completed manuscript when the guidelines request "Queries only" will not bode well with an editor.

❑ **I have included my contact information.** This is especially important when you are submitting e-mail queries. Many writers assume that the editor, agent, or publisher will just push the reply button on the e-mail transmission. Do not make an editor's job any harder than it already is. Whether they can easily hit the reply button or not, it is professional practice to always provide your contact information in a location that is easily accessible.

❑ **I have matched the correct query letter with its corresponding envelope for each submission.** If you are sending out multiple submissions, be sure to match the correct query letter with the right editor, agent, or publisher. Double-check the address and ensure you have included everything that has been requested by the guidelines.

❑ **I have recorded where each submission is going.** Using one of the query tracking submission techniques discussed in the previous section, it should be easy for you to document the details of each of your submissions. Before you send any queries out, be sure to record the statistics associated with each. Remember, these data may include: title, word count, genre, market, pay, date sent, response time, due date, and publication date.

❑ **I have made a digital or hardcopy of everything I am submitting.** Do not rely on the agent, editor, or publisher to keep a copy of your submission. In fact, there is a possibility that your submission might get misplaced, and the editor, publisher, or agent might request another query from you. Take the necessary precautions of making a digital or hardcopy duplicate of all the materials you submit with your query.

The art of querying is not just about the letter; it is also about the submission. Knowing how to submit your query using the writer's guidelines and following industry standards are the best ways you can increase your chances of getting past the slush pile, into the hands of an attentive agent, publisher, or editor, and on your way to assignment and publication.

Chapter 12

When Query Letters Are Not Required

t is possible to secure a writing assignment without having to submit a query letter. This chapter identifies and illustrates several scenarios where query letters might not be required and what to do when that happens. Of course, these scenarios are more the exception than the rule. As a beginning writer, expect to spend a good portion of your writing career submitting queries, so it is best to perfect the art. More experienced writers often can circumvent the query process because they already have an established relationship with an editor or they already are getting regular assignments from various editors and markets.

Do not assume these scenarios always hold true. They are more the exception than the rule. If you are not sure when it is necessary to query, it is best to refer to the writer's guidelines of the publication or publishing house.

Scenario 1: You Have Established a Rapport With Your Editor

You might have noticed a running theme throughout this book has been how to make it easier on your editor. Once you have turned in a handful of articles to a publication and established a rapport with the editor, you will become an asset to that editor. You turn in your assignments on time. You give the editor what he or she is looking for. You do not whine or complain. You are professional and respectful. And most important, your writing is clean and reliable. These are all good criteria for an editor not requiring a query letter from you.

If the editor comes to like you and appreciates your working relationship, you might soon enjoy the scenario that all writers dream about: the day when your editor calls on you to do a rush assignment or the e-mail from your editor asking for help to fill in an uncommitted section of the next issue.

Scenario 2: The Publication Guidelines State "No Query"

Writer's guidelines are the primary source of information for writers who want to know whether they need to submit a query. Inexperienced writers might assume all publications require a query letter. The best approach is to check the publication's guidelines because there are instances where the publication clearly states it does not need or accept queries. If the publication states a query is not needed or accepted, chances are, they want the full article or manuscript.

Scenario 3: Submitting to an Online, Small-Readership Publication

A reputation often proceeds itself. Not all online, small-readership publications are the same, but in general, many of these publications do not pay and therefore do not require a query letter submission. New writers tend to migrate to these markets to get a byline or bio and build a clip file. This can be a good avenue to break into to give your writing career a jump-start, but it is often low or no pay, and you will need to branch out into bigger markets as you advance in your career.

Scenario 4: Submitting Short, Out-of-the-Ordinary Pieces

Short and out-of-the-ordinary pieces such as poems, fillers (i.e., smaller pieces of content such as short stories, statistics, or humor used to fill in gaps in a publication), flash fiction (i.e., a style of literary fiction where the author uses a short form of storytelling), greeting cards, and jokes often are too short to warrant a query. Most editors, agents, and publishers can skim these pieces faster than they would be able to read your query. There is a good market for this type of work, but try not to make this your primary source of income simply to avoid the query process.

Scenario 5: The Publisher Wants a Book Proposal Instead

If you are considering writing a book, you will be expected to send a query letter to sell your book idea. But in some cases, the publisher will skip the query and ask for a book proposal.

A proposal is a much more detailed version of the query. Instead of one page, the proposal is generally 30 to 40 pages long. With this many pages, you will need to cover more territory than in the query letter. Instead of pitching an idea, you will also need to provide information about your competition, a preliminary market analysis, and a couple of sample chapters. Also, look at some of the following resources for examples of book proposal sections:

- **How to Write a Book Proposal (www.hiwrite.com/pro.html)** – A comprehensive writing website that addresses topics such as book proposals, literary agents, query letters, and writing styles. Focus primarily on the link to book proposal examples.

- **Alder & Robin Books, Inc. (www.alderbooks.com/howto.html)** – A plain and basic website, it provides a good description of preparing a book proposal and provides links to various sample book proposals.

- **Absolute Write (www.absolutewrite.com/novels/book_proposal.htm)** – An authoritative, industry website that covers all things writing related. The specific link is to an example book proposal used by an author to sell more than 30 nonfiction books.

Key elements of the book proposal

If mastering the art of querying was not enough, now you will need to learn how to craft a winning proposal. *A sample proposal is included in Appendix D.* Consider the query as a sprint race and the book proposal as the endurance race. The proposal will require more thought and time into developing the entire strategy for your book. Five components always go into the book proposal. Depending on the publisher, there might be more, but these five should never be excluded:

Synopsis – *[synopsis page count: 1–2]* The synopsis serves the same purpose as the hook of the query letter. The function of the synopsis is to provide detail about the book's content, structure, tone, and design. Because you have two pages to work with, you can further develop anything unique about the book, such as what solution it offers to the audience, the importance of the topic, and what can the reader expect to take away from the book.

A good approach to developing your synopsis is to start with a strong, concrete opening and fill in the details later. Even though you have more room to develop your ideas in the proposal, the editor still wants to be engaged and captivated by your story. The synopsis is your sales pitch, and the editor will be asking two things while reading these first two pages:

- Will the audience want to read this?
- Will the audience buy this?

There are several ways to address these questions and increase the editor's confidence in your idea. In your synopsis, cover these important elements:

- Mention the book's relevance to a current trend or in-demand topic.
- Discuss the book's value to the audience.
- Write the synopsis in the tone you will use to write the book.
- Demonstrate how the book will stand out on the shelf from similar books.

The key to crafting a solid synopsis is to develop your idea clearly so the editor can understand what you are pitching quickly. In addition, you want supporting evidence that will validate that your idea is a good one and that people will want to read it.

Table of contents – *[table of contents page count: 1–2]* Gone are the days of a simple, short-and-sweet table of contents. Studies show that readers skim the table of contents to determine whether they will continue reading the book. If your table of contents does not provide some insight into what the reader can expect, chances are they will return your book to the shelf. The trend is to be as descriptive as possible with some tables of contents providing a brief summary of the chapter.

Do not be shy about drafting a comprehensive table of contents in your book proposal. Now is the best time to provide creative and descriptive chapter titles to show the editor you have put some thought into it. Editors realize that the chapter titles might change as the book evolves, but at this point in the proposal stage, all the editor wants to see is what you have envisioned for the book.

The primary purpose of the table of contents for the book proposal is to demonstrate that you are organized, you have covered the essential aspects of the topic you are proposing, and you have a plan of attack to present the information. If you structure the table of contents strategically in the beginning, you will find that by the time you receive your book contract, the writing will come much more easily.

Chapter summaries – *[chapter summaries page count: 4–5]* The table of contents sets the stage for how the book will be organized, but editors want more detail. Chapter summaries are an expanded version of the proposed table of contents. This section of your proposal provides brief descriptions of each chapter and discusses what each will cover. This will serve as a blueprint for developing the content when you are ready to write.

Sample chapters – *[sample chapters page count: 10–20]* Depending on the publisher, you might have to submit both chapter summaries and one or two sample chapters. When submitting your sample chapters, do not include the Introduction or Chapter 1 because these are often viewed as too introductory or elementary and do not get into the meat of the subject matter. It is best to include a chapter from the middle of the book. Whether you are writing a fiction or nonfiction book, you will need to have some chapters completed. When including sample chapters in your proposal, these are not rough drafts or outlines; these are completely written chapters you will be submitting with your manuscript.

Put your best foot forward with these chapters and ensure they are top-notch. This is where the agent, editor, or publisher will get a feel for your writing style. These highly polished sample chapters are the evidence you will be able to deliver on your proposal.

Market analysis – *[market analysis page count: 3–6]* In this section of the book proposal, you provide the platform for marketing and promoting the book. With many publishing companies expecting most authors to conduct a large portion, if not all, of the marketing, it is an extremely important exercise to develop a comprehensive market analysis. This section of your proposal will consist of the following four components:

- **Competition:** Identify at least four to five books that are currently selling in the same market and on the same subject matter. Provide basic statistics about the book and a little bit of information about the book's sales pattern. Do not go overboard and tout too much about these books because it might take some of the limelight and steam away from your proposal. The goal is to show the editor there is a market for the topic and readers are buying the information. Find the balance that demonstrates you have done your homework by acknowledging the competition, but you are proposing a unique solution to an identified need.

- **Platform:** Demonstrate you have plans for visibility. This involves identifying how you will handle or initiate book signings, workshops, seminars, websites, blogs, conferences, and other visibility outlets.

- **Promotional plan:** List various things you intend to do to market and promote your book. In this part of the plan, you will want to list radio and TV appearances, newspaper and magazine articles, website development, workshops and conferences you will attend, direct mail promotions, and other promotional activities to get the word out. If you are a new writer and do not have any of these items secured, you can start building your promotional tools, or you can write a detailed description of how you intend to promote yourself and your book. Book publishers will market and promote well-known authors, but for thousands of other writers, self-promotion is the only outlet. Experienced writers often have a better understanding of how to position themselves and their work in a given industry. However, for beginning writers, the work to promote yourself and your book begins by establishing a website or blog, using social networks such as Facebook and Twitter, book signings, book trailer videos, radio interviews, and other creative ways to spread the word.

- **Demographics:** Identify your audience. The demographics section of your book proposal clearly defines your target reader and characteristics of that group. You will need to list identifiers such as gender, age, income, education level, nationality, and any other characteristics that show you understand your reader.

Qualifications – *[qualifications page count: 1–2]* Showing credentials can cause the up-and-coming writer some anxiety. Whether you are drafting a query or a book proposal, as a novice writer, you will have focus on showing you are qualified in other ways. Consider this a crash course in creative writing.

If you do not have a lot of experience or samples of previous work to provide, consider focusing your qualifications on areas such as your education, your associations and affiliations, your personal experience with the topic, any industry contacts, or your network. Without drawing too much emphasis on your lack of qualifications, the key is to draw the editor's focus to your expertise through references to professional or personal experiences relevant to the subject of your book.

If you have credentials, be sure to include them. Place qualifications that are most relevant to the book first. If you have room, add more information to substantiate your experience and expertise.

Regardless of the type of qualifications you have, a good exercise is to write a one- or two-paragraph author's biography. Reference books in the topic you are proposing, and see what other authors have written. Draft one for yourself, and refine it as you gain more credits and clips throughout your writing career.

Publishing companies are in the business of selling books. They look for good, solid proposals that offer a good read and a good sale. Make your proposal a good fit, and you can both benefit — a win-win situation.

Query Letter Anomalies

Editors, publishers, and agents greatly appreciate writers who follow the rules and submit good query letters. A large part of what makes a good query letter is the time and effort you have spent preparing it according to the guidelines and editor's wishes. If you spend a fair amount of time in the writing business, you will become more comfortable with the query process. As with many procedures and guidelines, there are usually a few outliers. The same is true with queries.

The message throughout this book has been to focus on crafting the best query letter possible and follow certain rules. Ignorance is not a valid excuse to break querying rules.

However, there are three special cases where query letters do not fall into the standard guidelines. The key is to research and know the rules first; you can learn to adjust them to your specific situation. The following are two instances where querying does not fall into the standard guidelines:

Quick-pitch queries

Proceed with caution with this type of query because it is primarily used when you have an established and good rapport with an editor, publisher, or agent. A quick-pitch is a type of query used when you want to quickly run an idea by an agent, publisher, or editor to see if he or she is interested. This can be another way of getting around writing a full query because you can often get a quick answer from the editor whether he or she wants to proceed with your idea. (Note: Even if your editor, agent, or publisher likes the idea you pitch, he or she still might want to see a query.)

The common mechanism for submitting quick-pitch queries are via e-mail and are usually no more than three to five lines in length. Even though it is a quick-pitch, it should still contain all the necessary information editors, agents, and publishers require to make a decision. Quick pitches are similar to the elevator pitch or a 20-second coming attraction. They are written in a way to demonstrate pertinent information so an editor can make a quick, relevant decision.

Advantages of quick-pitch queries

- Quick-pitch queries are just that — quick — which makes them easy for writers to formulate and submit.

- Quick-pitch queries are easy to read and reply to.

- Quick-pitch queries are more likely to receive a quick response, which helps the writer either start on the assignment quickly or move on to another query project.

Disadvantages of quick-pitch queries

- Quick-pitch queries usually are not a viable option for beginning writers because they usually do not yet have a working relationship with an editor, publisher, or agent.

- Quick-pitch queries are not a sure-fire way to get around writing a full-fledged query letter.

Multiple-pitch queries

Just as with the quick-pitch query, multiple-pitch queries are a series of smaller pitches presenting several ideas in one submission. Presenting multiple-pitch queries is another situation where it is good to already have an established relationship or rapport with an agent, publisher, or editor. Pitching multiple ideas can be tricky because the editor will want to be sure that you are capable of handling one or more of the topics you have presented.

As with any of these types of queries that go against the traditional rules for query letters, the editor, agent, or publisher might request a full query even after you submit a multiple-pitch query.

Advantages of multiple-pitch queries

- With multiple-pitch queries, editors can have a selection of several article ideas in one submission.

- Multiple-pitch queries provide writers with an increased chance of getting several assignments out of one query.

Disadvantages of multiple-pitch queries

- Multiple-pitch queries are more successful if you already have an established relationship with an editor, agent, or publisher.

- An agent, publisher, or editor will rarely accept all the topics you pitch.

- Multiple-pitch queries rarely provide an editor, agent, or publisher with all the detail about any particular topic.

- A writer usually has to be seasoned or well established to successfully use the multiple-pitch query.

Even if you have found a way to get around preparing a full query letter, you will not be able to escape the basic, general rules of submitting quick pitches, proposals, or e-mail submissions. Editors, agents, and publishers have specific guidelines they want every writer, novice and seasoned, to follow. These guidelines do not go away because you now have a working relationship with an editor who is sending you lucrative assignments. The goal, throughout your career, should be to perfect your craft of writing continually, learn the art of querying, and project a professional attitude in everything you do.

Chapter 13

What to Do While You Wait

The typical response time from submission to notification is anywhere from two weeks to six months. This can feel like a long stretch of time, but you can do several things while you wait for a response. Although follow-up is essential, this chapter emphasizes the importance of waiting the allotted time before following up so as not to exasperate editors and putting the entire project at risk. Make good use of the time after submission to work on additional queries, incorporate valuable lessons learned from rejection letters, and prepare for the work you already might have been assigned.

Follow-Up Is Essential

Do not be afraid to follow up on a submission. Every writer, at some point in his or her career, has struggled with the question: How long should I wait for a response? If you have not heard anything back from the editor, agent, or publisher in three months, then it is permissible to send a letter asking about the status of your submission and the assignment. There is a mandated response time, which can vary from publication to publication. Check the guidelines first to see if this time has passed. If so, then you can follow up. When you do decide to follow up, be sure your inquiry is professional and friendly. Also, consider these additional points of interest:

- **Use e-mail whenever possible.** Most editors, agents, and publishers do not have the time to entertain phone calls. And regular mail seems to be getting slower. E-mail is a good way to get a quick response and make better use of your time. However, proceed with caution. Refer first to the publication's guidelines before assuming e-mail is the best option.

- **Do not spend too much time following up.** Follow up is good and often necessary in this business of querying, but be careful not to spend too much time with follow-ups. There are literally thousands of outlets for you to pursue to get published. The more time you spend sending follow-up letters, the less time you will have to spend on new queries or previously assigned projects.

- **Be brief and direct.** This is not another one-page query letter. It is a simple follow-up. Be brief and get to the point. Do not forget to include pertinent contact information to make it easier for the publisher, agent, or editor to get back to you.

Use your best judgment when it comes to following up. There is no hard-and-fast rule for when to follow up and how many times. The best approach is to wait at least as long as the guidelines. If you are hard-pressed for time, send only one follow-up letter. If the editor, agent, or publisher does not respond, it is time for you to move to the next.

```
Sample Follow-up Letter
to an Article Query

Dear Mr. Huckabee:

I wanted to send you a quick note to see if you have
had a chance to review my May 26th query "How to
Know if a Literary Agent is Right for You," a how-
to article that helps writers determine whether a
literary agent is a good option to pursue.

I am excited about the opportunity to work on this
piece but wanted to wait the six-week response time
(as per in the guidelines) before pitching the idea
to other magazines.

I appreciate your time and consideration, and look
forward to hearing from you.

Best Regards,
Donna M. Murphy
```

Write and Send More Queries

Sending out many queries to different publications keeps the writer in practice and increases the chances of publication. If you can sell one idea, you can sell more. The key to building a steady income and securing assignments is to find consistent customers to buy your material. Start with a smaller number of publications to pursue rather than becoming overwhelmed with trying to submit to every possible publication that is relevant to your topic. Choose three to four receptive publications or publishers, and exploit these markets as effectively and efficiently as possible.

Make submissions a priority. As you gain more experience, the number of queries you submit also will increase. Your querying skills will continue to improve, and you will begin to fine-tune your submission approach.

Handle Rejections Professionally

Rejections are a reality. It happens quite frequently, and it happens to everyone, including experienced and seasoned writers. The reasons for the rejection are as vast and varied as the topics being submitted. So, try not to jump to personal conclusions too quickly. There are times when the rejection is not because of poor quality, but rather based on situations like the following:

- **Wrong timing.** Fads come and go, seasons change, and editor's tastes change too. Timing is a subtle type of rejection, but it is still a real and common reason for an editor, publisher, or agent to reject your query. Content often is secured well in advance of its publication date, so what you pitch today might not be "in" — but it might be in 18 months.

- **Space limitations.** Many publications are limited to the number of articles they can publish in an issue. Doing the math, if an editor is allowed to publish 15 articles in the next issue, and they receive 575 queries, then 560 of the queries will receive rejections. Not all these rejections will be based on poor quality, confusing pitches, or unprofessionalism. Many of them will be rejected on the grounds of not enough space.

- **Repeated topics.** This is a common reason for rejections and can be a challenge for writers. It can be like hitting a moving target for a writer to pitch something fresh and new to a publication when you do not know what the editor, agent, or publisher already has on file.

- **Already published.** Part of an editor's job is to find and publish content that will be new and interesting to the intended audience. New in this publishing industry can be anywhere from six months to two years. It can be difficult for a writer to keep track of all the topics that have been published. So getting a rejection because something similar already has been published is common.

Of course, there is the possibility that your query letter has been rejected because of the quality, lack of focus, or inexperience. If this happens to be the case, do not ignore it. Accept it, learn from it, and begin to hone your skills before sending the idea to another publication. The sign of a good writer is often demonstrated in their understanding that there is always room for improvement and skills development.

The difference between a published and unpublished writer is this: The published writers did not give up after receiving dozens of rejections. They kept trudging through and honing their skills until they landed an assignment. Whatever it takes; you might have to go back to the drawing board and rework your query. An agent might ask you to go back and revamp your manuscript — several times. Regardless of the repetition you experience with your queries, the best advice is three-fold: Keep trying, stay professional, and continue to develop your skills.

What else might have gone wrong?

You might be submitting dozens of queries and receiving dozens more rejections. You have followed all the instructions and are trying to craft a solid, professional, and captivating query. But something is still wrong. Remember that querying is an art that requires continual learning, personal critiquing, and constant revisions. Look deeper, and see if your query letter might fall into one these categories:

- **Too long.** Remember this one-page, concise letter is presenting an idea. You do not have to sell every idea you have and everything that you have done in your writing career. Keep it simple, focused, and one page.

- **Too short.** This refers more to the content rather than the length. You understand that the length should be kept to one page. However, do not leave your pitch open ended. Be sure to explain your idea completely and have an end in mind. Find a way to express that to the editor, agent, or publisher in your brief query letter.

- **Typos, ouch.** Checking for typos is often left as the last thing writers do before they submit the query letter. You probably have gone through the letter it once, but go through it twice or three times. Another good approach, if you have time, is to put your query letter aside for a day and then come back to it with fresh eyes to check for typos and grammatical mishaps.

- **Things went askew.** Going off on a tangent is a very common thing for writers, especially when they have several ideas brewing, or they are excited about the opportunity. If you need a formula, use one query letter to sell one idea at a time. This approach will help you focus and will prevent your pitch from going astray.

- **Unrequested or unrelated clips.** Sometimes newbie writers submit clips thinking that the editor will be impressed. If the editor did not request the clips, submitting them will only show that you cannot follow instructions. Also, if you submitted clips that were unrelated to the proposed piece or did not quite demonstrate that you had the right experience, this can have a negative impact.

- **Unfamiliar with the publication.** To gain a solid understanding of the publication to which you are submitting, you really need to be familiar with it. To write a tailored piece, you need to understand the publication's tone, audience, and writing style. Read the masthead, study the advertisers, and learn all you can about the values and objective of the publication.

- **Good article, weak credentials.** In section four of the query letter, you stated your credentials and provided reasons for why you were the best candidate for the job. Maybe your article idea was good, but your credentials were weak. Look carefully at how you present yourself to the reader. Did you convey clearly why you are the one writer that should get this assignment?

- **You are pitching an outdated idea.** It can be difficult to pitch a new idea with the number of publications circulating out there. But to be competitive in this industry, you need to be able to generate fresh ideas.

What to glean from rejections

As much as you would like to forget about the sting of the rejection letter and move on to the next, you can glean a lot from the response. The more queries you send, the more possibility of rejections. But, you also be will able to group these rejections into three categories: 1) You might receive a rejection letter that just has checkboxes with very general descriptions from the rejection; 2) some rejection letters will offer minimal feedback; and 3) others will provide you with enough detailed information to help you improve for the next submission.

By identifying in which category your rejections fall, you will be able to glean the help you need from an editor, agent, or publisher quickly without a one-on-one session. Reviewing the rejection letters that fall into the last two categories will be the most helpful for you to improve your skills and learn what not to do or what to do for the next submissions.

Be thankful for any feedback you receive with your rejection letters. It could be a good sign that an editor sees potential in your work and is willing to provide constructive feedback to help you submit another query in the near future. Think of it this way: Editors are so busy sorting through the mounds of query letters that cross their desks. If they have taken the time to comment and offer feedback on your letter, this is very often a positive sign and a good indication that they are trying to help you.

You might receive responses from an agent, publisher, or editor that could have been avoided. If you receive any of these responses, heed the warning, reference the writer's guidelines, and be sure to avoid these the next time around:

- We do not publish that genre.
- The piece is too long (magazines) or too short (books).
- Your submission is unagented.
- We do not accept e-mail queries.
- We do not accept queries without clips.
- Query only please.
- This piece is not right for our audience.
- We do not accept freelance material.

All of these situations could have been avoided by careful dissection of the writer's guidelines. If the guidelines were unclear or did not address these situations, then it would be wise to document it for future reference.

When to respond to a rejection letter

Although it is not common practice to respond to all rejection letters you receive, there are three exceptions to the rule:

- **You are referred to another agent, editor, or publisher.** In this situation, you will want to craft a polite and professional letter thanking the editor, agent, or publisher who referred.

- **You are asked to make changes and then resubmit.** Count your blessings, and get started on making the required changes. But first, send a brief and polite letter of thanks letting the editor, agent, or publisher know that you have received his or her feedback.

- **Your query was rejected, but the editor is open to other ideas.** This is another good sign that you are in the running. Send the editor a brief thank-you letter to let him or her know you appreciate the opportunity to present additional ideas. Do not spend any more time wallowing; start working on crafting more topics to submit.

Other Relevant Correspondence

As you continue to develop your writing career, you will realize that no two assignments are the same. That is why you need to remain flexible in your approach to query letters. Depending on the editor, publisher, or agent, a query letter alone might not completely do the job; you might need another type of correspondence to close the loop of follow-up on outstanding assignments.

Cover letters

A cover letter is the perfect tool for when you want to introduce yourself and your submission with brevity. While a query letter should be no more than a page, cover letters should be no more than half a page; about three paragraphs should be sufficient. In such a case, your article topic or manuscript is the focus of the submission, not the cover letter. So, it does not need to function as a stand-alone sales piece. A cover letter takes the place of a query letter; you do not need to send both.

Regardless of the person to whom you are submitting, a superior cover letter has certain traits. These traits can be considered guidelines for you to follow to ensure your cover letter has the most impact:

- **Write to someone specific.** As with your query letter, research the name of the person to whom you will be submitting your package. Avoid using generic salutation, such as: "To whom it may concern" or "Dear Sir/Madam." If you have not taken the time to address the right person, do not submit until you can track that information down.

- **Ensure your cover letter is error free.** This also means spelling the editor, agents, or publisher's name correctly. Call and verify the spelling, or see if you find the name on the publication's website, if possible. Also, review your letter several times, and remove all typos, grammatical errors, and anything else that should not be there.

- **Personalize your letter.** Form letters are not impressive to most reviewers; so, do not use them. With technology today, it should be simple for you to personalize your cover letter to an agent, publisher, or editor. To minimize the impact of mass mailing, try to send out your letters in smaller batches. Targeted mailings to a carefully selected group of prospective publishers, editors, and agents can be extremely effective. If you cannot customize or personalize your cover letter in some way, do not send it.

- **Make good first impression.** Your first contact with an agent, editor, or publisher always should be professional. This comes across not only in the tone of your letter, but also in the appearance of your materials. Use professional-looking letterhead, a common, readable font, and simple black and white typefaces, and do not handwrite the letter or envelope.

- **Target the audience.** If you have done your homework, you will know to whom to address your letter, how to present your idea clearly and succinctly, and how to speak to the appropriate genre or target audience. Included with your targeting is information about your relevant background and experience that shows you could handle the assignment.

- **Provide a clear closer.** Keep your closing brief, but be sure to be clear about what you will do next. Show that you can take the initiative, but do not be forceful. It is a balance between following the guidelines and demonstrating your professionalism.

Because a cover letter is a short-format correspondence, you will need to craft it in a way that will make the agent, editor, or publisher feel confident about what else has been included with the submission. A typical cover letter consists of three paragraphs: the introduction, a biography, and a conclusion.

- **Introduction** – This paragraph describes what you are enclosing with your submission and why. Do not mince your words or try to be hyper-eloquent with your first sentence. State clearly and simply what you are sending with this submission. For example, "I am enclosing my proposal, *Successfully Managing Your Career to While Navigating an Uncertain Economy*, for your review and consideration." Next, provide a qualifying sentence or two describing what relevance your submission has to either the publication or your personal or professional background.

- **Biography** – This paragraph can be a challenge for new writers who do not have an extensive background, but it also can prove difficult for experienced writers because the paragraph needs to be as brief as possible. The biographical paragraph should describe succinctly your writing experience, what you have published, and how much you have published in the topic or genre to which you are submitting. Also, include information about your expertise or background related to your manuscript or article topic. Remember, if you do not have the experience pertinent to your submission, your best approach is to say nothing.

- **Conclusion** – The third and final paragraph should be brief and should cover any closing remarks you feel are important to reiterate and stress before closing the letter.

The key to a successful cover letter is to keep it brief, concise, and save the meat for the manuscript, proposal, or short story that follows.

Sample Cover Letter

Dear Ms. Witherell:

Enclosed is my book proposal, *Successfully Managing Your Career While Navigating an Uncertain Economy*. It is a powerful career management guide that walks mid-career professionals through the various stages of managing a successful career even in an uncertain economy.

I feel this book can be a perfect companion for professionals who have been off-ramped from the workforce highway or who want to re-engineer a career to better suit their growing professional goals and aspirations.

Thank you for your time and consideration of my submission. I look forward to your response.

```
Best Regards,
Donna M. Murphy
[address/phone/e-mail]

Enclosure:
Proposal, Successfully Managing Your Career While
Navigating an Uncertain Economy
SASE
```

Thank-you notes

Believe it or not, editors, publishers, and agents rarely receive confirmation that they are doing a good job. It can often be a thankless job. So, imagine what a short, simple, "Thank you" from a good writer can do for an editor's attitude while he or she stares at a heaping review pile. Before sending off your thank you, consider these brief points of etiquette:

- Send thank-you notes right away.
- Be clear about what you are grateful for.
- Focus on the editor, agent, or publisher.
- End with an unrelated comment.

Sample Thank-You Note

Dear Mr. Miller:

I wanted to send a quick note thanking you for the quality work you did on the article I pitched to you for 21st Century Professionals. I appreciate how you maintained the essence of the piece I submitted while capturing the tone and voice of your audience. I believe it turned out quite well.

Thank you for the time and effort you put into producing high-quality content. I hope your readers can benefit from the information and request more.

I look forward to the opportunity to work with you again in the near future.

Best Regards,
Donna M. Murphy
[address/phone/e-mail]

If you are confident that an e-mail thank you will be sufficient, think again. Although expressing your appreciate and gratitude through e-mail might seem simple and effective, it does not show as much time and effort as a hand-written note or carefully crafted letter. A helpful hint for thank-you notes is to have a stock of thank-you cards already on hand, so you can pull one out and write a quick note. The bulk packs are more cost-effective, but you might consider thematic cards that relate to the topic or industry in which you are writing.

A brief word of caution: Be careful not to send too many thank-you notes or letters. Too many can be perceived as "brown-nosing." You do not have to send a thank you with every query or every acceptance, but do send them periodically as a reminder to your agent, editor, or publisher that you appreciate the work he or she does and appreciate his or her confidence in giving you assignments or publishing your work.

Complaint letter

Just like any other form of business, writing relationships do not all go smoothly or productively. There will be times where you and the publisher, agent, or editor will not agree or work well together. Conflicts, disagreements, and gripes will arise and are to be expected. The rule is still the same as it has been with all aspects of query letter preparation and ultimate publication: be careful to treat these, and all situations, in a professional manner. Whether you are doing the complaining or you are responding to a complaint, follow these helpful guidelines:

If you are the one complaining, state your issue in the most polite and constructive way possible.

- Clearly state the complaint or what you are upset about.

- Provide evidence, facts, and anecdotes to substantiate your reason for the complaint.

- Clearly state the outcome or resolution you would like to see.

- End with an upbeat request for an acceptable solution.

- Convey your desire for positive relations in the future.

If you are responding to an editor's, agent's, or publisher's complaint, the first thing you will need to decide is whether you want to continue relations with the editor, agent, or publisher. If you decide that you are following through with the response, use these tips to prepare a constructive and professional letter.

- Before sending off your letter, gather your thoughts, think things through, and stay calm.

- Read the complaint letter carefully to ensure you have not overreacted or misinterpreted the tone or purpose.

- Determine the purpose of your response; what do you want it to achieve?

- Clearly summarize the issues first, so the other party understands you have not misread or misunderstood their complaint.

- Remove your emotions from the letter, and keep it factual.

- End with a plea for an agreeable solution,

- Convey your desire for positive future relations,

When sending a complaint letter, consider using the approach where you state the complaint in between compliments or niceties. You might consider adding a little bit of humor or comic relief to convey that you are not offended to a point from which you cannot recover.

Sample Complaint Letter

Dear Ms. Thomson:

Thank you for running my article, "Strengthening Your Brand for the 21st Century." I enjoyed working on this piece and would enjoy the opportunity to work on similar projects in the future.

You already might have noticed the mistake in the website address provided as a reference for the readers. Because it was a primary resource, I wanted to bring it to your attention in case you are considering submitting a correction in your next issues. I would hate for readers to go to an inappropriate or irrelevant website to look for answers to their questions.

I referred to the original submission I sent over and was relieved to know that the mistake was not on my end.

I think the article turned out well with the exception of the website mishap. Again, I appreciate the opportunity to work on this assignment and hope that you will consider me for future work.

Best Regards,
Donna M. Murphy
[address/phone/e-mail]

It is never easy to face complaints, whether it is your complaint or the editor's complaint. Nonetheless, as a professional writer, it behooves you to handle these just as you would any other correspondence. How you handle this type of communication will have an effect on future assignments with other editors and writers.

Chapter 14

You Have Landed the Assignment. Now What?

I t is important for you to respond quickly to an editor after he or she makes initial contact with you. You will learn the importance of being responsive and open to the editor's feedback and ideas, meeting deadlines, and getting paid. The more assignments you land, the better you have become at querying. This chapter will show you how to take it up a notch and how to turn down assignments when you are overloaded.

If this is your first assignment, do not panic. Getting an assignment can create some anxiety, which is normal. But, do not let this anxiety paralyze you from getting down to the business of writing. If time allows, let the excitement of getting your first publishing gig settle in overnight. You can be more prepared and alert after a good night's rest. If you do not have the luxury of time, go ahead and do your celebratory dance, scream and shout, or call your friends and family. Acknowledge the victory, take a brief break, and then turn your focus back to the task.

The first order of business will be to send an acceptance or acknowledgment letter to the editor, publisher, or agent.

Responding to an Acceptance Letter

Sending an acceptance letter is the professional way to respond to an editor, agent, or publisher who has offered you an assignment. Your letter should start by clearly stating your intention to accept the assignment and reiterate what you intend to provide. Even though an acceptance letter is usually brief, it should be skillfully written. This acceptance letter will set the tone for how you will conduct yourself during the assignment and possible future assignments if your editor, agent, or publisher feels you are a valuable member of his or her writing team. When planning your acceptance letter, consider these helpful tips:

- Keep it brief, simple, polite, and professional.

- Address your letter to the editor, agent, or publisher who made the assignment.

- Discuss the specifics of the assignment (e.g., working title, word count, pay rates, and payment terms).

- Acknowledge or reiterate your responsibilities and obligations to the project.

- If appropriate, mention the skills and experience you bring to the assignment.

- Express your appreciation and excitement about the opportunity you were offered.

Sending an acceptance letter is not mandatory, but it is highly encouraged. When you send this type of letter, you are showing your professionalism and respect for the editor, publisher, or agent. Taking the time to send such an acknowledgment goes a long way in making the editor, publisher, or agent feel comfortable and confident about his or her decision to offer you the assignment.

Sample Acceptance Letter #1: Confirmation of Writing

Dear Mr. Frank:

I am extremely pleased that you have accepted my query for [Title] and have offered me the assignment. I will deliver a 1,500-word piece to by July 28th, and I understand that you will pay $750.00 upon acceptance of my work.

Thank you again, Mr. Frank, for having confidence in me and offering me this opportunity. If there is any additional information you need from me, please let me know, and I will send it along as soon as possible.

```
I look forward to working with you on this excit-
ing project.

Sincerely,

Donna M. Murphy
[address/phone/e-mail]
```

Time to Celebrate!
But Now the Work Begins

Now that you have had a moment to celebrate, however brief, the time has come for you to begin the real work. Your first step for deciphering the requirements of your assignment is to make a list. Identify the things you clearly understand and can handle. Next, make a list of the things from the assignment that you think you know or you can deduce. Finally, identify those items in the assignment that you do not know. The items in this last category need to be addressed first. Do some additional research to see how many of them you can answer yourself. If you have any questions or issues left, it might be time to send a letter or e-mail to your agent, editor, or publisher asking to clarify these outstanding issues.

While you are assessing the assignment and going through the requirements, consider these tips:

- **Do not panic, and do not put things off.** Panic can cloud your judgment and your ability. You do not want to get into a state of paralysis on your first assignment. Instead, take the professional path by breathing and focusing. Start your assignment as soon as possible. Taking a proactive approach to managing your assignment will allow plenty of time for unexpected obstacles.

- **Keep your assignment at the forefront.** All the time and effort you put into getting the assignment should help you prepare and succeed with the task. Start by skimming the assignment and noting or highlighting anything that jumps out at you. Next, reread the assignment carefully to uncover anything that is particularly important. Finally, take out a piece of paper, and begin jotting down ideas that come to mind. Do not confine yourself; just let your thoughts flow, and write down everything, even if it seems out of the ordinary.

- **Seek out directive verbs.** When an editor, agent, or publisher gives you an assignment, first look for directive verbs that tell you what you need to do to craft a good response. Common directive verbs include: illustrate, show, compare, contrast, show, describe, discuss, explain, etc.

- **Know your purpose and your audience.** Audience is a critical element in any writing assignment. Spend some time analyzing the background of the intended audience including personal, educational, and professional factors. Once you are clear about the purpose and intended audience of your assignment, it will be easier to craft a query letter with the right structure, tone, and word choice.

Be Responsive and Open

Take an active role and a proactive approach by being responsive and open to brainstorming and corrections. Editors often have an idea of what they are looking for. It is their job to manage and protect the outcome of the assignment. Editors, agents, and publishers do not intend to make your life miserable; they are not out to get you. They are focused only on producing the best possible piece of material for a hungry audience.

If they offer you an assignment, do not fall into the trap of thinking you will not have to rewrite, tweak, or adjust your article. The editor liked your idea; now it is time to develop it into what is appropriate for the targeted reader. Regardless of how much time an editor, publisher, or agent might invest in critiquing your work, the writing is still your responsibility. Strive to submit the best possible product you can.

Embrace idea and brainstorming sessions

Work *with* your editor, agent, or publisher, not against them. They liked your idea from the query letter; now, use this time constructively to develop ideas and participate in brain-storming sessions. Make this a two-way dialogue; do not just wait for the editor to tell you what he or she wants. Stay in-volved, offer suggestions, and think about how you can help your editor, agent, or publish-er succeed.

This will go a long way in de-veloping a strong relationship, which could lead to more op-portunities for work. Your brainstorming might involve suggesting graph-ics, sidebars, illustrations, or photos to help the article. Resist the inclina-tion to feel slighted if editors do not use all of the suggestions. This is often a repetitive process, and the goal is a tightly written and focused piece.

Use constructive criticism as a way to improve

The job of an editor, agent, or publisher is to secure high-quality content and match it with the appropriate audience. Your job is to provide the high-quality content. Very few writers can produce that caliber of content on the first try or even the second. So when an editor, agent, or publisher comes back with a response such as: "Why this approach?" or "Have you considered this?" or even "This does not work well here," do not despair or get discouraged. The publisher, editor, or agent knows what he or she is looking for; he or she has a vision of the article, short story, or book. It is your task to work with your editor, agent, or publisher to line up his or her vision with your writing.

This relationship often does not come easily at the beginning. Sometimes it takes a while for a writer and an editor to establish a rapport. Nonetheless, this is business, and you should proceed with that notion. Constructive criticism is inherent in this industry. Use the feedback you receive as a way to improve your writing and the craft.

Meeting Deadlines is a Must

Deadlines will be a major part of your career as a professional writer. The more assignments you secure, the more pressure you might feel from the deadline of each. You might be a world-class writer and produce good work, but if you do not meet your deadlines, you could harm your reputation in the industry.

That is why you need to be careful about how many assignments you accept, and you need to learn how to manage your time effectively. Meeting deadlines is necessary in the line of business. There are steps you can take to try to mitigate double-booking, overlapping deadlines, and bottlenecks. However, no matter how diligently you might plan your schedule, life seems to get in the way at times. If this is the case, keep the lines of communication open with your agent, editor, or publisher. Give them enough time to be able to adjust the schedule, find an option, or fit your piece into another issue.

In the meantime, follow these steps to help you successfully meet and manage your deadlines:

- Consider deadlines a serious matter and make them a priority.

- Keep a list of each project and its respective deadline.

- Get in the habit of setting your own internal deadlines to provide a cushion.

- Keep a two-way dialogue with your editor; this can go a long way toward minimizing obstacles.

- Learn the art of saying "no," especially when faced with projects that have unreasonable turnaround times.

- Break down your project into smaller, more manageable pieces.

- Block out or reserve adequate sections of time in your schedule.

- If you have exhausted all your possibilities and you absolutely cannot meet your deadline, try to negotiate a second deadline, and be sure to meet that one.

Your reputation as a solid and reliable writer — one whom an editor, agent, or publisher can rely on for future assignments — is based on the quality of your work and your ability to meet deadlines. So, give your reputation and your bank account a fighting chance by meeting those deadlines.

Getting Paid

As you may recall from Chapter 2, pay rates and payment terms should be indicated in the writer's guidelines for the publication you are pursuing. If you are at the point where you are expecting to get paid, then you ideally have worked out the terms and payment arrangements with your agent, editor, or publisher.

If you have received your payments on time, consider yourself fortunate and continue to seek out editors, agents, and publishers who have the reputation of paying their writers on time. However, there will be times where you may have to nudge your publisher, editor, or agent to receive payment for a completed assignment.

If you find yourself in this situation, approach your editor, agent, or publisher under the premise that you are helping them out rather than placing blame. In the case where you are working with a larger publication or publishing house, the editor might not be responsible for payment processing; it most likely will be the accounting department. There might be times where the editor, agent, or publisher is responsible for cutting the checks but forgot or is behind.

Regardless of the situation, your best approach is a short, concise e-mail that politely mentions the oversight. Give the editor, publisher, or agent the benefit of the doubt. This will set a professional tone that will help to secure on-time payments for future assignments. Before doing anything drastic, consider these few points:

- **Reread the contract.** First rule: reputable editors, agents, and publisher will establish a contract with you for your assignments. If you do not get a contract, even a simple one, then find another editor, publisher, or agent to work with.

- **Understand the terms.** There are two basic terms of payment for assignments; *pay on acceptance* and *pay on publication*. Before contacting your publisher, editor, or agent about getting paid; double-check the terms to which you agreed.

- **Diversify your outlets.** Try to rely on more than one or two sources for your writing income. Diversifying your markets and publications will help to minimize the variation in payment and rates.

- **Lessen your risk for next time.** Selecting more reputable publications will reduce your risk of getting burned or dealing with late payments. If you are not confident enough yet to pursue some of the heavy-hitters, increase the amount of research time you invest in the less established publications.

- **Invoice sooner.** If your editor, agent, or publisher accepts invoices, be sure to invoice sooner rather than later. The minute your assignment has been accepted, send out the invoice. Be sure to include payment terms on your invoice so the publisher, editor, or agent knows how long they have to submit payment before penalties kick in.

- **Follow up.** If your payment terms are net 15 days, follow up on day 16 and arrange a payment schedule if they need it. Start your follow-up efforts by e-mail first, then through letters, and finally by phone, if it reaches that point.

Getting paid on time by an editor, agent, or publisher is a matter of establishing and negotiating terms in advance. Sometimes this is not possible, but it does not hurt to ask or try to get as much down on paper as you can before agreeing to do the assignment. Establish the financial boundaries during your first meeting with your agent, editor, or publisher. This is often an uncomfortable subject to broach, but think of it as preventive medicine for your professional writing career. Clear communication up front is essential for future financial dealings.

How to Turn Down an Assignment Tactfully

It is hard to imagine that you would ever want to turn down an assignment. Saying "no" can be one of the hardest things to do, especially if this is your primary or sole source of income. To work at an optimal level and produce quality work, there may be times where you will need to decline a project graciously. Look at five circumstances where walking away might be a good decision:

- **You cannot finish the job.** You are already swamped. With another assignment coming in, you are not sure you can manage it. Making matters worse, the job might be for a publication you have been querying for the past 18 months. Now is the time for you to step back, take a deep breath, and carefully consider your options. The ultimate goal is to provide the editor with your best work. If you honestly do not think you can finish the job or put forth your best writing, it would be a disservice to the editor and to your reputation to accept it.

- **You have been given an unreasonable deadline.** This will depend upon your current workload and your time-management skills. Editors work under tight deadlines and often expect you to do the same. However, if the assignment is complex or you have too much on your plate, it would be difficult for you to do a good enough job in the time allotted. Before turning down the assignment, ask the editor if he or she can give you more time. If not, then decline, professionally.

- **Your assignment is not well defined.** If an editor, publisher, or agent cannot describe what needs to be done in a succinct and clear fashion, proceed with caution. A vague assignment about "dogs as pets" could use up several volumes, and you potentially could be writing for the rest of your career to fill the pages. Get clarification and confirmation from the editor about the exact slant of the assignment. If he or she refuses to provide clear, simple instructions, it might be time to walk away.

- **Your relationship with the editor is difficult.** You might be spending more time fighting with your editor than you are working on the assignment. If you continue butting heads, it might be time for you to find another editor to work with.

- **You will not work for the negotiated amount.** When you are first starting out, it is tempting to take all kinds of assignments. It can be your right of passage into the large, more lucrative markets. However, when the time comes in your career to step things up a notch, you might decide you do not want to work for pennies anymore. Some writers have established their own per-word minimum and try to negotiate this rate for assignments. If you cannot come to an agreement on a reasonable rate, spend your time more productively searching for better-paying assignments.

Whatever your reason for declining an assignment, be sure to use tact and honesty when addressing the editor, publisher, or agent. Use the following tips to prepare an appropriate letter or e-mail to decline an assignment:

- **Acknowledge receipt of the assignment.** Thank the publisher, agent, or editor for their confidence in your ability to do the job. Let them know you appreciate the assignment.

- **Clearly explain your reasons for declining the assignment.** Say "no" clearly so there is no confusion about whether you are doing the assignment. Also, express your regret for having to decline the assignment. Use your judgment about whether to provide a brief explanation. You do not want to sound like you are making excuses, but sometimes it helps to provide the agent, editor, or publisher with some background, if it is appropriate.

- **Be enthusiastic and positive about your skills to leave opening for future work.** Although you may not be able to complete the current assignment, make the editor, agent, or publisher feel comfortable about assigning you future assignments.

- **If possible, offer to find or provide an alternative.** Try to provide an alternate solution so the agent, editor, or publisher does not have to do all the work to find another option. They might have to anyway, but at least you have given them something to consider before they go searching for another writer.

Sample Letter to Decline an Assignment

Dear Mr. Steffen:

Thank you for your letter. I appreciate the confidence you have in me to handle an assignment of this nature. Regrettably, I am unable to accept the assignment at this time to meet your November 15th deadline.

If, however, the assignment is not time-sensitive, I should have some breathing room at the end of the month. At that time, maybe we could discuss other alternatives or a possible reassignment.

Best regards,

Donna M. Murphy
[address/phone/e-mail]

> **CAUTION:** Be careful telling an agent, publisher, or editor that you are declining or refusing the assignment because you are busy with other work. It might give the impression that you are too busy to be able to handle multiple assignments. If the piece is not time-sensitive, offer your services later.

Your approach to declining an assignment should be brief but feel upbeat. You want to give the editor, agent, or publisher the feeling that you are reliable and can handle the assignment under normal circumstances. Being able to set boundaries often will increase their respect for you.

Regularly turning down assignments is not good business practice. However, in the cases where you feel it would be beneficial to you and the editor, turn down the assignment professionally and move on. Doing so might just prove beneficial to your relationship with the editor, agent, or publisher and to your career.

Some Parting Thoughts on Querying

This book has focused on how to write query letters and following industry standards to minimize rejections. However, there will come a time when you receive an offer. What you do after this exciting milestone will dictate the success of your future assignments. First, do not let the shock of your first offer distract you from the reality of what is to follow. Consider it an accomplishment to receive your first assignment and continue striving to reach your ultimate destination of getting published.

Once you have gotten over the hurdle of your first published piece, it will be up to you to continue developing your skills, increasing your reputation in the industry, and building a solid foundation for future success. The next few sections will discuss briefly some additional ideas you might consider as you delve deeper into your writing profession.

Consider selling a column

If you find that you are writing more than three articles for the same publication in a year, you might want to ask the editor to assign you a regular column. Being a regular columnist can be a great way to create a steady income stream.

Another way to sell a column is through "self-syndication," which means offering a regularly published series to several different publications that are not in direct competition with each other. The whole purpose of selling a column is to distribute a topic to a broader audience. Here are a few items to consider when pursuing the path of self-syndication:

- **What is your topic?** For a column to be successful, it has to have a broad enough reach that it could potentially cross regional boundaries. For example, topics such as health tips, parenting, weight loss, and management are universal topics. If you intend to start as a local columnist, you might need to start with a local topic specific to your region. Do not worry, because the experience alone will help you branch into other topics and a broader audience. Select a topic you are passionate about but also that has a wide audience appeal. To gather ideas, go to bookstores, and look at the best-selling nonfiction books. What is popular in cooking, how-to, history, parenting, retirement, finances, business, and travel? If you have an interest or background in any of these areas, consider writing a unique column about it, and pitch it to a local or regional newspaper.

- **What is your market?** Finding a market will not be the problem. Narrowing down your search to a city, state, or region will be your biggest challenge. There are numerous local, alternative, and specialty newspapers just in your current city. Now imagine if you expand your search to the state, then the region, and then ultimately the nation. And, with the Internet so ingrained in our society, you have dozens of electronic "newsstands" on the Internet to pursue. The best resources to use to start your search on various newspapers include: *Gales Directory of Media Publications* and *The Annual Editor & Publisher International Year Book*. Both of these publications can be found in most libraries.

- **What are your terms?** Once you have settled on a topic and narrowed down your market, you will want to set the terms of your column. These terms will include items such as column length (How many words? 750 to 1,000 words is usually optimal), column frequency (How often will the column run? Daily, weekly, biweekly, monthly?), and rights (What type of rights will be offered by the publication?). The first two issues, column length and column frequency, are easy to negotiate and agree upon with the editor. However, the third item, rights, is often a challenge because many markets are placing increasing demands on writers for their rights. Unfortunately, the trend for many publications is to ask writers for all rights to their columns. Try to retain as many of your rights as possible with a column. The goal with self-syndication is to gain the widest possible distribution for a single piece. If you can sell the same piece to 50 newspapers for $75 an article, you already have multiplied your income and possibly the readership substantially.

- **What is your rate?** Along with establishing your terms of selling your column, you will want to determine the minimum rate you are willing to accept. Smaller newspapers still offer as little as $10 per column. This may seem miniscule at first, but this amount can add up quickly if you can sell your column to several newspapers. Do some research to see if you can uncover what the going rate is for self-syndication. Some writers ask for a minimum rate based on the column (e.g., $25 minimum per column). Others ask for a minimum rate based on the word count (e.g. 40 cents per word). And still others ask for a minimum rate based on a word count per number of subscribers (e.g. 75 cents per word per 1,000 subscribers).

The Self-Syndication Package

The primary negative aspect of syndication is that it can be costly to prepare and submit your proposals to various editors. Many editors still prefer submissions to be sent by regular mail instead of e-mail. This increases costs tremendously because you are trying to syndicate in as many publications as possible across a particular state or region. Your expense will be in postage, printing, paper, and envelopes. If you land a self-syndicated column, it will be well worth the investment. Preparing a self-syndication package is similar to preparing a query package or a proposal package. The primary elements for the self-syndication package include:

- **The column query** – You should be well versed in preparing a query; the column query will be similar. In a column query, you want to describe the proposed column and list the terms you are offering (length, frequency, rights, and rates).

- **Sample columns** – If you do not have sample of previously written columns, make up two to three sample columns showing what the proposed syndication will look like. Try to make it authentic as possible, but do not give the editor the whole concept.

- **Clips** – Provide clips that are relevant to the column you are proposing. Ensure that the clips have a writing style and tone similar to the one you intend to use in the column. The goal is for the editor to get a feel for your writing ability and to assess if the tone is appropriate for the intended audience.

- **Supporting materials** – If you think it will add weight to your submission, provide supporting materials that validate and substantiate your ability to write a column successfully. This might include your credentials in the topic, any testimonials you may have received from other editors, agents, or publishers from previous work, or awards you have received.

- **A self-addressed, stamped envelope (SASE)** – Many editors now prefer a postcard to a SASE. It is an easier way for them to respond by simply checking the most appropriate feedback option.

Sample Response Postcard

Date: _____

Dear Donna:

Thank you for submitting your query for the column titled "Practical Career Management Tips for Women."

_____ We would like to use your column on a monthly basis under the following terms:

- We will pay a fee of $ _____

- We will offer one-time, non-exclusive rights

_____ We are interested in your column but would like to further discuss your terms and rates.

_____ We regret that we cannot use your column.

(Signed): _____

Editor's Name: _____

Allow at least a month lead time to hear from your prospects before following up. Remember, editors are busy people, and they are receiving similar packages from other writers in astronomical amounts on a daily basis. If you do not hear from an editor after you have submitted your information and followed up, do not waste any more time; just continue to move forward and focus on the next prospect.

Develop a strong personal brand

Regardless of writing goals, you are a brand. That is a reality of being in business, whether for an agent, editor, or publisher or for yourself. As a professional writer, you create an in-demand product: content.

Developing a strong personal brand can be a challenging aspect of a writer's career. In an increasingly competitive market, personal branding is imperative, but equally intimidating. To be successful in the writing industry and to continue developing your career as a professional writer, you will need to develop a reputation that complements your writing skill. Here are some tips for building up your brand:

- **Be unique.** In this type of industry, being a copycat is probably one of the worst offenses against your colleagues. There is nothing wrong with gaining inspiration from others, but work on developing a uniqueness of your own. You will have your own writing style, and your brand needs to convey that same style. Work with a branding expert or read a handful of the personal branding books available at your local library or bookstore. Spend some time thinking about what you want to convey about yourself, your work, and your reputation.

- **Consider using a pen name.** One path to follow when developing a personal brand is to write under a pen name. This is particularly common in the fiction genre. Some writers use a pen name to avoid revealing their identity. Other writers use a pen name to enhance the brand of their writing style and genre focus.

- **Specialize in a genre.** Very few writers have been successful writing in multiple genres. It will be difficult for you to straddle two or more genres if there is no connection between the two. A safer route is to specialize in one genre and build your reputation within it.

- **Be consistent.** Consistency is what brings loyalty. If you continue to follow through on your promises and produce what your readers expect, they will come to rely on you. You will create your own personal following, and they will look to you and your writing to meet their needs. One of the primary components of a strong personal brand is your ability to be and remain consistent. That does not mean you have to stagnate. It means you have to remain true to your commitments and continue to stand on the uniqueness you developed from the beginning.

- **Be authentic.** The public can be brutal when critiquing works of art. Just read some of the reviews written about the movies that come out in the theaters. Also, read some of the reviews written about newly released fiction books by some of the nation's best-selling authors. Not all best-selling authors get glowing reviews every time they publish new books. Regardless of the reviews (positive or negative), your goal is to be authentic. Your authenticity is what will keep your readers coming back. Know when to admit your mistakes and faults. Let your readers see a little bit of your humanity so they can connect with you and feel that they know you.

- **Manage your brand.** As the saying goes, "If you do not manage your brand, someone else will." Keep reinventing and managing your personal brand. It should grow with you throughout your career. If you do not manage it, others will take it and run with it. The result might be something that does not represent you well.

It will be harder to change your audiences' mind about you once someone else has redefined your brand for you.

A few online resources for you to reference include:

- The Personal Branding Blog® (**www.personalbrandingblog.com/ authors-publishers-everyone-needs-to-brand**)

- The Grammar Girl's lesson in personal branding for authors (**blog. publishedandprofitable.com/2010/09/15/the-grammar-girls- lessons-in-personal-branding-for-authors**)

- Personal Brand Express: An Action Plan for Authors (**http://www. savvyauthors.com/vb/showevent.php?eventid=385**)

Do not mistake branding for your logo, website, or stationery. Your personal brand is more about the way you carry yourself: in speech, in presentation, and in your actions. Your personal brand comes out in how you do business with clients, colleagues, editors, agents, and publishers. It is important to your career to take care of your personal brand. It is the face the public sees; it is how they experience you without sitting down face-to-face over dinner to experience you live and in person.

Learn to write faster

As a newbie, you might spend more time laboring over every word and every sentence because you want things to be just right. As you become more skilled with querying and writing assignments, you will learn what to focus on first and what to tweak and perfect later.

Some writers spend time waiting for the right inspiration, the right block of time, and the right environment. If you wait for all the elements to be perfectly in line, you will be wasting valuable time. An effective way to increase your writing time and maximize your productivity is to develop and adhere to a writing routine. This writing routine might look something like:

- **Inspiration and idea time:** This is the time you allocate for thinking, brainstorming, and gathering snippets of inspiration. This time might require you to be away from the TV, the computer, and other people. You might have heard of stories from people who get their best ideas while they are in the shower or on a walk. The goal of the inspiration and idea time is to allow for purely brain-based freethinking.

- **Researching time:** Once you have obtained inspiration and gathered new ideas, there might be additional research needed to further develop an idea. Before hopping on the Internet or taking a trip to the library, write out your plan of attack. Develop a checklist or bullet points of the questions you need to answer or the problems you need to solve. Jot down relevant keywords or word strings that will help to refine your search. Once you find the information you need, clip, extract, or copy and paste it to a document for future reference. Do not forget to cite the source.

- **Planning time:** Your planning time involves writing your outline or creating a mind map of how you intend to approach your assignment. You can fill in the details to this rough outline later, but, at least, you will have a basis from which to start developing content.

- **Content development time:** With your research facts and outline handy, it is time to start writing. The objective of content development time is to write; do not worry about editing or filling in the facts. If there is a word or statistic you do not have at this time, just highlight it and keep going. The idea during this time is to keep the flow going. Write as long as you can, and stop when you get tired. Writing when you are tired drains your creative juices and your ability to write fast.

- **Editing time:** Start by reading aloud what you have developed. It might seem uncomfortable for you at first, but reading aloud helps you quickly identify errors or parts that need to be restructured. After you have identified sections that have errors or need rewriting, go back to the areas you highlighted and begin filling in the information or facts. Once you have everything filled in and fixed, do another edit. If time permits, see if you can have another person edit it before you submit.

- **Down time:** Before starting this sequence all over again, give yourself a break. Take some time to be away from the grind, or you will burn out. Use your down time to focus on you and your personal goals. Maybe go to the gym, spend time with your family, go out with friends, or do some volunteer work. The purpose of the down time is to refuel and prepare to start your writing routine again.

Practicing this writing routine will help you write faster, better, and easier in the future. It might be a slow start at first because you are not used to it. Every writer has his or her own system, but having a guideline to start from can help you transition into your own personal tool. The trick or secret behind writing faster is about being organized and prepared. Creating a sense of structure to your writing and your writing schedule allows ideas to flow easily and quickly.

Conclusion

ny writer will tell you that the path to publication starts with the quintessential query letter. As you have learned throughout this book, the goal is to craft a query letter that is strong, focused, captivating, and inspirational. You want the editor, agent, or publisher to stand up, take notice, and be prompted to ask for an article, a manuscript, or a book proposal.

In the writing industry, a well-crafted, compelling query letter sent to the right editor, agent, or publisher becomes the effective sales tool to pitch an idea for a magazine article or a topic for a nonfiction book for the trade.

All the tools you need have been compiled in this book. Even if you cross all your "t's" and dot all your "i's," the rejections will come. Rejections are part of this business. However, if you continue to practice and refine your art of querying, the day will come where you will see your name printed as a byline in a magazine article or published in a literary journal.

While doing your research, you will come across various stories of writers who landed an assignment on their first try or writers who did not get work until after two years of pounding the pavement. Regardless of the varied stories you read, your goal will be to find a balance between the strict rule following and the rebellious rule breaking to define your own art of querying. Querying, and ultimately writing, is a personal endeavor. As mentioned before, an editor, agent, or publisher can provide guidance and all the possible feedback they can, but you ultimately will be responsible for the writing, querying, preparation, and submissions.

The best approach to crafting a solid query letter is to learn the industry, understand the guidelines, and be professional through it all.

Happy querying!

Writers' Associations

Academy of American Poets (**www.poets.org/index.php**)
The Academy of American Poets was founded in 1934 with the mission to support American poets at all stages of their careers and to foster the appreciation of contemporary poetry.

American Christian Fiction Writers (**www.acfw.com**)
ACFW consists of authors, editors, agents, publicists, and aspiring writers and was organized in 2000 under the name of American Christian Romance Writers (ACRW). In 2004, the group changed the name to American Christian Fiction Writers (ACFW) in response to the diverse needs of its members, who write across many genres.

American Crime Writers League (**www.acwl.org**)
The ACWL was formed in the late 1980s by a group of writers who wanted a private forum for exchanging ideas.

American Society of Business Publication Editors (**www.asbpe.org**)
Founded in 1964, the American Society of Business Publication Editors (ASBPE) is the professional association for full-time and freelance editors and writers employed in the business, trade, and specialty press.

American Society of Journalists and Authors (**www.asja.org/about.php**)
Founded in 1948, the American Society of Journalists and Authors is the nation's professional organization of independent nonfiction writers.

Asian American Journalists Association (**www.aaja.org**)
Founded in 1981, the Asian American Journalists Association (AAJA) is a nonprofit professional and educational organization with more than 1,400 members today. AAJA serves Asian Americans and Pacific Islanders by encouraging young people to consider journalism as a career, developing managers in the media industry, and promoting fair and accurate news coverage.

Association of Young Journalists and Writers (**www.ayjw.org**)
The Association of Young Journalists and Writers is a nonprofit organization with its mission as promoting reading, writing, journalism, and serving the community. The organization was established as The Association of Young Journalists under Section 402 of the Not-For-Profit Corporation Law as a successor to the Forum of Young Journalists, which was created in 1981.

Association of Author's Representatives (**www.aaronline.org**)
The Association of Authors' Representatives is a not-for-profit membership organization, which is active in all areas of the publishing, theater, motion picture and television industries and related fields.

Authors Guild (**www.authorsguild.org**)
The Authors Guild has been the nation's leading advocate for writers' interests in effective copyright protection, fair contracts, and free expression since it was founded as the Authors League of America in

1912. It provides legal assistance and a broad range of web services to its members.

Backspace (**www.bksp.org**)

Backspace is an online writers' organization with more than 1,400 members in a dozen countries. A third of the members are agented and published and include nearly a dozen *New York Times* best-selling authors. Backspace is predicated on the idea of writers helping writers, which is accomplished through discussion forums; an online guest speaker program in which agents, acquisitions editors, and best-selling authors regularly conduct question-and-answer sessions with the group; advice; how-to articles from publishing experts on this website; as well as our real-world conferences and events.

CineStory (**cinestory.org/wordpress**)

CineStory is a nonprofit educational association dedicated to providing new screenwriters with opportunities to work with committed industry professionals on a personal basis in order to raise the level of their craft and the marketability of their projects.

The Electronic Literature Organization (**www.eliterature.org**)

The Electronic Literature Organization was founded in 1999 to foster and promote the reading, writing, teaching, and understanding of literature as it develops and persists in a changing digital environment.

Editorial Freelancers Associations (**www.the-efa.org**)

EFA is a national not-for-profit organization, headquartered in New York City, run almost entirely by volunteers. Its members, experienced in a wide range of professional skills, live and work in the United States and a variety of other countries, including Canada, England, France, India, Ireland, Israel, and Japan.

EPIC: Electronically Published Internet Connection™
(www.epicauthors.com)

EPIC, Electronically Published Internet Coalition, was established in 1998 to provide a strong voice for electronic publishing. Once an authors' organization, EPIC™ has expanded to include hundreds of professionals from all facets of the electronic publishing industry: authors, publishers, editors, artists, and others. Its members work together in a unique collaboration between authors and publishers to further the industry.

Historical Novel Society (www.historicalnovelsociety.org)

The Historical Novel Society, founded in 1997, promotes all aspects of historical fiction. It provides support and opportunities for new writers; information for students, booksellers, and librarians; and a community for authors, readers, agents, and publishers.

Horror Writers Association (www.horror.org)

The Horror Writers Association's mission is to promote and protect the careers of professional horror writers and those seeking to become horror writers. HWA also uses its reputation and affiliations to raise the profile of the horror genre in the publishing industry and among readers in the public.

HTML Writers Guild (www.hwg.org)

The HWG was founded in 1994 and is the leading training organization for the Web-design community, with more than 150,000 members in more than 160 countries worldwide. In 2001, the guild joined with the International Webmaster's Association to form IWA-HWG, the professional association for the growth of the professional Web-design company and individual.

International Food, Wine, & Travel Writers Association (**www.ifwtwa.org**)

The International Food Wine & Travel Writers Association (IFWTWA) is now a global network of journalists who cover the hospitality and lifestyle fields and the people who promote them.

International Women's Writing Guild (**www.iwwg.com**)

The IWWG, founded in 1976, is a network for the personal and professional empowerment of women through writing and open to all regardless of portfolio.

Media Bistro (**www.mediabistro.com**)

Mediabistro.com is dedicated to anyone who creates or works with content, or who is a non-creative professional working in a content/creative industry. That includes editors, writers, producers, graphic designers, book publishers, and others in industries including magazines, television, film, radio, newspapers, book publishing, online media, advertising, PR, and design. Its mission is to provide opportunities to meet; share resources; become informed of job opportunities, interesting projects, and news; improve career skills; and showcase your work.

Military Writers Society of America (**www.militarywriters.com**)

MWSA is an association of more than 800 authors, poets, and artists, drawn together by the common bond of military service. Most of its members are active duty military, retirees, or military veterans.

Mystery Writers of America (**www.mysterywriters.org**)

Mystery Writers of America is a writers association for mystery writers and other professionals in the field. MWA watches developments in legislation and tax law, sponsors symposia and mystery conferences, presents the Edgar Awards, and provides information for mystery writers. Membership in MWA is open to published authors, editors, screenwriters, and other professionals in the field.

National Association of Independent Writers and Editors
(**www.naiwe.com**)
NAIWE is a professional association for writers and editors. It exists to help members succeed, and its unique focus on creating multiple streams of writing income can make it happen.

National Writers Association (**www.nationalwriters.com**)
The NWA provides education and an ethical resource for writers at all levels of experience. This organization sponsors annual contests, offers members contract reviews, manuscript critiques, research findings relevant to writers, editing services, a professional freelancers directory and more.

The National Writers Union (**www.nwu.org**)
The National Writers Union UAW Local 1981 is the only labor union that represents freelance writers. It represents freelancers in all genres, formats, and media.

Native American Journalists Association (**www.naja.com**)
The Native American Journalists Association serves and empowers native journalists through programs and actions designed to enrich journalism and promote native cultures.

Novelists, Inc. (**www.ninc.com**)
Novelists, Inc. (Ninc) was founded in 1989 as an organization for published authors of popular fiction. The only requirement for membership is that an author must have published at least two novels with a qualifying market.

Poetry Society Of America (**www.poetrysociety.org**)
The Poetry Society of America, the oldest poetry organization in the country, was founded in New York City in 1910 by a prominent group of individuals — poets, professors, editors, and passionate readers of poetry who were distinguished in other fields.

Romance Writers Of America (**www.rwanational.org**)
Romance Writers of America (RWA) was chartered in 1981 to serve as a nonprofit trade association for romance writers. The mission of Romance Writers of America is to advance the professional interests of career-focused romance writers through networking and advocacy.

Science Fiction and Fantasy Writers of America (**www.sfwa.org**)
SFWA is a professional organization for authors of science fiction, fantasy, and related genres. SFWA informs, supports, promotes, defends, and advocates for its members.

Sisters in Crime (**www.sistersincrime.org**)
Sisters in Crime has 3,600 members in 48 chapters worldwide and offers networking, advice, and support to mystery authors. We are authors, readers, publishers, agents, booksellers, and librarians bound by our affection for the mystery genre and our support of women who write mysteries. Sara Paretsky and a group of women at the 1986 Bouchercon in Baltimore founded Sisters in Crime.

Small Publishers, Artists, and Writers Network (**www.spawn.org**)
SPAWN provides opportunities for everyone involved in publishing. SPAWN encourages the exchange of ideas, information, and other mutual benefits. This site provides information on writing and publishing and links to research sources, publishers, printers, and the media.

The Society of Children's Book Writers and Illustrators (**www.scbwi.org**)
Founded in 1971 by a group of Los Angeles-based children's writers, the Society of Children's Book Writers and Illustrators is one of the largest existing organizations for writers and illustrators.

Western Writers Of America (**www.westernwriters.org**)
Western Writers of America, Inc., was founded in 1953 to promote the literature of the American West and bestow Spur Awards for distinguished

writing in the western field. The founders were largely authors who wrote traditional western fiction, but the organization swiftly expanded to include historians and other nonfiction authors, young adult and romance writers, and writers interested in regional history.

Writers Guild Of America (**www.wga.org**)

The WGA represents writers in the motion picture, broadcast, cable, and new technologies industries.

Appendix B

Writers' Resources

Absolute Write

www.absolutewrite.com

Absolute Write is a one-stop, comprehensive website for writers of all levels, and offers articles and information about fiction, nonfiction, screenwriting, freelancing, and copywriting. Absolute Write also provides information about editing, publishing, agents, and market research. The site also offers links to classes, software, and a large and active online community of writers and publishing professionals.

Agent Query

www.agentuquery.com

The Internet's most trusted and FREE database of literary agents, Agent Query offers writers a literary touchstone. Agent Query offers the largest, most current searchable database of literary agents on the Web — a treasure trove of reputable, established literary agents seeking writers just like you.

AP Stylebook Online

www.apstylebook.com

The AP Stylebook is a style manual produced by Associated Press as an industry-standard handbook for writers, editors, students, and public relations specialists. This stylebook provides fundamental guidelines for spelling, grammar, punctuation, and usage.

Author Meeting Place

www.authormeetingplace.com

Author Meeting Place is designed for authors to meet and greet other authors in their close proximity.

Chicago Manual of Style Online

www.chicagomanualofstyle.org/home.html

The Chicago Manual of Style is the most used and trusted style guide for writers and the publishing industry. The history of *The Chicago Manual of Style* spans more than 100 years, beginning in 1891 when the University of Chicago Press first opened its doors.

Duotrope's Digest

www.duotrope.com

Duotrope's Digest is an award-winning, free writers' resource that lists more than 3,375 current fiction and poetry publications. This resource can be used to search for markets that may make a fine home for the piece you just polished. It offers other free services to writers and editors, including a free online submissions tracker for registered users.

Elements of Style

www.bartleby.com/141

Asserting that one must first know the rules to break them, this classic reference book is essential for any student and conscientious writer.

Intended for use in which the practice of composition is combined with the study of literature, it gives in a brief space the principal requirements of plain English style and concentrates attention on the rules of usage and principles of composition most commonly violated.

Free Management Library™

http://managementhelp.org/businesswriting/index.htm
c/o Authenticity Consulting, LLC
4008 Lake Drive Avenue North
Minneapolis, Minnesota 55422-1508

The Free Management Library by Authenticity Consulting, LLC, is provided as a free community resource. The library offers free, easy-to-access, online articles to develop yourself, other individuals, groups, and organizations. Over the past 15 years, the library has grown to be one of the world's largest and well-organized collections of articles and resources. The library features approximately 650 topics, spanning almost 10,000 links. Each topic has additional recommended books and related library topics.

Grammar Girl — Quick and Dirty Tips™ For Better Writing

www.grammar.quickanddirtytips.com
Whether you want to brush up on something you learned long ago in school, improve the way you manage your household, or develop professional skills to advance your career, Quick and Dirty Tips experts are here to help. In blog posts, podcasts, and newsletters, the Quick and Dirty Tips experts break down complex subjects to make them simpler and provide examples so you can easily see how to apply this new knowledge to your daily life.

Literary Market Place

www.literarymarketplace.com

Information Today, Inc.

143 Old Marlton Pike

Medford, NJ 08055

Literary Market Place (LMP) is the directory of America and Canadian book publishing. For more than 50 years, LMP has been the resource consulted by practically everyone looking for industry data — whether they are publishing professional, authors, industry watchers, or those seeking to gain entry into the world of publishing.

Poets & Writers

www.pw.org

P.O. Box 422460

Palm Coast, FL 32142

Phone: 386-246-0106

Poets & Writers, Inc., is the primary source of information, support, and guidance for creative writers. Founded in 1970, it is the nation's largest nonprofit literary organization serving poets, fiction writers, and creative nonfiction writers.

Publisher's Marketplace

www.publishersmarketplace.com

Cader Books, Inc.

2 Park Place, #4

Bronxville, NY 10708

The biggest and best dedicated marketplace for publishing professionals to find critical information and unique databases, find each other, and to do business better electronically.

Renegade Writer

www.therenegadewriter.com

This blog is an extension of the book. It is all about how to develop a querying style that works for you, overcome freelancing fear, get motivated, figure out your own systems for getting and doing work, earn more money as a freelancer, boost your freelance writing career, and reach your writing dreams.

U.S. Copyright Office

www.copyright.gov

101 Independence Ave SE

Washington DC 20559-6000

202-707-3000

The Copyright Office is an office of record, a place where claims to copyright are registered and where documents relating to copyright may be recorded when the requirements of the copyright law are met. The Copyright Office furnishes information about the provisions of the copyright law and the procedures for making a registration or recordation, explains the operations and practices of the Copyright Office, and reports on facts found in the public records of the office. The office also administers the mandatory deposit provisions of the copyright law and the various compulsory licensing provisions of the law, which include collecting royalties.

The Well-Fed Writer

www.wellfedwriter.com

Official website of Peter Bowerman, author of *The Well-Fed Writer* and various other self-published books. The Well-Fed Writer website offers e-books, teleseminars, an e-newsletter, a blog, mentoring, and industry links.

Writers.com — Writers on the Net

www.writers.com

Writers on the Net was founded in 1995 to serve the international community of writers on the Internet. The classes and services are used by aspiring writers and professionals from Alaska to Australia and take place either on an educational website or via e-mail lists. There is no set time the students must "meet" online. The courses offer extensive communication and interaction between students and instructors. Because this exchange of ideas is exclusively through text, the medium the student is trying to master, the class itself is a means of learning. Writers on the Net does not require students to purchase books or any other materials for its courses.

Writer's Digest

www.writersdigest.com
F+W Media, Inc.
4700 E. Galbraith Road
Cincinnati, Ohio 45236
513-531-2690

Since 1920, *Writer's Digest* has chronicled the culture of the modern writer and continues this great tradition through relevant first-person essays, interviews with bestselling authors and profiles with emerging talent. *Writer's Digest* also features practical technique articles, and tips and exercises on fiction, nonfiction, poetry, and the business side of writing and publishing.

Writer's Digest University

www.writersonlineworkshops.com

Writer's Digest University is a Web-based writing instruction developed by Writer's Digest. WD University combines the best of world-class writing instruction with immediacy of the Internet to create a state-of-the-art learning environment. WD University provides a traditional workshop setting — including peer review, instructor feedback, a community of writers to share ideas and solutions, and hands-on writing practice — without the hassle of commuting, parking, or filled classrooms.

The Write Jobs

www.writejobs.com

The Write Jobs™ is a specialty job board and career resource for journalism, media, publishing, and writing professionals. Write Jobs is part of Writers Write, Inc.'s network of resources for creative professionals that includes Writenews.com and Writerswrite.com.

The Writer Magazine

www.writermag.com

The *Writer* magazine has been providing inspiration and step-by-step solutions for writers of all levels since 1887. Each issue offers helpful advice for improving your writing, before-and-after examples, practical solutions to common writing problems, profiles on selected literary magazines, and tips from famous authors.

Writers' Market

www.writersmarket.com
F+W Media, Inc.
4700 E. Galbraith Road
Cincinnati, Ohio 45236
513-531-2690

WritersMarket.com is the Internet's most comprehensive guide to getting published. Since 1921, Writer's Market has been the "freelance writer's bible," providing contact information for thousands of editors and agents, tips on manuscripts formatting, query letter clinics, and more.

Writer's Weekly

www.writersweekly.com
Booklocker.com, Inc.
P.O. Box 2399
Bangor, ME 04402-2399
Fax: 305-768-0261

WritersWeekly.com is one of the oldest and most respected websites dedicated to freelance writing. This freelance writing e-zine has been published continuously since 1997, and is part of the Booklocker.com, Inc., family of businesses, which includes the e-publisher and online bookstore, Booklocker.com.

Writers Write

www.writerswrite.com
Writers Write® is the Internet's largest writing site, consisting of thousands of Web pages. With author interviews, articles, an extensive guidelines database, an online community, and comprehensive resources for all types of writing, WritersWrite.com is home to The Writer's Blog.

Successful Query Letters and Synopses

Successful Query Letter: Memoir

Dear Ms. Gardner:

I was born and raised in the Fundamentalist Church of Jesus Christ of Latter-Day Saints, which was lead by Warren Jeffs and whose compound in Eldorado, Texas, was recently raided. In this raid, they have removed more than 400 women and children they believe to be under abuse or eminent threat of abuse. These events have been dominating the headlines for the past week now. As events unfold, the public is becoming increasingly curious about what life is like inside this cult.

Other books have been written about life inside polygamist cults like the FLDS Church, and they have become bestsellers. Irene Spencer (my aunt) wrote *Shattered Dreams*, which is a bestseller. Carolyn Jessop's *Escape* is also another popular book on the subject.

What makes my book stand out is that it is the first of its kind from the perspective of a young man growing up in a polygamist cult. It isn't full of dark stories of abuse, although abuse is addressed in it. It is filled with stories of the humorous things that were part of being in a large family like ours. The goal is to make the reader fall in love with my family before dealing with the abuses so that the impact on the reader's emotions is greater. It is also an inspirational Christian story about the healing power of Christ to reconcile the pains of the past. It is about how I could eventually see my value through Christ's eyes and to be able to put the past behind me, even to the point of being able to forgive my own father, who was an abuser and pedophile.

The book begins in the office of my psychiatrist where I am seeking help to keep from acting on my homicidal thoughts and feelings toward my father. I use the psychiatrist's office to explain my family's background in Mormonism (I am a seventh generation Mormon) and how the FLDS Mormons came to be. I then use a flashback to present my life growing up in this cult. Toward the end, I come back to the psychiatrist's office where he helps me come to grips with my feelings and I move on from there in real-time. I get married, have a son, and then come to faith in Christ where I learn the power of forgiveness so profoundly that it compels me to forgive my father. The book ends with the events surrounding my father's funeral and the conclusions that I draw from it.

I look forward to hearing from you.

Yours truly,
Brian J. Mackert

Successful Query Letter: Nonfiction Anthology

Dear Mr. Sternfeld,

"Well-behaved women rarely make history," said Laurel Thatcher Ulrich.

That's because well-behaved women don't rescue men in the Wild West, discover Radium, or achieve Hollywood stardom after being fired from countless chorus-line jobs. Well-behaved women don't speed 300 miles/hour around a racetrack, trek in the Egyptian desert in full Victorian garb – and they certainly don't soar into the mysterious unknown.

Several biographies describe women who didn't behave and made history – but few anthologies provide real-life applications for readers.

What can we learn from the divas, outlaws, and entrepreneurs who pursued their passions? What do they have that many of us lack? Juice, life force, energy, passion, vision, and the ability to embrace change. We have juice but life drains it. We have dreams, but our mothers, partners, kids, jobs, and our own personalities can override them. We get rejected, depressed, anxious, and scared… and we stop living even though we're still breathing.

SEE JANE SOAR! 200 WHO WEREN'T WELL-BEHAVED: FOLLOWING THEIR HEARTS, MAKING HISTORY:

- Presents brief, accurate profiles of historical and contemporary women from all cultures and nationalities.

- Emphasizes personality traits, achievements, and struggles. Each profile includes quotes from the woman and direct life applications for the reader.

- Highlights 10 different categories: outlaws, divas, athletes, politicians, explorers, entrepreneurs, etc. Readers can easily access subjects that interest them.

This book offers more than a link to history. It inspires women to change and grow, to achieve their goals - whether that means earning a Ph.D., losing that last 10 pounds, or asking for a bank loan. Readers will see themselves in the lives of these women who courageously pursued their talents and dreams. They'll learn that Annie Oakley didn't shoot photographs and Annie Leibovitz didn't shoot targets because they followed their own hearts, minds, and souls.

SEE JANE SOAR will encourage women to accept and nurture who they truly are.

SEE JANE SOAR has the potential to morph into a calendar or daily journal for holiday or first-day-of-school gifts. A "soar" series is possible: 200 girls who didn't behave and changed history - or 200 Canadians, seniors, athletes, teachers, people with disabilities, people with diseases, and so on.

My degrees in education and psychology give me a solid background with which to research and write this book. I lived and taught in Africa for three years and traveled worldwide — I know how exciting it is to soar!

And I write. My publications include articles for *Woman's Day*, *Flare*, *Reader's Digest*, *Glow*, *Alive*, *Esteem*, *Good Times*, *Today's Health and Wellness*, and *cahoots*.

Let me know if you'd like to review a full book proposal.

Yours truly,
Laurie Pawlik-Kienlen

Successful Query Letter: Christian Literary Fiction

Dear Victoria:

What happens when a lost man finds Christ, only to lose his soul?

The first person novel, *MAMMOTH MOUNTAIN* (100,000 words) is a cross between *The Catcher in the Rye* and *Good Will Hunting*. Set in the early 1980s, it follows four years in the life of Drew, a pot smoking, thieving womanizer who's coming to terms with his violent upbringing by an alcoholic father, a man who may not be his biological father.

Twenty-one years old and new to Mammoth, he continually brawls with a powerful Olympic ski racer but has an even more dangerous nemesis inside his head. Over four years, Drew's roller coaster life takes him to the Pacific Northwest, Maui, and Mexico but he always returns to Mammoth Mountain. With the help of an old friend, he barely pulls through his mental breakdown in a cave on Maui and becomes a father himself, vowing to do a better job than his father did.

MAMMOTH MOUNTAIN is a "Rated R" Christian novel.

I have had more than twenty stories and editorials published in: *The San Diego Union Tribune*, *The Surfer's Journal*, *Surfer Magazine*, and *Surfing Magazine*. My collection of short stories, *Zen and the Art of Surfing* is now in its eighth printing. In 1998, five of the stories were originally published in *The Surfer's Journal* (20,000 copies), and the Julian Paz Foundation now publishes the entire collection through a grant. There are currently three magazines that are going to run more stories from the collection: *SurfMor* (a new magazine), *The Surfer's Path* (based in the U.K.) and *Ocean* magazine. You can read an excerpt of the collection at my website, and I'd be happy to send you a copy of *Zen and the Art of Surfing*.

Sincerely,
Greg Guttierez

Successful Query Letter: Erotic Romance

Thank you for responding to my e-mail query so quickly! Here are the first five chapters and synopsis for *MINE, ALL MINE*, a single title erotic romance that is a perfect fit for Kensington Brava. I believe your agency would be ideal for representing the project.

MINE, ALL MINE is the erotic story of desire, passion, and unrequited love in San Francisco and the rolling hills of Tuscany. Lily Ellis has been deeply in lust with Travis Carson for well over a decade. But since Travis likes his women bold and sassy, not meek and size 14, she knows her feelings will never be anything more than bathtub fantasies with Travis's name on her lips. But all it takes is one special night at a fashion show in San Francisco, one very special dress, and the wonders of Tuscany to change Travis's feelings for Lily forever.

My first novel, *Authors in Ecstasy* (published by Ellora's Cave under the pseudonym Bella Andre), received a 4.5 star review in the March 2004 edition of *Romantic Times* magazine.

My publishing experience also includes several novellas with Ellora's Cave and two non-fiction books on the music business. I am a member of RWA and a graduate of Stanford University.

Thank you for your consideration. I look forward to hearing from you.

Sincerely,
Bella Andre

Successful Query Letter: Chick-Lit Novel

TULLE LITTLE, TULLE LATE
By Kimberly Llewellyn

Life's Too Short — And So Are My Skirts
A Very Funny, Very Sexy, Very Newfangled Chicklitty Book

Synopsis

"Life's too short and so are my skirts" is the new motto for NINA ROBERTSON after she realizes she's been putting her current life on hold, waiting for her "real" life to begin. Life is what's been happening while she was off making premarital plans, which fell through the butt cracks of reality. With the help of her gal-pals, she decides to set a new plan in motion. Her friendships with the gal-pals are genuine… in the sense that they all love each other, but don't necessarily always get along, which is closer to the real thing, right? Who needs brainless-but-supportive cheerleader friends, anyway? Their relationships are the kind where alliances are formed, friendships broken, secrets betrayed, and lives altered forever… and this is all during happy hour!

Right… back to Nina's grand plan. First, she must stop pining over her ex-fiance, JEREMIAH, the famous jet-setting journalist who broke her heart… twice. ("I didn't let him go… he chewed off his own arm and ran!") Then she's gotta start playing "catch-up" with career, friendships, and sex. She must cultivate herself for a change. But can this just-turned-30-year-old succeed at getting up to speed and on the fast track without crashing and burning from life's – ahem – little detours? (Oh yeah, throw in one skeptical mom, to boot.)

Okay, so maybe Nina's having a pre-quasi-mid-life crisis. Yes, she's upset that she's not where she "should" be in life, but she's simply freaking out about it ten years sooner than everyone else. It makes sense. See, everyone else has sped past her in the life-departments of career position, marriage prospects, and – hell, even having a little spare cash in the ol' checking account. Yeah, she's a little behind. Speaking of behinds, she'll have to work on that, too, if she's to start dating again.

Straightening out her life doesn't happen simply. How can it, once she's humiliated when she gets caught snared in her arch rival cousin's wedding gown at the woman's own bridal shower? (This is a good time to add that the cousin calls off the entire wedding because of Nina… long story.)

Then a promotion is up for grabs at the ad agency/ PR firm where Nina works as an assistant. She's got to fight for it big time and beat out the "shoo-in." Part of earning the promotion includes "babysitting" a Zsa-Zsa-Gabor-cop-slapping actress who's in town to make a comeback movie and needs help with her PR nightmare. Of course, the movie star makes Nina's life a living hell. But Nina must endure and do her job fabulously well for the next few weeks… all in time for the company's annual gala affair. It's an event where the promotion announcement will be made. An event where she must have the perfect date by her side to save face. No pressure, right?

Marathon dating doesn't come easy. See, when it comes to heartache, Nina is a bleeder, despite her lighthearted smart-alecky exterior. Her breakup with Jeremiah has left her reeling and she finds it impossible to suffer the dating scene – until she literally stumbles across DANTE. Okay, so maybe this guy hemorrhages his handsomeness all over the place. But he can usually be found straddling his motorcycle and behaving in a way indicative of a rudderless, rebel lifestyle.

Falling for Dante is as smart as running with scissors in the dark and drunk. He's the epitome of what Nina doesn't want right now. Not with all she's trying to accomplish. But she can't help herself each time she gets sidetracked by this guy, who's all hell-bent on showing her that she's wrong in attempting to lead her life in one direction, according to convention. He feels she should fly by the seat of her panties. And Nina is torn. She's having feelings for this guy, who's feeling cool stuff for her, too. Oh, hell, why does being so bad have to feel so good?

From soup to (Dante's) nuts, the obstacles Nina faces are mounting:

(1) She's in knots trying to keep in line the aging fruitcake movie actress, especially when the woman ends up in jail. (2) She also must keep the peace with her friends. These gal-pals make matters worse for her under the guise of "just tryin' to help." With friends like these, who needs therapy? (3) She can't help but be seduced by her often polemic, but always passionate, run-ins with Dante, the stud muffin on a chopper. (4) Oh, right, then there's the evil "shoo-in" guy sabotaging her efforts for promotion at the ad agency every chance he gets. (5) Cue the ex-fiance. Now's as good a time as any to mention that Jeremiah the jockey-journalist comes back from reporting on a dangerous assignment overseas and wants to get back together with Nina.

With Jeremiah home, Nina entertains the notion of getting back together with her repentant Geraldo-wanna-be. It would be so easy to just set her life back on its original course. After all, who knew that living life would be so much work? But she also entertains the notion that she enjoys her free-spirited romps with Dante, despite their polar-opposite views on, well, everything.

Okay, so maybe she does more than "entertain" both notions… she "entertains" both men.

The plot thickens… and so does her waistline.

Believing she "may be" a little pregnant (yeah, yeah, either you are or you aren't, unless you're in denial, then it's a definite "maybe"), Nina must make some serious choices. She needs to decide whether to tell both fathers (an egg can be dually fertilized, can't it?) about her possible pregnancy. She also must decide whom to bring to the gala since both men insist on escorting her. And, she must figure out how to get the evil "shoo-in" guy to hang himself by his own devices, revealing his incessant sabotaging in time for the gala-soiree. Finally, she must get the attention-craving movie actress to behave herself once and for all.

A couple things turn around for Nina. She comes to terms with her relationships with her mom and her friends. Then she sees a softer side to the movie actress, who's actually sympathetic to Nina's plight, and a bond is formed. Nina also discovers she's not pregnant. Nevertheless, the non-birthing experience makes her grow anyway, and she sees things in a new light.

She finally informs both men in her love triangle that she intends to go alone to the gala… she's learning to be happy with herself and where she is right now. She discovers that always worrying about the future has been keeping her from enjoying the present. The urgency to be where she thinks she "ought" to be in life has lessened; some things simply can't be rushed.

Does this stop the two competing men from showing up at the gala anyway? No. Both men are decked out in tuxes when they make their appearances at the affair and attempt to win her affections. She doesn't need this right now. So far, at the gala, things don't look good for her promotion. And the two men causing a testosterone-filled scene aren't helping matters.

One thing is good however. While she's juggling these two boy-toys, her previous efforts pay off in getting the evil "shoo-in" to bite himself in the ass with his rotten antics. His ploys finally backfire, getting him caught red-handed sabotaging Nina. As for Dante, well, Nina discovers he's harboring a shocking secret of his own.

Nina is ultimately offered the promotion; she accepts. But when she gets an ultimatum from both Dante and Jeremiah, telling her to choose, she asserts that she chooses neither. They must leave the gala now. Dante takes the news like a man, showing much greater chivalry and dignity than Jeremiah, who mouths off at her, spitefully revealing his true colors, and storms off.

Okay, so some parts of Nina's life are "getting there." Others, well, they ain't so good. She's lost Jeremiah again. That makes it three times now. But she's certain it will be the last, especially after she finds out why he wanted to get back together with her. Apparently, when he bagged out on their engagement, the tabloids caught wind of this and tore him to pieces for being a coward. They had a field day when they macheted his machismo in their papers, and he'd become desperate to rectify his big bad rep. Imagine, going through those pains all in the name of a job…

Nina realizes Dante was right (at least to a degree) about the way she's been running her life. While she doesn't totally agree with his non-directional ways, he has helped to show her that she doesn't need to be so worked up about extreme societal convention.

She knows living her life falls somewhere between the two. If only she had the chance to tell him.

She gets that chance as she leaves the gala. Dante is waiting in the shadows for her. He's sitting on his motorcycle, oozing sexuality in that suave rented tux of his. He's genuinely concerned to see if she's all right; he also wants to see if she needs a lift home.

Admittedly, she's happy Dante stuck around; it says a lot about the guy's character. She informs him how she realized that much of what he believes about life turned out to be right on the money. He corrects her, saying his beliefs were only partly true when it comes to leading your life without direction. He tells her he also came to the gala tonight to let her know something. He feels the time has come to stick around for a while and open up his dream business of a vintage motorcycle shop and touring motor club. But he wants to know one thing… does he have something worthwhile to stick around for?

She unceremoniously hikes up her sequin gala gown, straddles the back of his motorcycle, and wraps her arms around his waist. "Hell if I know," she answers happily, "but for now, let's just ride."

Successful Query Letter: Mystery Novel

SWIFT JUSTICE
By Laura DaSilverio

Synopsis

When CHARLOTTE "CHARLIE" SWIFT, former Air Force investigator turned barely solvent PI, confronts an armed woman in her office first thing Monday morning, she knows the week is going to suck. And when she finds out she must accept the woman, GIGI GOLDMAN, as her partner in Swift Investigations, she hatches a plan to get rid of Gigi. (LES GOLDMAN, Gigi's husband and Charlie's silent – emphasis on *silent* – partner, embezzled funds from his businesses and decamped to Costa Rica with his personal trainer, leaving Gigi nothing but the house, the Hummer, and half-interest in Swift Investigations.) A pampered socialite in her fifties, Gigi doesn't strike Charlie as investigator material and she resolves to "persuade" the woman to give up on PI work by assigning her all the most tedious and grubby tasks.

Meanwhile, a client turns up with a missing person case that challenges even Charlie's investigative skills. MELISSA LLOYD found a baby on her doorstep with a note asking her to take care of it for a few days. Not unnaturally, in Charlie's opinion, she wants to find the mother who, Melissa confesses, is her daughter. Piece of cake, Charlie thinks, until she asks for the daughter's name and description, only to hear that Melissa doesn't know because she's never met her. Huh? Turns out, Melissa got pregnant as a teen and gave the baby girl up for adoption. Apparently, the now sixteen-year-old has located Melissa and ditched her own infant on the doorstep. Find the teen and give the baby back, Melissa orders Charlie.

Following clues culled from the one-of-a-kind blanket BABY OLIVIA came swaddled in, Charlie sallies forth from Colorado Springs to interview a goat herder/artist in Larkspur and a wine shop owner in Denver. Her queries net her the name of the girl who left the baby with Melissa, and she heads home triumphantly, only to learn from a police detective buddy, that the body of a Jane Doe fits the description of Charlie's missing teen. Charlie e-mails the detective the photos she got in Denver and receives confirmation that the dead girl is ELIZABETH SPROUSE, Melissa Lloyd's daughter, Olivia's mother, and the city's 27th homicide of the year. When Charlie breaks the news to her client and shows her the photos, Melissa faints. Revived, she tells Charlie she knows the girl in the photos. Calling herself Beth, and saying her husband was a soldier deployed in Iraq, the girl has done piecework sewing for Melissa's interior design business for the better part of a year.

Charlie figures she's done her job by locating Olivia's mother, but Melissa changes her assignment: find the baby's father and off-load Olivia on him. This task proves much harder as Charlie delves into Elizabeth's life, talking to her high school counselor, her best friend, and the parents who adopted her as an infant. The father is a pastor in the style of an Old Testament prophet, and the mother is a cowed homemaker. When Elizabeth ran away, her father was plotting an arranged marriage for her with a 45-year-old member of his congregation with the money and connections to get Pastor Sprouse his own TV show. The alleged fiancé, Seth Johnson, an immensely rich and politically powerful rancher, vehemently denies having sex with Elizabeth and threatens Charlie with unnamed consequences if she investigates him further. In fact, no one Charlie talks to can point to a potential father for Olivia. All of them, however, agree Elizabeth was obsessed with finding her birth mother. Charlie locates the PI Elizabeth hired to find her mother and the PI says the girl seemed a little "off" in her motives. She wasn't looking for a joyful Hallmark reunion, the PI opines.

As Charlie's frustration mounts, she must deal with the results of Gigi's catastrophic attempts at investigation, including burning down the organic fast-food joint where she was undercover as the mascot, Bernie the Bison, and blowing up a meth lab during the botched surveillance of an alleged adulterer. Each time, she manages to solve the case and generate positive publicity for Swift Investigations. Exasperated by the woman's refusal to quit (despite a broken arm), Charlie gives Gigi summons work to do and continues unraveling Elizabeth's surprisingly complex life.

Charlie thinks she's making progress when she discovers Elizabeth was trolling surrogate mother sites on the Internet. Olivia's father must be STEPHAN FALSTOW, Charlie decides, the male half of a couple Elizabeth met via a surrogacy site. Interviewing Mrs. Falstow dashes that theory: Elizabeth was already pregnant when she met the Falstows. They agreed to pay her expenses in return for permission to adopt Olivia. JACQUELINE FALSTOW, desperate for a baby, has longed to know the baby's fate since learning of Elizabeth's death. Suspecting Charlie knows where the baby is, she follows her to a meeting with DETECTIVE MONTGOMERY (who threatens to arrest Charlie for second-degree kidnapping if she doesn't reveal the baby's location) and then almost to Melissa Lloyd's front door. Charlie, realizing she's being followed, traps Mrs. Falstow in a cul de sac and confronts her. Charlie, annoyed with herself for almost leading Falstow to the baby, continues to the Lloyd house and meets IAN LLOYD, Melissa's husband. He'd run into Elizabeth only a couple of times and still doesn't realize that Olivia is Melissa's granddaughter. He's never wanted children, however, and is eager to see the last of Olivia. (He thinks Melissa is taking care of her for a friend.)

An urgent phone call draws Charlie away from the Lloyds and by the time she's finished persuading the Pine Creek Golf Course manager not to press charges against Gigi for drowning a cart while trying to serve a summons, Melissa Lloyd has fired her. Why, Charlie asks? She sees past Melissa's concocted explanation and realizes the woman loves Olivia and wants to keep her. She's confessed the truth to her husband and is no longer interested in locating the baby's father. Accepting her fee and driving back to the office, Charlie ponders the women who desperately want Olivia – Janet Falstow, Elizabeth's adopted mother, and Melissa Lloyd – and the men who could, conceivably, have fathered the baby: Stefan Falstow (who knew Elizabeth earlier than his wife suspected), PASTOR SPROUSE (who several people suspect of abusing his step-daughter), the high-school counselor, the lawyer who runs a shady practice introducing pregnant teens to rich parents desperate enough to buy babies, or SETH JOHNSON (with three failed marriages behind him and an obsession with producing an heir). To stop Charlie's investigation of his affairs, Johnson threatens to put her out of business by buying out her partner (Gigi) and buying up her mortgage and foreclosing at the first opportunity. Charlie must, against all her instincts, beg Gigi to stay on as her partner and not sell out. The women take the first tentative steps toward friendship.

Just as Charlie reaches her office, trying to come to terms with not being able to close the case, Melissa calls. Olivia has been kidnapped! Charlie immediately calls Detective Montgomery and, convinced she knows who has kidnapped the baby, heads to the Falstow house with Gigi. It soon becomes obvious Janet Falstow did not take the baby. As Charlie's sifting through all the data she amassed during the investigation, Montgomery calls to say Melissa denies a kidnapping took place. The police suspect she's lying and Montgomery wants Charlie to talk to her. On the way to the Lloyd house, the pieces fall into place for Charlie, and she calls Melissa to ask where Ian is. Melissa initially refuses to believe her husband could have taken the baby, but agrees to activate his truck's antitheft GPS tracker.

Charlie and Gigi locate Ian and Olivia at a Walmart south of Colorado Springs. (He stopped to purchase a car seat and diapers, not having planned his kidnapping very well.) He wasn't going to hurt the baby, he assures them when they trap him; he was going to take her across state lines and leave her at a fire station or hospital. Once Melissa told him Olivia was Elizabeth's baby, he knew her DNA could connect him to Elizabeth and her death. Her accidental death, he hastens to add. When Elizabeth birthed Olivia and decided to keep the baby, she needed money to get away from Colorado and the sure-to-be-furious Falstows. She called Ian and threatened to tell Melissa about their brief affair if he didn't help her financially. He met her at a secluded location, planning to persuade her, he says, to give up the baby. But she didn't have the baby with her (having dropped it off at Melissa's). Elizabeth shocks him by saying she plotted their affair as revenge against Melissa for abandoning her. She'd tracked her birth mother down, with nebulous ideas for revenge that crystallized when she met Ian. What better revenge than to sleep with Melissa's husband? Appalled, he punches Elizabeth and she falls, breaking her neck on his F-150 bumper.

Knowing the police are on their way to the Walmart, Ian tries to escape. Sprinting to the back of the store, he hijacks a Fluffy-Whip truck from the loading dock, with Charlie in hot pursuit on foot. Gigi appears in the Hummer, and Ian wrecks the truck to avoid a collision. Whipped cream oozes into the parking lot, and customers frolic in it as the police arrive to take him into custody.

In the end of *SWIFT JUSTICE*, the 80,000-word first in a PI mystery series, Melissa ends up with the baby while Ian awaits trial. Charlie and Gigi capitalize on the publicity generated by the successful case and move forward to their next case as partners.

Successful Query Letter: Young Adult Novel

Synopsis

REVOLUTION, SIZE SMALL
By Loretta Nyhan

Sixteen-year-old TRUDIE MORESCO is increasingly unhappy living in the shadows of her larger than life parents: FIONA, a local celeb known for her eco-activism, and TONY, an adrenaline addict serving Doctors in Crisis in Africa. She experiments with ways to create an identity separate from that of her parents, mainly, exploring her interest in photography and flirting with EMIL, a recent immigrant and Fiona's intern. Emil likes Trudie, but stops the romance before anything serious happens: He's still getting over someone from back home. Someone who, as Trudie later learns, happens to be a boy.

After a night of drinking, Trudie's growing frustration culminates in a really dumb decision. She breaks into the property of CLINTER FLETCHER, a real estate developer intent on ruining her mom's plans for a community garden, and etches her feelings onto his Lincoln Navigator with her Swiss Army knife. Luckily, the Gross Hills Police Department has a program for "good kids who do stupid things." Instead of standing in front of a judge, Trudie can work off her debt to society by working *for* Mr. Fletcher, painting one of his investment properties.

On the first day of her prison sentence Trudie is not met by Mr. Fletcher, but by CONNOR, his troubled stepson, and Trudie's ideological opposite. Surprisingly they work well together, and as a tentative friendship develops, Connor gives Trudie glimpses into the lives of the secretive Fletchers.

Her friends think Trudie's stumbled into the perfect opportunity to spy on behalf of her mother's activist group. Trudie agrees but becomes conflicted when she senses Connor likes her in the way she wishes Emil would.

As Trudie spends less time with her friends and more with Connor, his roundabout stabs at asking her out develop a certain appeal, and she agrees to have dinner at his house. Afterwards, Connor offers Trudie some information Fiona could use to fight Clint's bid on the community land. Though the evidence is pretty circumstantial, alerting the zoning board would assure a win for Fiona and destroy Clint's ability to build anywhere in Gross Hills.

Trudie struggles with what to do. After watching her mom tirelessly lead the community on the two-year garden campaign, failure would be devastating but might bring her father home from Africa. Connor seems to have a score to settle with his stepdad, making Trudie feel like a convenient way to get the job done. She needs help but has fallen away from the people who could best offer it. Fiona is distracted and silently grieving for a marriage put on hold; Trudie's best friend nurses hurt feelings after Trudie refused to share the details of her relationship with Emil, and Tony's communication with her practically consists of one-line e-mails and a link to his Facebook page. Trudie shares her information with the person of last resort, who refuses to tell her what to do, and instead advises Trudie to do what she feels is right.

Trudie attends the board meeting, with a manila envelope as her contribution to the hearing. After the board decides in Fiona's favor, a member of the committee hands the folder to Fiona, telling her the contents really showed the committee the garden's potential. Fiona opens it and finds a hand bound album of photos depicting herbs from her garden: dill bursting like fireworks on the Fourth of July, lavender swaying in the breeze, soft and hazy chamomile, and, finally, a mint plant Trudie shot with her 1968 Pentax on a day Emil left her alone on the contested patch of land to think.

To celebrate the win, the group heads back to Trudie's house for a party. As people set up tables and light candles in the garden, Trudie feels a little overwhelmed and heads up to her room for a breather. She enters her darkened room to find Tony sitting on her bed, 20 pounds thinner, with knobby knees and stories to tell. They head down to the party, and while Tony and Fiona get to the business of working out their relationship, Trudie does the same with both Emil and Connor. Nothing is completely settled, but as Trudie has learned, when presented with an either/or decision, it's perfectly appropriate to make your choice from the small space between the two. She realizes this as she takes Connor's hand, and they join the party, together.

Successful Book Proposal

A Proposal for

Modern Traditions:

Inspiring Ideas for Incorporating
Yesterday's Customs into Today's Wedding

by Gina Cunningham

Table of Contents

Introduction

Overview   1

Markets and Spin-offs   4

Promotion   5

Competitive and Complementary Books   8

About the Author   11

The Outline

Chapter Summary   12

Sample Chapter

Chapter 7: The Ceremony

Supplemental Material

Press Clippings Featuring the Author

Cunningham / *Modern Traditions*   1

INTRODUCTION

Overview

Engaged couples want weddings that blend tradition and personal style. They are looking to the

past for inspiring ways to transform a modern wedding into a meaningful experience.

Modern Traditions will be the first book to present traditional cultural wedding elements with a twist; updated and reinterpreted for today's couple. The book will outline cultural customs, rituals, and symbolism from around the world associated with music, dance, food, ceremony, design, and decor and provide inspiring ideas for readers to adapt traditions to their wedding.

Modern Traditions will help brides and grooms design a signature wedding that reflects their style as a couple by defining ways to honor their heritage, adopt a custom, update a tradition, or create a new ritual to personalize their wedding and pay elegant tribute to what is meaningful to them.

Industry publications and professionals note the trend toward incorporating, updating, and "borrowing" wedding traditions. *Bride's* magazine reports, "Couples are choosing to observe centuries-old traditions, updating them to reflect their own personalities. And more couples than ever before are including ethnic customs from their heritages in wedding celebrations." *Modern Bride* magazine observes in their 2002 report, "Couples are borrowing traditions from their own heritage or other cultures [for their wedding]." *Bridal Guide* writes, "Many couples select traditions from a variety of cultures because the idea resonates with them. They like the symbolism behind these acts and incorporate them [into their wedding], regardless of the heritage." The book will provide a much-needed resource in the fast growing wedding design market. *Modern Traditions* will appeal to:

- Couples wanting to incorporate aspects of each other's culture into the wedding

- Couples looking for a guide to provide practical and stylish ideas for incorporating traditional elements into the wedding

- Couples looking for ideas to personalize their wedding

- Couples wanting to add meaningful elements to their wedding

- Couples wanting to differentiate their wedding from others and create a unique celebration

- Wedding coordinators, designers, event planners, and catering managers looking for new ideas and inspiration

As a wedding coordinator and designer, the author has planned numerous celebrations incorporating her clients' cultures and personalities. From Irish handfastings to African-American ribbon tying, the author creates inspiring events for couples. The author will present ideas from her diverse portfolio and create new designs gathered from extensive cultural research.

Vibrant photographs of design elements, sidebars with real couples' stories, references to celebrities' wedding designs, checklists outlining updated ideas, and a complete resource list will add value and visual appeal.

The finished manuscript will contain 250 pages, including 20 pages of back matter, 73 photographs, and 19 black and white photographs, and one chart. The book will be divided

into three sections: ceremony, design, and celebration, with 18 chapters, five design element
inserts, and ten couples' stories. The manuscript
will be completed six months after the book advance is received.

The author will ask the following authorities to
write an introduction or cover quote:

- Colin Cowie, celebrity wedding designer,
  author, and television host

- Maria Melinger-McBride, wedding designer,
  author of *The Perfect Wedding* and *The Perfect
  Wedding Reception*, contributing editor for
  Bride's magazine.

Cunningham / *Modern Traditions*   3

- Vera Wang, celebrity wedding fashion designer
  and author

- Carley Roney, author *The Knot Guide to Wedding
  Traditions and Vows*, creator TheKnot.com

Back matter will include a resource list, a
chart of traditions by culture, recommended reading, author's biography, and a form for the readers to note their design ideas, photo credits, a
feedback request form, and index.

Cunningham / *Modern Traditions*   4

Markets

More than 2.4 million couples marry each year in
the United States according to *Modern Bride*. The

Great Bridal Expo reports that weddings are a $92 billion per year industry. Gerard Monaghan, president of the Association of Bridal Consultants, adds that wedding inquiries are up 25 percent since September 11, 2001, and states, "[according to a survey of 2,600 professional wedding coordinators] there is a growing demand for weddings celebrating heritage."

According to the Great Bridal Expo, wedding customers are 90 percent female, age 25-34, college graduates, with an average combined income level of $75,000. Engaged consumers are recession proof, constantly renewing, and have high immediate needs. Couples purchase wedding items at bridal fairs, wedding salons, event showrooms, and stationary stores, and via the internet. A bride spends more than 100 hours designing the wedding. Brides turn to design books, wedding experts, bridal magazines, and television shows for inspiration.

Markets for the book include engaged couples and members of the hospitality industry: wedding designers, coordinators, and venue catering managers.

Spin-offs

Modern Traditions will be the first in a series of six wedding design books including:

- A Heritage Wedding: Culturally Inspired Designs to Personalize Your Wedding

- Elegant Themes: Stylish Designs to Personalize Your Wedding

- Defining Your Wedding Style: How To Reveal Your Personality to Design a Unique Celebration

- Inspired Ideas for Designing an Elegant Wedding on a Minimal Budget

- Stylish Ideas for Designing a Destination Wedding

Cunningham / *Modern Traditions*   5

Promotion

The author will do the following to help the publisher promote the book:

Publicity Campaign

Expand the author's current publicity campaign by hiring a public relations firm with expertise in book promotion to obtain national television interviews and magazine and newspaper features.

Media Kit & Video

Expand the author's current media kit. Press kit will include the author's biography, headshot, book cover jacket (galley), author Q&A sheet, Rolodex card, book reviews, and press clippings. Author will hire award-winning videography company Blvd. Video Productions to produce an 8-minute video featuring author interviews and wedding design highlights and produce 1,000 Rolodex cards with "wedding expert" headline to be sent to media and journalists. Author will commission Century Guild Press to create a letterpress media box to hold the press kit, video, and tie-in promotional items. Author will make press kit and her media contact list available to the publisher.

Send Books to Opinion-Makers

If publisher supplies copies of the books, the author will mail 25 books to leading wedding industry opinion-makers.

Author Magazine Articles and Column

Pitch author-written feature articles to media contacts at national wedding magazines including *Martha Stewart Weddings, Bridal Guide, Modern Bride*, Conde Nast's *Brides*, and *Elegant Bride*. Pitch a "Modern Traditions" column to *Elegant Bride Magazine*.

Cunningham / *Modern Traditions*   6

Television Special

Approach production company contacts to produce a television special based on *Modern Traditions*. With the author's association with Lifetime Television, the network would be a good placement for the show.

Obtain Appearances on Design Shows and Wedding Shows

Contact design and wedding shows to be a featured expert. Shows include: *Martha Stewart Living* (CBS), *You're Invited* (Style Network), *Weddings of a Lifetime* (Lifetime Television), *InStyle Wedding Special* (NBC), and other current wedding shows in production.

Bridal Fairs

Author will provide 20,000 book postcards (with book cover and purchase information) to The Great Bridal Expo. The postcards will be used as "bag stuffers" and handed to attendees at 18 national bridal fairs located in: Philadelphia, New York City, Washington D.C., Baltimore, Long Island, Boston, Detroit, Dallas, Miami, Atlanta, Fort Lauderdale, San Francisco, Anaheim, Los Angeles, Denver, Phoenix, Cleveland, and Cincinnati. Author will give The Great Bridal Expo 36 copies (two copies per city) of *Modern Traditions* to be given as prizes to attendees. Author will conduct "Modern Traditions" workshops at select bridal shows.

Cunningham / *Modern Traditions*   7

Wedding and Event Industry Conferences

Author will attend, speak, and sell books at the four leading wedding and event industry conferences each year: The Special Event (sponsored by the International Special Events Society), The Business of Brides (sponsored by the Association of Bridal Consultants), Event Solutions, and the National Association of Catering Executives.

Website

Expand the author's current website to include an updated author appearance schedule for television and magazine features, creative wedding ideas and tips, links to bookseller's website to purchase the book, author's biography, press page (for media to contact the author), resources for purchasing wedding items associated with the book, and a monthly contest to win a one-hour telephone consultation with the author. Promote the book online with "live chats" or interviews with AOL's writer's club, Amazon.com writer interviews, barnesandnoble.com, theknot.com, weddingchannel.com, modernbride.com, and Martha Stewart Weddings online.

Cunningham / *Modern Traditions*   8

Competitive Books

No competitive books currently on the market explore cultural customs and provide updated interpretations and ideas for incorporating them into the wedding design. Books that would most closely compete with *Modern Traditions* are:

The Knot Guide to Wedding Vows and Traditions: Readings, Rituals, Music, Dance, Speeches, and Toasts by Carley Roney, Broadway Books, 2000, paperback, 200 pages, $15.00. A bestseller in Theknot.com series. Provides cultural and religious wedding suggestions. Book does not provide design ideas or update traditions. Topics are limited to wedding readings, toasts, speeches, ceremony vows, and music selection.

A Bride's Book of Wedding Traditions: A Treasury of Ideas for Making Your Wedding The Most Memorable Day Ever by Arlene Hamilton Stewart, Hearst Books, 1995, 4 printings, hardcover, 300 pages, $18.00. Details the history of marriage and the origins of wedding custom. Only covers English and American traditions. Provides only a few design ideas. No photos.

Timeless Traditions: A Couple's Guide to Wedding Customs Around the World by Lisl M. Spangenberg, Universe, 2001, paperback, 232 pages, $22.50. An extensive, though not exhaustive, collection of cultural wedding traditions, sorted by country. Customs and traditions are outdated and impractical. Author does not provide design ideas or suggestions for updating customs for the modern bride. No photos.

Cunningham / *Modern Traditions*   9

Complementary Books

Wedding Rites: The Complete Guide to Traditional Weddings by Michael P. Foley, St. Augustine Press, 2002, hardcover, 256 pages, $35.00. Book provides a comprehensive collection of wedding music, readings, vows, prayers, ceremonies, and blessings from various religions around the world. Religious customs compliment *Modern Traditions* cultural customs.

Complementary Books by Publisher:

Wedding design, wedding planning, and wedding etiquette books are good companions to *Modern Traditions*.

Chronicle Books: *The Anti-Bride Guide* by Carolyn Gerin, *Wedding Showers* by Michele Adams, *The Wedding Planner* by Genevieve Morgan, *Weddings for Grownups* by Caroll Stoner.

Crown Books: *Martha Stewart's Wedding Planner* by Martha Stewart, *Priceless Weddings* by Kathleen Kennedy, *Bride's Wedding Book* by Elizabeth Hilliard.

Adams Media Corporation: *The Everything Wedding Book* (series), *Loving Vows* by Barbara Eklof, *The Creative Wedding Idea Book* by Jacqueline Smith.

Sterling Publishing: *Wedding Flowers* by Iain Thomson, *Wedding Decorations on a Budget* by Jo Packman, *Wedding Toasts and Vows* by Bette Matthews, *Wedding Style* by Sy Snarr.

HarperCollins Publishing: *The Perfect Wedding Reception* by Maria Melinger-McBride, *The Perfect Wedding* by Maria Melinger-McBride, *Wedding Details* by Mary Norden, *Legendary Brides* by Letitia Baldridge, *How to "I Do"* by Holly Lefevre, *Emily Post's Weddings* by Peggy Post.

Berkeley Publishing Group: *Words for the Wedding* by Wendy Paris, *The Wedding Guide for the Grownup Bride* by Shelley Christiansen, *The Wedding Wise Planner* by Suzanne Kresse.

Hearst Books: *Town and Country Elegant Weddings* by Stacey Okun, *A Romantic Wedding Planner* by *Victoria Magazine*, *Creating a Beautiful Wedding* by *Victoria Magazine*.

Random House, Inc.: *With This Ring* by Joanna Weaver, *This is Your Day* by Lisa Weiss, *Real Weddings* by Sally Kilbridge.

Michael Friedman Publishing Group, Inc.: *Centerpieces and Table Accents* by Kathy Passero, *A Wedding Workbook* by Bette Matthews, *Cakes* by Bette Matthews, *For Your Wedding* (series).

Steart, Tabori & Chang, Inc.: *Bouquets: A Year of Flowers for the Bride* by Marsha Heckman, *The Perfect Wedding Cake* by Kate Manchester, *A Perfect Home Wedding* by Kerry Eielson.

About the Author

As a celebrated wedding designer, coordinator, and owner of Wedding Design Studio in Los Angeles, I create and produce distinctive weddings for couples. My diverse portfolio includes both celebrity couples (actors and prominent sports figures) and everyday couples. I have been featured on several episodes of Lifetime Television's *Weddings of a Lifetime*, *The Today Show*, and *Good Morning, America*. I author a bimonthly column on theme weddings in *Inside Weddings Magazine* and speak to more than 50,000 event professionals at conferences each year. My blog, Designing Poetic Weddings, receives more than 5,000 hits per day, and I have a database of 85,000 subscribers for my monthly e-newsletter. I have been featured in *Elegant Bride Magazine*, *Bridal Guide*, *Condé Nast Bride's WeddingBells*, *The Knot Wedding Pages*, *InStyle Magazine*, *Martha Stewart Weddings*, and *The Los Angeles Times*.

Cunningham / *Modern Traditions*   12

THE OUTLINE

Chapter List

Acknowledgements

Introduction

Chapter 1: Getting Accustomed

SECTION ONE: CEREMONY

Chapter 2: Custom Tailored – *Wedding Attire, Rings, and Accessories*

Chapter 3: When December Snows Fall Fast – *Wedding Location, Date and Time*

Insert 1: The Ties That Bind – *Wedding Knots*

Chapter 4: Embracing the Sun – *Rites of Passage and Pre-Wedding Celebrations*

Chapter 5: Quill and Ink – *Invitations and Programs*

Insert 2: To Speak of Love – *Poetry, Quotes, and Readings*

Chapter 6: Angels on Horseback – *Wedding Transportation*

Chapter 7: Ceremonia – *The Ceremony Elements*

SECTION TWO: DÉCOR AND DESIGN

Chapter 8: Walking Among The Stones – *Ceremony Décor*

Chapter 9: Lavender and Edelweiss – *Bouquets and Boutonnieres*

Chapter 10: Of Branches and Ivy – *Wreaths and Garlands*

Insert 3: Illumination – *Candles and Fire*

Chapter 11: Cattails and Harvest Wheat – *Setting the Table*

Chapter 12: Of Heaven and Earth – *Design Details*

Insert 4: A Sweet Life – *Honey*

Chapter 13: Red Boxes and Wishing Stones – *Gifts, Favors, and Keepsakes*

SECTION THREE – CELEBRATION

Chapter 14: Fiddlers, Pipers, and Ragamuffins – *Music, Dance, and Entertainment*

Chapter 15: Wild Berries and Whiskey – *Food and Wine*

Chapter 16: To Taste Abundance – *The Cake*

Insert 5:   Rosemary for Remembrance – *Herbs*

Chapter 17: Dancing on the Embers – *Reception Customs*

Chapter 18: Bringing Your Wedding Vision to Life

Design Forms

Resources

Recommended Reading

Chart of Customs by Culture

Index

About the Author

Send Suggestions Page

```
SECTION ONE — CEREMONY


Chapter 1

Getting Accustomed

  The first chapter discusses why couples include
traditions in their weddings, then goes on to give
readers an understanding of how to incorporate
traditions into the wedding. It outlines universal
elements and provides options for honoring one's
culture, updating traditions, blending cultures
and traditions, borrowing traditions, and creat-
ing new traditions. The chapter explains the im-
portance of intent in creating new rituals and
gives "how-to's" for getting started, finding in-
spiration, selecting items, and designing the flow
of elements to run smoothly. The author provides
specific ideas for sharing the significance of the
traditions with the wedding guests. The chapter
concludes by encouraging readers to explore and
identify what is important to them as a couple.


Chapter 2

Custom Tailored: Wedding Attire, Rings, and Acces-
sories

  Chapter two outlines traditional wedding attire,
accessories, and rings by culture and provides
stylish ideas for incorporating and updating ele-
ments. The chapter begins with wedding clothes:
dresses (colors, style, embroidery, symbolism,
fabrics, and patterns), heirloom gowns, groom's
attire, wedding attendant's clothes, and shoes;
and then discusses hairstyles, special tokens,
veils and headpieces, accessories, handkerchiefs,
```

and ribbons. A section on rings: types of rings (including Claddagh, Gimmal, posie, Celtic, Luckenboot, crested,

gemstones, precious stones, birthstones, keeper rings, regard rings, and Fede rings), engraving rings, and meanings associated with rings completes the chapter. "A Couple's Story" features Melissa and David: A Wedding with English, Asian, African-American, Israeli, and Celtic elements.

Chapter 3

When December Snow Falls Fast: Wedding Location, Date, and Time

In Victorian times, falling snow on a couple's wedding day was believed to signify a happy marriage. "When December's snow falls fast, Marry, and true love will last" – Old English folk rhyme.

The chapter outlines traditional wedding sites and selection of the wedding date and time. Traditions are listed by culture; ideas are provided for incorporating and updating them. Items included in the chapter are: outdoor weddings, historical venues, sacred places, divination techniques using fortune-tellers and astrologers, benefits of seasonal wedding celebrations, and preferred days and time. "A Couple's Story" features Jennifer and Lee: A Wedding with Filipino and Irish Elements and a beach theme.

Special Insert 1

The Ties That Bind: Wedding Knots

Knots are one of the oldest and universal wedding elements. The special insert elaborates on numerous ways to creatively incorporate knots into the wedding. Highlights include: harvest knots, ribbon knots, bouquet knots, cookie knots, wrist knots, and handfasting knots.

Chapter 4

Embracing the Sun: Rites of Passage and Pre-Wedding Celebrations

On the morning of her wedding a Native-American bride greets the sun in a ritual representing her passage into a new life.

The chapter explores the universal practice of purification and transformation rituals, and provides ways to incorporate and update elements for the modern bride and groom. Highlights include henna and body painting, beauty applications, cleansing and symbolic baths, fragrant massages, wedding eve dinners, wedding showers, bachelor and bachelorette parties, engagement parties, and spiritual preparation ceremonies. "A Couple's Story" features Moira and Andrew: A Wedding with Native-American and French elements.

Chapter 5:

Quill and Ink: Invitations and Programs

With quill and ink, medieval monks inscribed the first paper invitations in calligraphy.

The chapter showcases invitation customs by culture, ways to elegantly update them, and the inclusion of cultural traditions. The chapter proposes ancient design options: engraving, calligraphy, letterpress, oral biddings, heraldry, coats of arms, emblems, and artwork; then moves on to items included in an invitation and program: myths, legends, family stories, photos and renderings, gifts and tokens, and the symbolism and significance of selected elements. The chapter closes by emphasizing the visual importance the invitation and program have on the wedding.

Cunningham / *Modern Traditions*   17

Insert 2:

To Speak of Love: Poetry, Quotes, and Readings

The special insert focuses on how to use poetry, quotes, and readings throughout the wedding design: invitations, programs, place cards, favors, toasts, and the ceremony.

Chapter 6:

Angels on Horseback: Wedding Transportation

A Corsican bride rides a white horse to her wedding ceremony. Along the way, she launches an olive branch down a stream to signify the abundance, peace, and happiness that will flow through her marriage.

The chapter will list traditional, unique ways couples, and their guests, are transported to the wedding: horses, carriages, sleighs, foot, and specialty vehicles.

Chapter 7:

Ceremonial: The Ceremony Elements

The chapter identifies cultural ceremony elements and suggests ways to update, borrow, and personalize them to create a meaningful and memorable event. The chapter begins with the bridal path, processional, and fire rituals, then details ceremony exchanges, sharing rituals, bindings and handfastings, offerings, and acceptance practices. The chapter concludes with unification ceremonies, rituals for honoring the family, symbolic tosses, and the recessional. "A Couple's Story" features Rebekah and Brooks: A Wedding with Celtic and Medieval elements.

Cunningham / *Modern Traditions*   18

SECTION TWO: DÉCOR AND DESIGN

Chapter 8:

Walking Among The Stones: Ceremony Décor

Stones long have been associated with wedding ceremonies and incorporated into the décor. To show her acceptance of the groom and commitment to the marriage, an Apache bride walks along a path of stones.

The chapter outlines traditional ceremony décor by culture and offers ways to create new designs.

Starting with the creation of the altar, the chapter then moves on to canopies, banners, circles, stones, and the aisle. Recommendations for ceremony gifts and guest participation are included.

Chapter 9:

Lavender and Edelweiss: Bouquets and Boutonnieres

Boutonnieres are a legacy from medieval times when a knight would wear a flower or other item to match his lady's' colors.

The traditional use and origin of bouquets and boutonnieres is discussed. A thorough list of flowers and herbs is presented by culture, country of origin, season, color, and associated meanings and symbolism. "A Couple's Story" features Monica and Bernd: A Wedding with

Cunningham / *Modern Traditions*   19

German, Southern, and African-American elements.

Chapter 10:

Of Branches and Ivy: Wreaths and Garlands

Wedding wreaths symbolize the circle of life. Ivy, representing fidelity, happiness, and marriage, and branches considered life's essence, are commonly incorporated into the floral design.

Chapter ten builds on chapter nine; elaborating on flowers and herbs used in wreaths and garlands.

Hair wreaths, door wreaths, plant talismans, and necklace garlands are discussed.

Insert 3:

Illumination: Candles and Fire

The special insert looks at the traditional, universal use of fire in wedding rituals and offers suggestions for bringing it into today's celebrations. Candlelit ceremonies, favors, and centerpieces are presented along with new traditions and ideas.

Chapter 11:

Cattails and Harvest Wheat: Setting the Table

Traditionally, wedding celebrations often were held during autumn, after the harvest. Cattails and sheaves of wheat, seasonal items, and fertility symbols were frequent décor elements.

Cunningham / *Modern Traditions* 20

The décor of the table is the focus of chapter 11. First, table styles, sizes, and room placement are examined, followed by a presentation of fabric treatments, linens, and napkins. Next, we look at centerpieces, dishware, and glasses. An investigation of table display items completes the chapter. "A Couple's Story" features Yu Mei and Jeffrey: A Wedding with Chinese and Latin elements.

Chapter 12:

Of Heaven and Earth: Design Details

Asian weddings abound with myth, symbolism, and balance: yin and yang, mirth and harmony, and heaven and earth – represented in the wedding décor by white paper tablets.

The chapter elaborates on the design details: furnishings, lighting, and artistic elements. Colors, their meanings and significance, are examined by culture. Cultural symbols – butterflies, feathers, and maypoles – are explored for inspiration and creativity. Designing place cards, using ribbons, and displaying hope chests round out the chapter.

Insert 4:

A Sweet Life: Honey

Another common wedding element, honey, is investigated in the special insert. Suggestions for bringing honey into your wedding in a playful and poignant way are provided. Ceremony tastings,

décor, favors, and menu items are included.

Chapter 13:

Red Boxes and Wishing Stones: Gifts, Favors, and Keepsakes

In an old Celtic tradition, guests throw pebbles into a river near the ceremony site, while making a wish for the couple. An updated version of this time-honored ritual will create a beautiful keepsake for the bride and groom: at the ceremony location, have guests place small stones, along with their wishes, in a glass container filled with water that you can keep in your new home.

The chapter identifies traditional gifts and favors for guests, by country, provides inspiring suggestions for including unique items, and expands on ways to create meaningful keepsakes. Guest writings, family ties, and charitable contributions are covered, along with dozens of distinctive ideas. "A Couple's Story" features Sumi and Matt: A Wedding with Indian and European elements.

SECTION THREE: CELEBRATION

Chapter 14:

Fiddlers, Pipers, and Ragamuffins: Music, Dance, and Entertainment

In a rural Irish custom, it is considered a sign of good luck if strawboys or ragamuffins "attend" the celebration and dance with the bride.

Cunningham / *Modern Traditions*   22

The chapter explores music, dance, and entertainment associated with each culture. Instrumentation, guest participation, and the hiring of entertainers are discussed. A comprehensive list of music and dances is included. "A Couple's Story" features Adrienne and Bud: A Wedding with Scottish and Hawaiian elements.

Chapter 15:

Wild Berries and Whiskey: Food and Wine

Honor your heritage, include a favorite beverage, or create a unique twist on an age-old cultural item by providing whiskey shots (a traditional celebratory drink of Ireland and Scotland) during the cocktail hour or as a champagne substitute in the ritual wedding toast.

The chapter outlines traditional drinks, wedding food, and dining customs by culture. The chapter begins with selecting the right type of meal service for your wedding: brunch, tea, breakfast, cocktails, dinner, or buffet and then expands on the ideas for the cocktail hour, lists sample menus, and suggestions on how to include family recipes. The chapter closes by exploring different cuisines for inspiration. "A Couple's Story" features Jane and Sachin: A Wedding with Indian and Irish elements.

Chapter 16:

To Taste Abundance: The Wedding Cake

The wedding cake or bread is used worldwide to encourage fertility, wish the couple a sweet life, and offer a taste of the abundance a marriage will produce.

The chapter focuses on traditional cakes by culture, helping the couple design one that represents their style and personality. The use of charms, trinkets, and ribbons is discussed along with selecting a filling and including a cake topper. The chapter concludes with the groom's cake.

Insert 5:

Rosemary for Remembrance: Herbs

The final special insert focuses on the age-old tradition of wedding herbs. Herbal significance and symbolism along with dozens of suggestions for incorporating herbs into the wedding are highlighted. Design suggestions include herbal rings for votives, wine glasses and candles, herbal ribbons and ties, centerpieces, bouquets, boutonnieres, favors, and tosses.

Chapter 17:

Dancing on the Embers: Reception Customs

At Belgian wedding celebrations, the bride and groom symbolically toss their past life onto the embers of a dying fire.

The chapter identifies reception traditions from around the world. Highlights include toasts, the sharing of food and drink, and customs that honor family and ancestors. "A Couple's Story" features Narelle and Jacopo: A Wedding with Australian, Italian, and Jamaican elements.

Cunningham / *Modern Traditions*   24

Chapter 18:

Bringing the Wedding Vision to Life

 The final chapter offers guidance for pulling all
the elements together and provides organizational
steps, resources, and design forms to complete the
process.

Sample Chapter(s)

Appendix E

Sample Revised Pages

This appendix contains an example of a successful rewrite. Read each draft carefully to see what types of changes the author made, and consider why he or she made these changes. The content has been reworked, and the grammar has been corrected.

Original Draft:

Unwillingly, I moved forward as the officer prodded me after the electronic hum sounded; then the large steel door slid open. Once I was inside, the door went the other way and locked with a loud and ominous sound that echoed throughout the whole corrections facility. Finding more than 3 feet of space between me and the other inmates was impossible in the overcrowded cell. I was scared, but it did not register because I was numb; still hearing the police officer yelling in my ear while putting on the handcuffs and charging me with a felony crime.

Just a short while ago I was asleep and dreaming in my bed unusually passed my normal waking hours. Yes, they were good dreams but not for long. At 8:45am my door was pounding with a thunder the likes of which I had never heard. It was so loud that I through the covers off and ran to the door thinking it was an emergency opening it quickly only to be grabbed, handcuffed and taken away in the squad car.

In the jail cell, I was in my light summer pajamas and bedroom slippers. Not exactly my preferred dress for incarceration. Most people think of their clothes as a fashion statement; right now I was just wishing for protection from the cold and danger. Just some blue jeans and a regular shirt would do. With what I had on now, one quick jerk in a struggle and my flimsy summer pajamas, thinner than a T-Shirt would just tear off as rags.

I was once rich and free, but no more. Now being in a jail cell with criminals and charged with a felony was the last thing I thought would ever happen to me. My one phone call did not get through. Emotions were no good now and self preservation was the only thought on my mind. Staying alive was my only focus.

Revised Draft:

It seems only a short time ago I was asleep in my bed, still dreaming long past my normal waking hour. And they were good dreams, but not for long. At 8:45 a.m., someone pounded on my door with a thunder the likes of which I had never heard. It was so loud I thought it had to be an emergency. I threw the covers off, bolted out of bed, and ran to the door. As soon as I opened it I was grabbed, handcuffed, and shoved into a squad car.

An electronic hum sounded and a large steel door slid open. Unwillingly, I moved forward as the officer prodded. Once I was inside the door slammed shut behind me and locked with a loud and ominous sound that echoed throughout the corrections facility. Finding more than three feet of space between me and the other inmates was impossible in the overcrowded cell. I was scared, but it did not register. I was numb — still hearing the sound of the police officer yelling in my ear while he shackled my wrists and charged me with a felony.

In the jail cell, I was still in my light summer pajamas and bedroom slippers. Not exactly my preferred dress for incarceration. Most people think of their clothes as a fashion statement; right now, I was just wishing for protection from the cold and danger. A pair of blue jeans and a regular shirt would do. With what I had on now, one quick jerk in a struggle and my flimsy summer pajamas, thinner than a well-worn T-shirt, would tear off in rags.

I was once rich and free, but no more. Being in a jail cell with criminals and charged with a felony was the last thing I thought would ever happen to me. My one phone call did not get through. Emotions were no good now, and self-preservation was the only thought on my mind. Staying alive was my only focus.

Glossary

Letter Writing and Publishing Terminology

Advance: The percentage of money paid to a writer by the publisher before publication

Agent: A professional who represents writers and markets creative works to publishers

All rights: When the publication owns all rights to the work but does not own the copyright

Assignment: A piece that a writer has been assigned to write by an editor or publisher for a pre-determined amount

Byline: The acknowledgment line that appears with the author's finished piece

Caption: A brief description that accompanies a picture, graph, diagram, or table

Clips: Published samples of writing submitted with queries to prospective publications. See also "tear sheets."

Copyright: Ownership by an author over his or her creation

Cover copy: Text that is printed on the cover of a book to convey concisely the contents of the book's interior

Cover letter: A brief letter accompanying a proposal, manuscript, or résumé introducing you and your credentials

Deadline: The date an assigned piece is due for submission

Draft: A completed version of piece that might need further revision, rewriting, or polishing

Editor: A professional commissioned to edit or write pieces for publication

Electronic submission: Submission that is made electronically, most frequently by e-mail but also by computer disks

Endorsements: Positive comments about a piece of work or writer that are used to promote the content or the writer's work and experience

E-query: A query that is transmitted electronically

E-zine: Electronic magazine; a magazine published online on the Internet or through e-mail

Fees: Money paid to a writer for services provided

Filler: Smaller pieces of content, often in the form of short stories, statistics, or humor, used to fill in the spaces or gaps of a publication. Fillers commonly range from a few sentences to no more than 200 words.

First Electronic Rights: The right to publish a written piece electronically for the first time

First Print Rights: The right to publish a written piece in the medium it is published in

Flash fiction: A style of literary fiction in which the author uses a short form of storytelling. The length is often fewer than 2,000 words but more than 75 words.

Flat fee: A lump sum amount paid to a writer after completion of an assignment

Formatting: The manner in which a manuscript is laid out and designed on the page

Genre: The type or category of writing (e.g. mystery, romance, science fiction, thriller, or juvenile)

Guidelines: Instructions for submitting work to a publication

Hook: A technique used in the lead paragraph of a piece to grab the attention of the read

Journal: A periodical that covers news or information in a specific area or industry

Kill fee: Payment made to compensate an assignment that was turned in but not used or published

Lead: The first paragraph of a query where the "hook" resides

Lead time: The time between getting an assignment and publication of the piece

Manuscript: An author's written copy of a book, article, or screenplay

Multiple submissions: Submitting more than one piece at a time to the same publisher, literary agent, or editor — also referred to as "simultaneous submissions"

Newbie: A new writer

Novel: A work of fiction more than 45,000 words

On acceptance: Payment given to a writer after the editor accepts the finished piece. This usually applies to nonfiction magazine articles.

On assignment: Writing a piece upon request of the editor, agent, or publisher

On publication: Payment given to a writer after the piece is published

On speculation/on spec: When an editor is not obligated to publish a piece that a writer was not officially assigned to develop

Outline: A bulleted list of sentences describing the major ideas to be covered in a piece

Payment: Compensation a writer receives from an editor, agent, or publisher for accepted work

Permission: A fee paid by an individual or publication that wants to reprint a writer's work

Pitch: A detailed description of an idea for a magazine, newspaper, or book

Print on demand (POD): Publishing and/or printing a book or books as they are requested

Proposal: Detailed summary of a book, which is usually nonfiction

Query letter: A one-page letter used to pitch an idea for an article or book to an editor

Reprints: Previously published work made available for publication in other magazines or journals

Rights: Ownership of all the various ways in which a creative work may be used, applied, reproduced, or printed

Rough draft: Often the first fully organized version of a piece

Royalties: A percentage paid monthly or quarterly to an author for sales, which is based on the cover price of the book

SAE: Self-addressed envelope (no stamp)

SASE: Self-addressed stamped envelope — sent with a query or proposal so the editor can mail it back to the writer

SASP: Self-addressed stamped postcard — sometimes sent with a manuscript submission to be returned by the publisher requesting notification of receipt

Self-publishing: A branch of the publishing industry in which an author publishes his or her own work

Serial: A type of publication is produced periodically (i.e., monthly, quarterly, annually). Common serial publications include magazines, newsletters, and newspapers.

Simultaneous submission: Sending a query, manuscript, or proposal to more than one publisher, editor, or agent at a time

Slant: The angle a writer presents as a way to write a specific piece

Slush pile: A common term used for unsolicited queries sent to editors or unsolicited manuscripts sent to publishers

Style: A writer's manner of expression by word choice, grammatical structures, literary devices, and other language elements

Subsidiary rights: Rights to publish a piece of work in a different format from the original work under contract

Submission guidelines: Instructions provided by the editor or publisher for submitting queries or manuscripts to the publication

Tear sheet: A sample of a writer's published work (see clips)

Terms: The deal made between the writer and the editor or publisher for publication of a specific work. The terms may include items such as:

rights purchased, payment schedule, and expected date of publication.

Unagented: A term used in the writing and publishing industry to describe a writer who is not being represented by a literary agent

Unsolicited: An article, manuscript, or proposal that was not requested by the editor, agent, or publication

Vanity publication: A form of publishing in which the author pays the publisher to produce his or her manuscript

Word count: The estimated number of words in a piece

Work for hire: The writer is commissioned to write a piece but does not receive a byline and does not get rights to the work

Writer's guidelines: A set of instructions to which a publication expects a writer to follow.

Author Biography

onna M. Murphy is technical and business communications specialist and published author who develops and designs customized products for print and online media. Business publications, process documentation, manuals, and presentations are her forte. Donna provides editorial and publication design services to a variety of industries including publishing, information technology, small business, career cultivation for women, and personal branding.

Before her communication and design work, Donna worked as a computer systems analyst, a Web content editor, a technical copywriter, and a communications instructor. Her clients have included HP, Motorola, GE, Texas Children's Hospital, and Shell. Donna has worked as an assistant editor to Atlantic Publishing Group, Inc., where she edited and coauthored *How to Open and Operate a Financially Successful Vending Business,* and *The Complete Guide to Windowsill Plants.*

Donna is also the author of two self-published books: *Organize Your Books in 6 Easy Steps,* and *The Woman's Guide to Self-Publishing.* She has authored and published numerous articles and resource booklets, which have been featured in various magazines, business journals, and online communities including *Real Women Real Issues,* Work.Home.You., *The Old Schoolhouse Magazine,* Suite101, Digital Women, iVillage, and Bizymoms.

Index

A

advance 325
AP Stylebook 118, 150, 264

B

blog posts 35, 41, 265
boilerplate contracts 174
book series 27, 34, 40, 41, 49, 89,
    100, 105, 179, 209, 243, 274,
    289, 298, 302, 303, 304

C

checklist 39, 194, 250
Chicago Manual of Style 118, 150, 264
clips 89, 155, 245, 325
consumer magazines 60, 61, 62, 64,
    65, 66, 95
cover letter 97, 219, 220, 221, 222

D

deadlines 22, 67, 164, 180, 181, 229,
    235, 236, 239

E

e-book 40, 49
Elements of Style 150, 264

F

five Ws 94, 125
flash fiction 326
frequently asked questions (FAQ) format
    39

G

ghostwriting 52
Google "Alerts" 30
grabber 103, 104
greetings and salutations 122

H

hook 48, 53, 54, 94, 100, 104, 121,
    124, 125, 126, 127, 128, 129,
    130, 154, 202, 327

I

inverted pyramid 125

K

kill fee 83, 327

L

literary agent 15, 103, 171, 172, 173, 174, 213, 327, 329
local slant 97

M

markets
  consumer magazines 60, 61, 62, 64, 65, 66, 95
  international 72, 73
  literary magazine 62
  literary magazines 63, 64, 70, 269
Meetup.com 38

O

online booksellers
  Alibris 29
  Amazon.com 29
  Barnes & Noble 29
  Booklocker.com 270
online databases
  QueryTracker 128, 193
  Submission Manager 193
  Writer's Database 19, 192
  Writer's Market 19, 62, 64, 79, 80, 95, 102, 184, 193, 269
online markets
  eHow.com 41
  Examiner.com 41
  e-zines 52, 60, 68
on spec 44, 166

P

payment terms 80, 231, 236, 238
PayPal 74

pen name 247

personal brand 152, 153, 247, 248, 249
podcasting 40
publishing rights 49, 70, 71
  all rights 51, 325
  electronic rights 52
  exclusive rights 51, 82, 246
  first North American serial rights (FNASR) 50
  first serial rights 50, 51
  nonexclusive rights 50, 51
  one-time rights 50
  reprint rights 51, 153
  second serial rights 51
  work made for hire 52
pull-quotes 89

Q

query
  "code of ethics" 20
  e-mail 156, 159
  local newspaper 98
  multiple-pitch 154, 209, 210
  nonfiction book 71, 99, 100, 103, 138, 204, 253
  novel 71, 94, 95, 99, 103, 104, 105, 106, 107, 108, 128, 138, 169, 170, 195, 275, 276, 277
  quick-pitch 208, 209
  sample letter 101, 104, 139, 169, 204, 213, 222, 224, 226, 231, 241, 245, 246, 294, 319

R

"reading fee" 54
rejections 214
repurposing 41
resources
  Absolute Write 35, 202, 263
  Adventures in Writing 128
  AgentQuery 175

Alder & Robin Books, Inc. 202
American Society of Newspaper Editors 68
Annual Editor & Publisher International Year Book 244
AP Stylebook Online 150, 264
Archetype 128
Association of
  Alternative Newsweeklies 68
  of Author's Representatives 58, 175, 256
Author Meeting Place 264
Bacon's Newspaper/Magazine Directory 66
Chicago Manual of Style Online 150, 264
Copy Law.com 53
Duotrope's Digest 193, 264
Editor and Publisher 68
Electronic Literature Organization 257
Encyclopedia of Associations 66
Every Writers Resource 63
Free Management Library 265
Gales Directory of Media Publications 244
Grammar Girl 150, 249, 265
HighWire Press 30
How to Write a Book Proposal 202
HTML Writers Guild 258
Keep Your Copyrights 52
Kirkus Reviews 64
Literary Market Place 150, 266
NewPages 63
Oxbridge Directory of Newsletters 66
Poets&Writers 63
Preditors and Editors 58
Publishers Marketplace 175
Publisher's Weekly 63, 175
Publist 72
QueryTracker.net Blog 128
Rachel Heston Davis blogs 128
Renegade Writer 267
Rights of Writers 52

Small Publishers, Artists, and Writers Network 261
U.S. Copyright Office 267
Well-Fed Writer 267
William Strunk's *Elements of Style* 150, 264
Worldwide Freelance Writer 72
Worldwide Freelance / Writing Markets 62
Write Jobs 269
Writer Beware 58
Writer Magazine 70, 269
Writer's Digest 62, 70, 101, 268
Writer's Digest University 70, 268
Writers' Market 269
Writers Net 175
Writers Weekly 62

S

sales letter 45
SASE 19, 62, 82, 88, 94, 116, 117, 137, 155, 162, 170, 195, 223, 246, 328
scams 53, 54, 55, 56, 58, 150, 56
  cyber-squatting 56
  vanity presses 55
self
  -branding 21
  -publishing 328
  -syndication 40, 243, 244, 245
SendBlaster Blog 157
sidebars 89, 234, 296
simultaneous submissions 82, 96, 327, 328
slush pile 44, 121, 131, 146, 197
software
  Duotrope 193
  PowerTracker 191
  SAMM 191
  Sonar 3 191
  Write Again 19
  Writer's Database 19, 192
  Writers Project Organizer 191

Writer's Scribe 19, 191
step-by-step booklet 39
subgenres 108, 109
submission
  guidelines 63, 64, 69, 75, 102, 162, 163, 167, 183, 186, 192
  tracking software 10, 19, 189, 190, 191, 192, 193
subsidiary rights 173
synopsis 7, 89, 103, 105, 106, 108, 170, 202, 203, 276

T

tear sheet 325, 329
trade journals 30, 64, 65, 66

U

unsolicited manuscripts 13, 173, 329

W

webinar 40
Wikipedia 70, 166
work for hire 329
"wow" factor 104
writer's groups
  Absolute Write 35, 202, 263
  Academy of American Poets 255
  American
    Christian Fiction Writers 110, 255
    Crime Writers League 255
    Society of Business Publication Editors 256
    Society of Journalists and Authors 256
  Asian American Journalists Association 256
  Association of Young Journalists and Writers 256
  Authors Guild 256
  Backspace 257
  CineStory 257
  Editorial Freelancers Associations 257
  EPIC, Electronically Published Internet
    Coalition 258
  Forwriters.com 35
  Goodreads 35
  Historical Novel Society 258
  Horror Writers Association 258
  International Food, Wine, & Travel Writers Association 259
  International Women's Writing Guild 259
  LibraryThing 35
  Media Bistro 259
  Military Writers Society of America 259
  Mystery Writers of America 35, 108, 259
  National
    Association of Independent Writers and Editors 260
    Writers Association 260
    National Writers Union 260
  Native American Journalists Association 260
  Novelists, Inc. 260
  Poetry Society Of America 260
  Poets & Writers 266
  Romance Writers of America 35, 261
  Science Fiction and Fantasy Writers of America 35, 261
  Sisters in Crime 261
  Society of
    Children's Book Writers and Illustrators 110, 261
  Western Writers Of America 261
  WritersBeat 35
  Writers
    Guild Of America 262
    on the Net 268
    Write 269, 270
writer's guidelines 18, 44, 49, 50, 61, 62, 77, 78, 84, 85, 97, 99, 102, 114, 116, 117, 155, 185, 195, 196, 197, 199, 200, 218, 236, 329
writing schedule 187, 188, 251